D0899920

RED
STACKS
OVER
THE
HORIZON

CAPTAIN ALBERT EDGAR GOODRICH 1826 - 1885

Founder of Goodrich's Steamboat Line, 1856

(From a painting made in Germany, 1870)

RED
STACKS
OVER
THE
HORIZON

THE STORY OF THE
GOODRICH STEAMBOAT LINE

by

JAMES L. ELLIOTT

WILLIAM B. EERDMANS PUBLISHING COMPANY
GRAND RAPIDS, MICHIGAN

To Phyl

FOREWORD

The name Goodrich was synonymous with travel by steamer on Lake Michigan for over seventy-five years. During this long span of time, literally millions of passengers were transported to and from the Lake ports in Michigan, Wisconsin, and Chicago.

As this book is being prepared, another thirty-four years have passed since the Goodrich Transit Company disappeared over the horizon. This means that it is now over a century ago that the first Goodrich steamer, the staunch and brave little *Huron*, first began to make her way up and down the west shore between Chicago, Milwaukee, Sheboygan and Manitowoc.

This volume is offered to the public in the hope that some of the excitement and pleasure enjoyed by those who, like the author himself, were fortunate enough to travel on those fine Lake steamers, will be transmitted to posterity. The author also hopes that for those who missed the thrill of a Lake trip or the excitement of an evening departure from a dock on the busy Chicago River, this book will be able to help them visualize the great mode of travel that has now virtually disappeared from our vast fresh-water inland seas. It seems timely that the history and ship record of Lake Michigan's largest and most famous steamship company be made available for all to read and contemplate.

With these thoughts in mind a book devoted solely to giving an accurate record of Captain A. E. Goodrich's Steamboat Line and its successors is offered for the public's interest and reading pleasure. To the author's knowledge there is no other such record available. Throughout the entire volume he has taken great care regarding the accuracy of dates and detail so that this record may be a lasting one.

ACKNOWLEDGMENTS

In the preparation of this story I had to spend a great deal of time traveling in search of facts, records and photographs. During these travels I came in contact with a great many persons in the Lake port governmental agencies, libraries, historical societies, museums, newspaper offices, and private homes who possessed information and pictures in their collections. All those whom I approached gave generously of their time and were most sympathetic to the task I had undertaken. While it would be impossible to name all these people individually, I would like to express my sincere appreciation to all who assisted me in the research.

I wish to give very special thanks to Father Edward J. Dowling, S.J., Harry W. Thorp, Jr., Captain D. J. McGarity, and Edward N. Middleton. These four men were kind enough to read the manuscript and give their valuable comments based on their own vast knowledge and experience.

Finally, to all those wonderful people such as Dora B. Goodrich; Janet Coe Sanborn, editor of the quarterly journal *Inland Seas;* Henry Barkhausen, present owner of the Carus Collection; Paul Sotirin and his very capable assistant Ruth Revels of the Marine Room, Milwaukee Public Library; William A. McDonald; John Otto; Henry Scheutte; Robert E. Lee, Curator, and his fine assistant Pat Labadie, of the Dossin Great Lakes Museum; Roy F. Valitchka, editor of the *Manitowoc Herald-Times;* Ted Roberts of Harris Trust and his capable secretary Sharon O'Loughlin; and a host of others, too numerous to mention, goes a very special and warm thank you. Without their capable assistance and encouragement, this story could not have been completed.

— J. L. E.

CONTENTS

Foreword   7

Acknowledgments   8

1. A Town Is Founded   11

2. A Steamboat Line Is Born   21

3. The Steamboat Business Grows   35

4. The Founding of the Goodrich Transportation Company   57

5. The Passing of a Great Leader   93

6. New Hands on the Helm   105

7. The Gay Nineties   139

8. Turn of a Century   153

9. A New Port-of-Hail   169

10. D. J. McGarity — A Great Goodrich Captain   199

11. The Last New Steamer   213

12. End of the Goodrich Dynasty   227

13. The Roaring Twenties   239

14. G & M Steamers Change Color   253

15. The Demise   271

    APPENDIX   283

    GOODRICH CAPTAINS   285

    LIST OF STEAMERS   289

    PREFERRED SHAREHOLDERS   299

    COMMON SHAREHOLDERS   301

    Bibliography   303

    Index of Names   305

S.S. A. D. PATCHIN — The first position held by Albert E. Goodrich on a steamer was as clerk aboard this side-wheeler in 1847.

Courtesy: Marine Review

Steam Packet A. D. Patchin.

Chapter One

A TOWN IS FOUNDED

In THE RECORDED STEAMBOAT HISTORY OF THE Great Lakes there is one man who has made a greater single contribution to its progress than any other. This man is Captain Albert E. Goodrich, founder of the famous Red-Stack line that carried his name for almost eighty years. His foresight and imagination marked him as a real genius in the planning and the operation of the steamboat business.

The fact that the Goodrich line was older than any other line, and outlasted and outgrew all competition, is mute testimony to the ability of its illustrious founder. At one time or another during its history, this famous Lake Michigan line owned or leased over fifty steamships of all sizes and types. No other passenger carrier on America's fresh-water inland seas came even close to this record.

Our story begins in the fall of 1834 on Lake Michigan. A heavy gale from the northwest was lashing the Lake into a white-capped frenzy and blowing before it the schooner *Post Boy*. Unable to come about, the schooner was in immediate danger of being driven on the lee shore in the southeastern corner of Lake Michigan. The schooner's master, Captain Wessel D. Whittaker, decided to run for the mouth of a stream known as State Creek in an attempt to gain shelter from the fury of the storm. *Post Boy* failed to gain her objective at the mouth of the stream and stranded on the beach a few miles from Michigan City, Indiana.

After she went aground, the heavy seas continued to pound the little schooner and the waves soon built a heavy deposit of sand around her hull. The terrific seas soon broke the ship's back and rendered her a total loss. When the storm was at its height, the temperature dropped rapidly and it became bitterly cold. The men aboard the *Post Boy* had little shelter from the lashing, freezing spray and spent a most uncomfortable night aboard the wrecked vessel. When the storm finally subsided, Captain Whittaker and his crew were able to use the schooner's small boat to make their way to shore. Then they walked along the beach to Michigan City.

On arrival at Michigan City, Captain Whittaker and his men secured transportation by stagecoach to the busy Lake port of St. Joseph, Michigan, for the purpose of reporting the loss of *Post Boy* to the insurance underwriters. At this time St. Joseph was the western terminus of one of the overland routes from Detroit and, as a result, was a very important Lake Michigan port, handling traffic from the East en route to Chicago and Milwaukee.

While en route to St. Joseph, the stage paused at the point where the Galien River joins Lake Michigan. Captain Whittaker was impressed with what he saw. In this location he foresaw the possibilities of a new city, complete with harbor and a busy port. Also he was not overlooking the opportunity of a handsome profit if his idea could be successfully carried out and the new community established.

At this time southwestern Michigan was just beginning to feel the effects of a huge real estate boom that swept the state and carried on into 1839 before the bubble burst. The Land Office that had been established in White Pigeon in 1831 was moved to Kalamazoo in early 1834 so that it could better handle the demand for Public Sale land. By 1836 the demand at the Kalamazoo Land Office was so great that a small tent city was erected to house all those who were eagerly seeking a Michigan homestead. In 1820 Congress had reduced the minimum price of Public Sale land from $2.00 to $1.25 per acre. The minimum-quantity purchase was, at the same time, reduced from one hundred and sixty acres to eighty acres. Under the new plan only one payment was allowed and this was to be in cash. Before that the purchaser was allowed four equal payments within one year of the purchase date.

Upon completion of his business with the office of the underwriters at St. Joseph, the crew of *Post Boy* was paid off and dismissed. Captain Whittaker then boarded the overland stage for Kalamazoo. On arrival he visited the Land Office and obtained maps and legal descriptions of the land surrounding the mouth of the Galien River. His idea still seemed sound to the dauntless captain, so he immediately arranged to purchase a large tract of the shoreside location. Following this transaction with the Land Office a large "S" appeared on the Land Office maps showing that the sections so marked had been sold.

Captain Whittaker returned to his home in Buffalo, New York, where he persuaded his friends, Jacob A. Barker and Nelson Willard, to invest the sum of $13,000 for an undivided fifty percent interest in the development of the new land.

The captain and his friends, together with a surveyor, then returned to the new site and proceeded to lay out streets, lots and public areas. The founders envisioned the new community rapidly becoming a most important Lake port. So certain were they of this that they decided to name the new community New Buffalo in honor of the thriving port city of Buffalo, New York, their former home.

One of the first purchasers of property in the new settlement was Russel Goodrich, a brother-in-law of Captain Whittaker. Mr. Goodrich had owned and operated a tavern at Hamburg, New York. Russel Goodrich purchased blocks two and twelve in the new development. He built a home on block twelve and erected a hotel and tavern on block two.

In 1836 the township was organized and the first election held, which was conducted in the Goodrich Hotel. Goodrich became very active in the planning and development of rapidly growing New Buffalo.

Russel Goodrich was born on September 4, 1796. On January 1, 1818, he married Comfort Marvin and the couple settled in Hamburg, New York, near Buffalo.

To this marriage were born a total of seven children. Twice in succession the happy couple was blessed with twins. The seven children and their dates of birth were as follows:

Jasper Goodrich, May 5, 1819
Joseph M. Goodrich, September 3, 1821
Edgar Goodrich, September 3, 1821 (died the same year)
Cordellia Goodrich, January 23, 1824
Cornellia Goodrich, January 23, 1824
Albert Edgar Goodrich, February 11, 1826
Catherine Goodrich, February 3, 1832

The sixth child, Albert E. Goodrich, like his brothers and sisters, attended the public schools in the area. There is nothing in the records to indicate that Albert was anything other than an average student. His keen interest in ships and shipping did, however, manifest itself at an early age.

Buffalo, New York, was already then a thriving and most important Great Lakes port. Located, as it is, at the extreme

JUNCTION OF THE GALIEN RIVER WITH LAKE MICHIGAN — It was here that Captain Whittaker first visualized the site of New Buffalo in 1835.

eastern end of Lake Erie, it was the scene of the earliest Lake steamships. The very first and famous steamer *Walk-in-the-Water* was built near Buffalo in 1818 and first operated on Lake Erie. It foundered in a gale on Lake Erie in 1821. After the wreck the boiler and engine were salvaged and used in the second Lake steamboat *Superior,* which was also built near Buffalo and which proved to be quite successful.

For many years Buffalo was the point of embarkation for the popular rail and water route from the East to Detroit and Chicago. This heavy concentration of Lake shipping at Buffalo made it quite natural that at an early age young Goodrich's interest would turn to ships. To whet his interest in Lake shipping further was the fact that his uncle was Captain Whittaker, who was a shipmaster of considerable reputation. Ships and their navigation being a first love with Albert, his uncle undertook to teach him the ways of the Lakes when he was still very young. Albert soon proved to be an eager and adept student.

When Russel Goodrich decided to move his family to New Buffalo, the long trip was made by boat. This was a very exciting event for young Albert because he was, even at the age of ten, determined to make a career for himself on the Lake boats. He dreamed of the day when he would become master and have command of his own ship.

The development of New Buffalo as an improved port progressed rather slowly. In the year 1839 a lighthouse was built there. The harbor itself received no major improvements, however, until 1848. In that year extensive improvements were undertaken and wholly financed by the Michigan Central Railroad Company.

At this point in our history the best, and certainly the most popular, route of travel from New York City and other cities in the East to Chicago and Milwaukee was by boat up the Hudson River to Albany. From Albany the long trip to Buffalo was accomplished via the Erie Canal or by railroad or a combination of both. From Buffalo the traveler embarked on a Lake steamer to Detroit. On arrival at Detroit, the Michigan Central was boarded for a tedious trip across Michigan, partly by rail and partly by overland stagecoach. The point of changing from rail to stage varied as railway construction worked its slow way across the southern section of the state. The last lap of the long journey was accomplished by a Ward Line steamer from St. Joseph, and later from New Buffalo, across the southern end of Lake Michigan to Chicago or Milwaukee, depending on the traveler's destination. The complete trip often required thirty-three to thirty-five days!

This same route was utilized by the United States Government for the movement of mail. As a link in this route the Ward Line carried sacks of mail between St. Joseph and Chicago. This

LIGHTHOUSE HILL, NEW BUFFALO, MICHIGAN — On this hill a lighthouse was erected in 1839.

Courtesy: John Otto Collection

gave Captain Ward the right proudly to display the words "U. S. Mail" on the white bows of the little Ward Line steamers.

Thousands of immigrants, after clearing the port of New York, made their way to new homesteads in the Midwest over this route. This number was swelled by those who found the rocky soil of New England unattractive and decided to try the more fertile soil of the newly developed Midwest. Many a newcomer to Illinois and Wisconsin had his first glimpse of his chosen new land from the deck of a Ward Line boat.

Construction work on the Michigan Central continued. The line pushed steadily west across the Wolverine State. The western terminal was extended to Kalamazoo until in 1848 the line reached Niles. On April 23, 1849, amid much rejoicing and celebration, the first train from Detroit entered New Buffalo. The point of embarkation for the last link of the combination rail-water-stage route was changed from St. Joseph to New Buffalo. Passengers could now travel from Detroit to Chicago in only thirty-three to thirty-six hours. Records indicate that over eighty thousand passengers were handled by the Michigan Central in the year 1848. This number swelled to over one hundred thousand in 1849!

For about two years New Buffalo was the western terminal for the railway. During this time the young little city really boomed. What had been a rather placid and quiet place became one of feverish activity as thousands of travelers arrived to make the relatively graceful change from the "cars" to the steamers and vice versa. The elimination of a stage ride over roads that were hardly improved trails did much to stimulate travel to the Midwest.

When Albert Goodrich became old enough to seek employment, his first job was as a clerk in his father's hotel. He remained at this occupation until he was offered a position as clerk aboard the side-wheel steamer *A. D. Patchin* in 1847. Chartered by the Ward Line, *A. D. Patchin* was owned by his uncle, Captain Harry Whittaker, who was also master.

At the close of navigation that year Captain Goodrich was awarded a number of contracts by the Michigan Central in connection with the extension of the line westward. These contracts proved to be quite profitable, and young Goodrich continued his association with the railroad company off and on throughout the construction period until the line finally reached its objective at Chicago.

About the time the railroad drew near New Buffalo Captain E. B. Ward placed three new steamers, *Pacific*, *Traveler* and *Cleveland* on the cross-lake route in preparation for handling all of the rail traffic from New Buffalo to Chicago and Milwaukee.

In his capacity as clerk and later as captain, Albert served on all three of these new Ward Line steamers. His early training with his uncle and his natural love of ships made him a happy and enthusiastic employee for Captain Ward.

In spite of the more convenient interchange at New Buffalo, construction work on the Michigan Central continued to push westward. On across the sand dunes at the south end of the Lake went the ribbon of steel. The company's objective finally to reach Chicago proved to be an expensive feat for the new line, however. Their rival, the Michigan Southern Railway was also pushing toward Chicago on a route just to the south of the Michigan Central. A host of grafting petty politicians were reaping a harvest from the intense rivalry between the two railway companies. The Michigan Southern won the race to Chicago.

The first train of the Michigan Central to enter Chicago did so on May 20, 1852, but not before the management had paid the staggering sum of $500,000 for a non-existent Indiana chartered railroad. Even then it was necessary to negotiate a long-term lease to use the Illinois Central Railroad tracks from Pullman to downtown Chicago. In spite of many obstacles and delays the objective was finally gained and as of May 20, 1852, a traveler could ride the 269 miles from Detroit to Chicago entirely by rail and on the same train! Thereafter the Michigan Central gained momentum rapidly and by 1855 it was doing an annual volume of over two and one-half million dollars.

Upon completion of the railroad to Chicago it was quite obvious to all in the steamship business that the lucrative cross-lake traffic, enjoyed by the Ward Line steamers, was in dire jeopardy. For a short time the line was fairly busy with some traffic for Milwaukee, but it was not long until the volume of business enjoyed by the fleet of staunch little white steamers fell off to practically nothing. The importance of New Buffalo as a Lake port suffered accordingly and it was never again an important factor in Lake shipping.

At this time the Ward Line enjoyed a nice volume of traffic from Detroit to ports on Lake St. Clair and Lake Huron. When the Lake Michigan cross-lake routes began to dwindle, Captain Ward decided to give up this segment of his business and concentrate all activity of the Ward Line at Detroit.

Then Captain S. Clement, a former Ward Line shipmaster, chartered the steamers *Traveler* and *Cleveland* from Captain Ward to enter the steamboat business. In 1854 he established operations at Chicago and began service to most ports on Lake Michigan.

Business became brisk with the Clement Steamboat Line and in 1855 the records show that they operated *Traveler, Cleveland, Arctic* and *Pacific* in their Lake Michigan service. All these

NEW BUFFALO HARBOR — Two piers extending into the Lake and built by the Michigan Central Railroad Company formed the first harbor at New Buffalo, Michigan.

vessels were chartered from Captain Ward. Later that year the steamer *Huron* entered the Clement service.

In 1856 Captain Clement and several former Ward Line employees decided formally to incorporate under the name Clement Steamboat Line. This took place at Chicago with Captain Clement as president and chairman of the board of directors. Other directors were George C. Drew, T. A. Turner, L. H. Kellog, J. Hutchins and Captain A. E. Goodrich. Captain Goodrich had been associated with this group and he was quite active in the affairs of the new corporation from the outset.

The Clement Line continued to operate out of Chicago to ports on Lake Michigan. For several years this line practically controlled steamboat traffic on the Lake and they did quite well financially.

Being a part of this fairly large group was not entirely to the liking of our ambitious young captain. He had long dreamed of having his own ship and his own steamboat line and this situation with Clement was far from that. Early in 1856, A. E. Goodrich sold all of his stock in the Clement Line and severed all relations with the company. That same year he and his friend and former associate with the Clement Line, George C. Drew, decided to cast their lot together and form a partnership.

Courtesy: John Otto Collection

NEW BUFFALO, MICHIGAN — An early scene on Whittaker Avenue, named after Captain Whittaker, founder of the city.

S.S. COMET — For several seasons this ship was commanded by Captain Pabst.

Chapter Two

A STEAMBOAT LINE IS BORN

AFTER THE FORMATION OF THE PARTNERSHIP BE-
tween George C. Drew and Captain A. E. Goodrich, they turned
to the task of securing a suitable ship with which they could enter
the steamboat business. Captain Goodrich appealed to his former
employer and old friend, Captain E. B. Ward, owner of the Ward
Line. An agreement was reached whereby the new partners
would charter the side-wheel steamer *Huron* from Captain Ward.
Since the discontinuance of the cross-lake service by the Ward
Line, *Huron* had been on charter to the Clement Steamboat Line
of Chicago.

Huron was a wooden side-wheel steamer rated at 348 tons
burden. She had been built in the Ward Yard at Newport, Michigan, in 1852. Newport, located on the shores of the St. Clair River,
is now known as Marine City. This sturdy ship was not large,
even by the standards of her day. She was 165 feet in length, had a
beam of 23 feet 6 inches and a draft of a little over 9 feet. Her
low-pressure boilers used cordwood as fuel and she carried the
walking beam, so familiar with vessels equipped with the vertical
beam engine, on her hurricane deck.

In general appearance she had a single mast forward, a single
black stack, and her hull was painted entirely white. Her name
appeared in large black letters on her paddle-wheel boxes. Arched
trusses, to add longitudinal strength to her hull, appeared topsides.
By all standards, *Huron* was a staunch and pretty ship in her

day. Under the very capable command of Captain Goodrich, they made a most dependable and popular combination.

When originally built for the Ward Line, *Huron* was intended for service from Detroit to ports on Lake St. Clair and on up the St. Clair River as far as Newport. Later her routes were extended to include Saginaw and other ports on lower Lake Huron.

On November 23, 1853, *Huron* struck some unseen obstruction in the Saginaw River and sank. Raised on December 12, 1853, she was towed to Detroit where extensive repairs, costing over $12,000, were made. Upon completion of these repairs she was transferred to Lake Michigan to assist in handling the cross-lake traffic given the Ward Line by the Michigan Central Railroad.

After the leasing of the *Huron,* Captain Goodrich began to make plans for routes, docks and port arrangements for his new steamboat service. One port of prime interest was Chicago. In 1856 property on the south bank of the Chicago River, just east of Michigan Avenue, was secured. This location was on land now occupied by the Michigan Avenue link bridge and extended eastward along the river for about a block and a half.

On this site a dock, some small sheds and a small office were constructed. From here the *Huron* sailed on August 10, 1856, carrying the first Goodrich excursion from Chicago to Milwaukee. Strangely enough, this same dock location was to serve the Goodrich interests for the next seventy-odd years!

Captain Goodrich sensed that the city of Milwaukee was destined to be a great trading center and an important Lake port. The country to the north of Milwaukee was being rapidly settled, especially the Manitowoc and Green Bay areas. Milwaukee was the logical gateway to serve this fertile and rapidly expanding territory. Docking space, sheds and another small office were secured on the Milwaukee River. This first Goodrich steamboat dock in the Cream City was secured at the East Water Street bridge. The docks were moved to the foot of Sycamore Street in 1859. There was no Sycamore Street bridge until 1890. Sycamore Street was changed to Michigan Street in the 1920's. The name "Goodrich's Steamboat Line" and the ports it served appeared in large black letters on the small wooden office.

At the outset *Huron* did not attempt to keep any regular schedule of sailings. At her normal rate of speed she required about ten hours to make the trip from Chicago to Milwaukee. Trips between the west-shore ports were made whenever the traffic warranted it.

At the time Captain Goodrich began service with the *Huron,* steamers were the only means of transportation between Chicago, Milwaukee and the west-shore Lake ports of Port Washington, Sheboygan, Manitowoc, Two Rivers and those located on Green

Bay. The railroad did not enter Manitowoc, for example, until about 1873. The early steamboat cargos consisted of livestock, both for the farms and the market, dried peas, beer, merchandise for the stores, specie for the banks, machinery and many other items required to sustain the life and comfort of the early settlers in rapidly expanding Wisconsin. New settlers, German, Polish, Bohemian and Scandinavian, were landed at Milwaukee and points north by the boatload. As early as 1855, there is a record of a boatload of new Bohemian settlers being landed at Manitowoc by the steamer *Huron*, then under charter to the Clement Line.

In the spring of 1857, Drew and Goodrich purchased the *Huron* outright from Captain Ward, for $16,000. Not long after this she began venturing north as far as Two Rivers. Manitowoc was an important port for Goodrich and in 1857 K. K. Jones was appointed agent for the line at that port. Pierpont and Hall were appointed agents at Two Rivers.

From the very beginning, Manitowoc was a lucrative port for Captain Goodrich's Steamboat Line. Even at this early date, shipbuilding was done there and it was a strategic location for the development of the east central part of the state of Wisconsin. Cordwood was always kept available on the docks for passing steamers.

On several occasions the little *Huron* weathered some lively blows on Lake Michigan. Word of her stability and the dependability of her captain and crew spread quickly. This did much to enhance the traveling public's fondness for Goodrich's Steamboat Line and *Huron's* illustrious young captain.

Travel on *Huron* was a true test of a passenger's patience and durability. Whatever food was consumed was brought aboard by the passengers themselves. Like all vessels of her day, the only cabin space available on *Huron* was for use only as a shelter from the rain and winds. Sleeping, if any, was done in the deck chairs or on the deck itself and passenger comfort was a term that had not yet been coined!

Traffic continued to be heavy with the new steamboat line and it was not until December 7, 1857, that *Huron* departed from the village of Manitowoc, bound down for Milwaukee on her last trip of that season. The press, in reporting this event, expressed the sincere hope that Captain Goodrich would return his service to the same area the following spring.

Return he did and the record indicates that *Huron* made her first call of the new season at Manitowoc on April 23, 1857. The arrival of the first boat of the new season was always the signal for a gala occasion. It usually meant that the local merchants would receive a new stock of merchandise and many things that had been in short supply all winter would again be plentiful.

It was announced in the May 3, 1859, issue of the *Muskegon Reporter* that the "low pressure steamer *Huron* will leave Muskegon for Grand Haven and Chicago on Tuesdays, Thursdays and Saturdays at 1:00 P.M. during the season of 1859." Captain Frederick Pabst was announced as her master.

June of 1860 found *Huron* back on the west-shore route. It was advertised that she would leave the North Pier at Manitowoc every morning at 8:00 for Milwaukee with stops at Sheboygan and Port Washington. On arrival at Milwaukee *Huron* made a close connection with *Gazelle*, Captain Butlin commanding, for Chicago. That year *Gazelle* ran opposite *Traveler* between Chicago and Milwaukee for the Clement Line.

Later *Huron* was again returned to the cross-lake service. On August 10 of that year *Huron*, under the command of Captain Sanford (Shanty) Morgan, was approaching Grand Haven. There were no pier heads at that time at the junction of the Grand River and Lake Michigan. A heavy sea was running and as *Huron* began to make her entry she struck a bar and was completely spun around, to the consternation of the throngs that had assembled to welcome her. Undaunted, Captain Morgan merely signaled "full astern" to his engine room and the brave little side-wheeler actually backed her way up the river to the dock to the amusement and wild acclaim of those gathered to watch her arrival.

RUSH STREET BRIDGE, 1861 — The Goodrich steamer *Comet* is shown approaching the Goodrich dock on the Chicago River.

Courtesy: Chicago Historical Society

S.S. HURON — This was the first Goodrich steamboat, acquired in 1856.

Huron was not only a very lucky steamer for Captain Goodrich, she was an excellent money-maker as well. During her career as a Goodrich boat, she steamed on all the routes and rendered wonderful service. Her name was a household term in all the homes located in or near the Lake ports at which she called.

The early Lake steamer provided one of the few forms of entertainment and recreation available to the early west-shore residents. For example, in July of 1860, the musical society of the village of Manitowoc chartered *Huron* for a picnic and excursion to Sheboygan. The steamer departed from the North Pier at 8:00 A.M. and returned at 10:00 P.M. that same evening. Tickets for the round trip were fifty cents.

When, in 1867, Captain Goodrich felt that *Huron's* usefulness to his steamboat line was at an end, the popular and brave little steamer was sold to Captain Cook and Mr. Trowbridge of Detroit, Michigan.

During the late summer of 1857, it had been increasingly difficult for the little *Huron* to keep up with the demand for her services. It now became quite obvious to her owners that the line must be expanded if they were to take full advantage of the traffic available.

On May 1, 1858, only two years after the beginning of *Huron's* service, the wooden propeller *Ogontz* was purchased. Commanded by Captain Flood, *Ogontz* was immediately placed in service on the west shore and operated on the same routes as *Huron*.

Ogontz was built at Ohio City in 1848. Rated at 343 tons burden she was, like *Huron*, a small steamer. She was painted all white and carried a single stack and mast. Captain Goodrich paid $5,600 for her but in actual service she never proved to be as dependable or as good a seaboat as *Huron*. In 1860 Captain Goodrich removed her engines and machinery and she was sold to W. Crostin for $500. Crostin converted her to a sailing vessel and she operated as such until she foundered in a Lake Michigan storm in 1862.

Following the acquisition of *Ogontz*, business for Goodrich's Steamboat Line continued to increase. The addition of the second steamer granted more flexibility of operation and the Goodrich reputation for dependable, safe service continued to grow by leaps and bounds. By 1859, something of a regular schedule was maintained between Chicago, Racine and Milwaukee with *Ogontz* making more and more frequent trips to the Green Bay ports. This brought Goodrich in direct competition with the Clement Steamboat Line.

In the spring of 1859, the North Pier at Manitowoc was leased from K. K. Jones, the Goodrich agent, by a group known as Johnston & Hodges who really represented the Goodrich interests. As the years went on, this property became the operating base for the entire Goodrich fleet.

In May of 1859 the partners searched the market for a third steamer to add to their growing operation. By this time they had become an important factor in the west-shore traffic and they realized that if this position was to be maintained they could not continue to refuse business because they did not have the ship capacity to handle the available traffic.

Once more Captain Goodrich went to his old friend Captain Ward for assistance. The wooden side-wheeler *Comet* was under construction at the Ward Yard at Newport. Captain Goodrich purchased her for $32,000 before she was completed and took delivery of the new ship on May 1, 1860. *Comet* was 158 feet in length, had a beam of 24 feet 6 inches, a draft of 9 feet and was rated at 351 tons burden. In size and appearance she was very similar to *Huron*. The *Muskegon Reporter* of May 4, 1860, had the following to say about the new steamer:

THE STEAMER COMET — This fine steamer is now making regular trips between Chicago and Muskegon, touching at Kenosha, Racine and Grand Haven. She was built at Newport, on the Saint

Clair River, by Captain Ward, of Detroit, for Messrs. Drew & Goodrich, of Chicago. She is a staunch, fast, and splendid looking steamer, and is, in every particular, well adapted for this route. Her cabins, or saloons, are large and elegantly furnished and all her accommodations for passengers are excellent. She has already proved herself a good sea boat and has, we believe, shown an average speed of 15 miles per hour.

She is commanded by S. W. Morgan, so well and favorably known here and elsewhere that any commendation from us would be superfluous. The clerk, Mr. Henry Goodfellow, and the steward, Mr. McGrane, are both strangers to us but are highly spoken of by those acquainted with them.

Messrs. Drew & Goodrich, the owners of the COMET, deserve success for their enterprise and liberality unbounded.

Comet proved to be a fine ship in every way. She caught the fancy of the public and during the years she served Goodrich, there was not another ship more popular with shippers and travelers alike. In 1861, the *Milwaukee News* had this to say about the assignment of Captain Frederick Pabst as shipmaster of the *Comet*:

Captain Fred Pabst, everybody's favorite, now has command of COMET. This steamer, under command of Pabst, late of HURON, has taken the place of HURON on the run to Manitowoc and Two Rivers.

COMET is neat, elegant and comfortable and is said to be the swiftest sailor on Lake Michigan.

Even as far back as when he commanded *Comet*, his third ship, Captain Goodrich was striving to make his steamers better, safer and more attractive. In February of 1861, *Comet* was sent to the shipyard for extensive overhaul. Her hull was divided into four watertight compartments and her interior repainted and refitted throughout. On April 4 of the same year, Captain Goodrich announced that *Comet* would make four trips north each week. Her days of departure from Milwaukee were Tuesday, Thursday, Friday and Saturday. Her new route was to include Keewaunee, Wisconsin, and this marked the first time that regular service was offered from Milwaukee to points north of Two Rivers. The story of the career of her illustrious Captain Pabst is a most interesting one.

Frederick Pabst was born in Thüringen, Saxony, in Germany, on March 28, 1836. His father Gottlieb and his mother Fredericka Pabst decided to migrate to Milwaukee in 1848. Frederick, then twelve years old, accompanied his parents, and during the long crossing of the Atlantic he became very fond of ships and was deeply impressed by the men who sailed them. This experience did much to shape his future life in the new country.

After a stay of only a few months in Milwaukee the father, mother and son moved to Chicago in 1849. That same year an epidemic of cholera swept the city and one of its victims was Mrs. Pabst.

Young Frederick worked as a waiter in the old Mansion House for a salary of five dollars a month. Later he secured a similar position in the New York House. His memory of the sea was still strong and he secured a position as cabin boy aboard a Ward Line steamer.

In addition to his regular duties as a cabin boy he was put in charge of receiving the tickets from the passengers as they left the steamer at one of her ports of call. His instructions from the steamer clerk were that no one should pass without presenting a ticket. Captain Ward, one of the most prominent steamboat owners in the business and owner of the boat on which Frederick Pabst was employed, attempted to leave the steamer without showing his ticket. He was stopped and thrust back by the husky young German. Even the offer of a bribe of a dollar failed to gain an exit for Captain Ward. He had no choice but to return to his cabin

Courtesy: Henry Barkhausen

THE GOODRICH DOCKS AT MANITOWOC — This photo was taken in 1920. The site was procured by Captain Goodrich in 1859.

where his temper eventually cooled off. He had to admire the integrity and courage of young Pabst and they became lifelong friends.

Frederick Pabst demonstrated a love and interest in his work aboard the Ward Line steamers that soon earned him rapid promotion. His intellectual curiosity and ambition earned him the title of captain aboard the *Huron* when he was only twenty-one years of age.

In 1858 he transferred to the Goodrich line and was soon a popular and dependable master under the direction of Captain Goodrich. At the beginning of the season of 1861 he was given command of the *Comet* and sailed her from Milwaukee to Two Rivers for the next two seasons.

In 1862 he married Marie Best, the daughter of Philip Best, then the head of the famous brewing firm of Jacob Best & Sons of Milwaukee. This was a very happy marriage and his reluctance to leave his bride for the long separations caused by being a Lake captain brought about his leaving the bridge of Lake steamers early in 1864.

Courtesy: Chicago Historical Society

THE FIRST GOODRICH OFFICE — This office was built on the south bank of the Chicago River at Michigan Avenue in 1856.

He entered the brewing business with his father-in-law. At the death of Philip Best he became head of the brewing firm and from this came the Pabst Brewing Company of today's fame. He passed away on January 1, 1904, at the age of 68. A successful and prominent man in his industry, he was equally respected for his civic interest in Milwaukee. He was the founder of the famous Pabst Theater, which is only one of his many civic accomplishments as one of Milwaukee's most distinguished citizens.

As the war clouds gathered, the first soldiers to depart from Manitowoc were the Manitowoc Guards. This local troop was called to active national duty with orders to proceed to Camp Randall at Madison for further training.

The evening of June 23, 1861, was the scene of feverish activity as the troops assembled at North Pier in Manitowoc to board the *Comet,* under the command of Captain Pabst. Just as it was getting dark the loading of the troops and their equipment was completed, the last tearful and sad farewells were said, and as the throngs on the dock continued to wave, the *Comet* cast off and moved out into the darkness of Lake Michigan on her first of many troop-carrying assignments during the Civil War. On several occasions she made the long trip from west-shore points to Cleveland, Ohio.

The winter of 1861 was a mild one and as late as December 20 of that year, the *Comet* was still giving regular service on the new route. This did much to build up her popularity and that of her well-liked master and Goodrich's Steamboat Line. Spring in 1862 came early and on April 1 the *Comet,* with Captain Pabst in command, arrived at Kewaunee to open the new season.

As an indication of how dependent the early residents of the west-shore ports were upon the Goodrich steamers and the men who manned them, we copy an announcement that appeared in the *Manitowoc Herald* in 1861:

John Fredericks, bartender on the steamer COMET will attend to all business in the line of purchasing goods, carrying parcels, doing errands, etc., between all ports from Two Rivers to Milwaukee.

On November 13, 1862, *Comet* was the subject of an unusual and interesting news story. At 3:30 A.M. *Comet* and her sister ship *Sunbeam* loaded the Provost Marshall General and a contingent of Federal troops. Their destination was Port Washington, the scene of a serious draft riot.

One of the few mechanical failures to occur aboard this reliable steamer took place on March 8, 1864. On that day she broke a piston rod and cylinder head. Repairs required a lay-up of about ten days and this inconvenienced many people because there was no other boat to take over her west-shore route.

Sunday night, July 1, 1865, found Lake Michigan lashed to a fury by a big storm. *Comet*, en route to Green Bay, was driven ashore on the rocks at Washington Island. The vessel was in grave danger from the pounding seas so her commander, Captain Gaylord, ordered her scuttled. She sank in about thirteen feet of water. Except for the loss of cargo, valued at $10,000 and covered by the Home Insurance Company, she suffered no great damage. After the storm subsided, she was pumped out and taken to Manitowoc for repairs.

Comet continued her colorful and very successful career as a Goodrich steamer until the close of the season of 1869. In November of that year the sturdy old side-wheeler was dismantled. Her engine, boilers, most of her machinery, and some of her cabin fittings were utilized in the construction of the new steamer *Corona*. The stripped-down hull was sold to Captain Cobb for conversion into a tow barge. Sale price was $1,000. None of the early Goodrich steamers contributed more to the company's reputation for dependability than did *Comet*. Throughout her life she was also a good money-maker for Captain Goodrich.

At the same time negotiations for the steamer *Comet* were underway, the wooden propeller *Wabash Valley* was purchased from Clinton Bank of Buffalo, New York. The deal was consummated on May 16, 1860, for the sum of $19,000.

Wabash Valley was then four years old. She had been built at Buffalo, New York, in 1856. The newest addition to the growing steamboat line was rated at 592 tons burden. In general appearance she was almost identical to the *Ogontz*. Her career with Goodrich was to be short-lived and perhaps her only claim to fame as a Goodrich boat was the fact that she proved to be "jinxed."

Her first assignment was the route from Manitowoc to the Green Bay ports. This was a new route for the Goodrich line and on July 4, 1860, under the command of Captain Douglas, *Wabash Valley* offered a special excursion trip to Green Bay. The purpose of the trip was to acquaint the passengers with the beauties of the Green Bay country. The regular fare was cut in half to encourage people to make the journey. In the announcement of the proposed trip Captain Douglas was referred to as a "whole-souled man and an experienced Captain." The excursion was well attended and the trip was made without incident. Later that summer *Wabash Valley* was caught in a bad storm and ended up on Thunder Bay Reef, suffering serious damage. After being refloated the hapless steamer was towed to Manitowoc for repairs.

In November of 1860, shortly after repairs were completed,

Captain Goodrich leased her to the D & M Railway for a few weeks as a replacement for their steamer *Detroit*.

On the night of November 21, the *Wabash Valley*, under the command of Captain Sanford Morgan, departed from Milwaukee at 8:30 P.M. on her first trip under the new lease to the railway company. At the time of departure the wind was light in a west-southwesterly direction. Captain Morgan shaped the course for Grand Haven, allowing 3/4 of a point leeway. At midnight he turned the ship over to his first mate and went below to get some rest.

During the night, due to the good weather, they made the anticipated running time. Shortly after 3:00 A.M. the mate made the light and then called Captain Morgan to the bridge. On arrival on the bridge, Captain Morgan inquired from the mate how the light was made and then shortly thereafter he himself saw the light flash. Later he thought the flash was caused by another vessel passing under his bows and going ashore. At this time the weather became quite thick due to snow and increasing winds, and a gale seemed to be in the making.

It turned out that the ship was actually off the entrance to Muskegon harbor instead of being near Grand Haven, their objective. The light at Muskegon was a fixed white light while the one marking the entrance to Grand Haven was a flashing light. Captain Evans of the *Comet* later made the statement that just a few nights before, he had approached Grand Haven and in the hour that he had observed the light, it had failed to flash even once.

In addition to the lighthouse at both places there were shore-stationed range lights. These were located quite similarly at both places but the range lights at Muskegon were not lighted during the summer. But having been lighted on this occasion added greatly to the deception. Said Captain Morgan, "I felt confident it was Grand Haven and was more assured by the range lights than anything else." If the captain had had any doubts he would have hauled off and awaited daylight in spite of the rising seas and the threat of gale-force winds.

The snow became heavier and as the steamer approached the shore the visibility dropped to almost zero. When the plight of the ship was discovered, it was too late to haul her off. The big seas carried her well up on the beach where she soon broke in two and became a total loss.

Captain Goodrich was among the thirty-six passengers that stormy, ill-fated night. All aboard were saved as was a lot of the cargo, most of which was stowed on her main deck. Captain Goodrich completely exonerated Captain Morgan and that famous gentleman went on to sail for Goodrich for many more years, becoming one of the most popular masters of his time. The

Courtesy: Marine Collection, Milwaukee Public Library

FREDERICK B. PABST — This popular captain of the *S. S. Comet* went on to fame in the brewing industry.

boilers, some machinery, and other salvageable equipment from *Wabash Valley* went into the construction of the new steamer *Sunbeam*. At the time of her loss *Wabash Valley* was valued at $28,000. Insurance paid to Captain Goodrich amounted to $14,831.67.

In 1861 Captain Goodrich purchased all of the interests in Goodrich's Steamboat Line held by George C. Drew. With this action he became the sole owner of the line, thus fulfilling his boyhood dream of owning his own steamboat company.

S.S. LADY ELGIN — The tragic loss of this elegant side-wheeler off Evanston, Illinois, on September 7, 1860, brought about a serious setback to the Lake passenger business.

Chapter Three

THE STEAMBOAT BUSINESS GROWS

Business on the Lakes continued to be good and the Goodrich line continued to gain momentum. While the loss of *Wabash Valley* was a serious blow, fortunately some of the financial losses were covered by insurance. The concentration of effort on the same routes was paying off for Captain Goodrich inasmuch as he was now enjoying the lion's share of the traffic volume from the ports he served. But then came the first major hurdle in the progress of the Goodrich company.

Passenger travel on the Lakes received a major setback with the tragic loss of the palatial steamer *Lady Elgin* during the stormy night of September 7, 1860. The accident occurred just a little north of Evanston, Illinois, about two miles off shore, in Lake Michigan.

On this fateful night the upbound *Lady Elgin* was rammed by a heavily loaded lumber schooner, downbound and sailing rapidly before the wind.

Lady Elgin, under the command of Captain Jack Wilson, had been chartered by an Irish political group from Milwaukee to attend a large political rally in Chicago. It was about midnight, on their return to Milwaukee, that the horrible collision took place.

The schooner *Augusta*, sailing without lights, plowed into *Lady Elgin* without any warning. Striking the steamer near the bow, the impact tore a huge hole in her hull just at the water line. *Lady Elgin* rapidly filled and sank beneath the waves of Lake

Michigan. Many went down with the ship to a watery grave. Other lives were claimed by the raging surf as they neared the beach on floating wreckage. A total of 287 persons were drowned in the rough waters of Lake Michigan on that terrible night.

The accident received country-wide attention in the press. Due to the political nature of the gathering there were many investigations and charges. Equally vehement counter-charges were made and the controversy made front-page copy in the press for a long time.

All of this publicity had a very sobering effect on the patrons of the Lake steamers. Passengers began to shun the boats and business fell off at an alarming rate. This slump in traffic caused the downfall of some of the smaller lines. The heavy freight traffic that Captain Goodrich had built up on his routes now stood him in good stead. It was the revenue from this freight traffic that permitted Goodrich steamers to maintain their regular schedules all through the serious slump in passenger patronage brought about by the sinking of *Lady Elgin*

For many years, prior to 1860, the Bates Shipyard at Manitowoc, Wisconsin, had built many splendid Great Lakes sailing schooners. This shipyard had been founded by Stephen Bates. Later in his career he was joined in this very successful venture by his son John Bates.

S.S. SUNBEAM — Originally built as *Victor*, her name was changed to *Sunbeam* when her original propulsion system was changed because it proved to be a failure.

Courtesy: Dowling Collection

It was at this time that Stephen Bates realized that the steamboat was rapidly gaining favor with Great Lakes ship operators and the fate of the Lake schooner was merely a matter of time. If the Bates Yard was to maintain its position in the shipbuilding trade, it was high time to gain some experience in the building of steamboats. Captain Goodrich was approached and as a result a contract to build a wooden propeller for the Goodrich line was awarded to the Bates Yard in late 1860.

The new steamer was christened *Union* upon her launching on April 10, 1861. Her length was 170 feet, beam 26 feet, draft 12 feet and she cost $19,000. Her first master was Captain William Dougall. The engines, machinery, and a lot of the fittings from *Ogontz* had been utilized in building her. *Union* proved to be a staunch little steamer but her career with Goodrich was a relatively short one. She was sold on August 1, 1862, to James H. Mead and J. F. Kirkland for $28,000. *Union* was one of the very few steamers disposed of by Captain Goodrich at a profit, in this case $9,000.

The building of *Union* by the Bates Yard was the beginning of what proved to be a long and close association between the Goodrich line and the Bates Yard and its various successors for many years to come.

As construction on *Union* progressed, Captain Goodrich was favorably impressed with the quality of the work being done by the Bates organization. Long before the construction was completed he awarded the Bates Yard another contract. This was for the construction of a wooden steamer of 400 tons burden. Originally called *Victor*, her name was shortly changed to *Sunbeam*. Building her cost Goodrich $50,000, and at the time of her launching she was heralded by the press as the most expensive and finest steamer on the Lakes.

The launching took place on a late afternoon. At the proper time the yard superintendent gave the signal to "cut away." The new ship shuddered and then started to move slowly down the greased ways. Suddenly she came to a stop and no amount of effort could get her to move that afternoon. Darkness overtook the project and the launching was postponed until the next morning. This hesitancy on the part of the new steamer to enter her element was almost like an omen of the fate that was to claim her on Lake Superior in the year 1863.

Victor was widely discussed by shipping men on the Great Lakes because of her unique and vastly different propulsion system. Known as the Whittaker propulsion system, it consisted of two side-mounted propellers. Captain Goodrich was noted for his zeal in trying new innovations on his steamers but unfortunately the Whittaker system did not prove to be a success and was soon re-

placed by paddle wheels powered by a vertical-beam engine with
the familiar walking beam on her hurricane deck. It was at this
time that she was renamed *Sunbeam*.

After the mechanical problems were solved, *Sunbeam* was
placed on a route from Chicago to Superior City, Wisconsin. As
she operated only in the summer season, this route called for
stops at all the west-shore ports, Mackinac Island, and the Soo.
Upon entering Lake Superior, *Sunbeam* was scheduled to call at
Eagle Harbor, Copper Harbor, Ontonagon and Superior City. She
began this new service on June 7, 1862. The steamers were the
only form of transportation to the vast Lake Superior country and
there were relatively few vessels making the long trip. Those
that did found themselves doing a capacity business at a handsome profit.

The first season the new Lake Superior route went well.
Sunbeam was able to operate until November 26 before the icy
hand of winter closed the route. Spring came late in 1863 and it
was not until July that the *Sunbeam* returned to Lake Superior.

Up to this point in the life of Goodrich's Steamboat Line,
Captain Goodrich had been most fortunate in not having any

S.S. SEABIRD — An artist's conception of the hapless steamer lost by fire
on Lake Michigan.

Courtesy: Marine Historical Collection, Milwaukee Public Library

major reverses such as the one that befell the owners of *Lady Elgin*. This fortunate and happy record came to an abrupt end as the tale of *Sunbeam* will reveal.

In the course of her regular schedule, *Sunbeam* departed from Ontonagon, Michigan, located on the south shore of Lake Superior, at 6:00 P.M. on Thursday evening, August 28, 1863. She was bound for Chicago and her next scheduled stop was to be Copper Harbor at the extreme northeast tip of the Keweenaw Peninsula. As the trim little side-wheeler made her way northeast, through the calm waters of Lake Superior, all was cheerful and cozy aboard. *Sunbeam* was commanded by Captain Dougall and her wheelsman was Charles Frazier of Superior, Wisconsin.

About 9:00 P.M. the wind swung into the northwest quarter and began to freshen at a rapid rate. The seas became heavier and began to slap hard against the hull, causing the ship to fall off her regular course. All night Captain Dougall fought to keep her head to the seas but the little steamer was taking a terrific pounding and it was getting more difficult to manage her. As the punishment began to take its toll on the straining hull, leaks started to appear. The water rose in the fireholds and finally, with her engines

Courtesy: Chicago Historical Society

S.S. PLANET — This ship was a leviathan in her time. Here she is shown at the Goodrich dock in Chicago in 1860.

stopped for the lack of steam, the ship lay dead in the water. In an attempt to give her steerage, the auxiliary sails were raised, but to no avail. Wallowing crazily in the troughs of the huge seas *Sunbeam* was indeed doomed. With reluctance Captain Dougall gave the order to abandon ship.

The crew managed to launch the two lifeboats that were still undamaged. Both were badly overloaded and this contributed greatly to the difficulty in keeping them from capsizing.

When the order to abandon came, Frazier was at his post in the wheelhouse. Because the steamer was completely on her beam ends, he had to break a window in the wheelhouse to escape. He found himself in the yawl boat when the chambermaid pleaded to be taken aboard. Frazier abandoned the yawl in favor of a large piece of the hurricane deck that floated by. He also retrieved a piece of the rigging and used the rope to tie himself to the piece of wreckage.

From this point of questionable vantage he saw the yawl boat capsize and its human cargo thrown into the raging, icy waters of Lake Superior. One by one, as their ability to cling to the overturned yawl diminished, his former shipmates slipped from sight and into their watery grave. Captain Dougall was among the occupants of the yawl who drowned while Frazier watched in helpless horror.

The next thirty hours were a test of endurance and a nightmare for Frazier. Often the waves would turn his improvised life raft completely over but by use of the ropes, salvaged from the rigging, he was able to reboard. Saturday afternoon the wind and the waves drove Frazier and his raft ashore among the boulders and rocks.

He managed to find shelter in a recess among the rocks where he was compelled to stay until Monday morning before the storm subsided sufficiently for him to leave his shelter.

Weak, benumbed, and nearly starved, he dragged himself back to the beach and started out to seek assistance. About midday on Monday he was found by a party of Chippewa Indians and two French explorers who were seeking survivors among the vast amount of floating wreckage.

Eventually Frazier made his way to Houghton where he obtained passage aboard the steamer *Planet* for Chicago. As the only person from the *Sunbeam* still alive, he was able to give Captain Goodrich a first-hand account of her tragic foundering.

The exact number of lives lost in the sinking of the *Sunbeam* is not known but it is generally believed to be about twenty-nine souls. Insurance on the lost *Sunbeam* netted Captain Goodrich $20,000. Inasmuch as the steamer was only a little over a year old, it can be readily seen that her loss presented a serious financial blow to Goodrich's Steamboat Line.

Lady Franklin, a wooden propeller of 342 tons, was built at Chicago by Jacob W. Banta, in the year 1861. In January of 1863 she was purchased by Captain Goodrich from John T. Edwards for $24,000. After less than two years of service in the Goodrich operation, she was sold to Captain Eber Ward in the process of a trade for the steamer *May Queen*. This transaction took place in May of 1865.

The wooden side-wheeler *Seabird* was purchased on April 21, 1863, from Captain E. Ward and others, for $36,000. First she was intended for use on the cross-lake route to Muskegon. This steamer of 638 tons burden was somewhat larger than the previous Goodrich boats. Built at Newport in 1859, she was four years old when transferred to the Goodrich fleet.

Her first assignment, under the Goodrich banner, was to the Chicago-Muskegon route. After only a month Captain Goodrich notified the city of Muskegon that he was discontinuing the service due to the shallow water caused by a sand bar at the harbor entrance. The steamers could not enter or leave the harbor without striking the bar and this made for a dangerous situation.

Even after the situation was corrected *Seabird* was kept primarily on the west-shore and Lake Superior routes where she became a well-known and popular sight.

In late March of 1868, the *Seabird* was brought out of winter lay-up at Manitowoc and made ready for the coming summer season. She was given a thorough going over and freshly painted inside and out.

During midmorning of April 8, 1868, she loaded passengers and freight for her first downbound trip of the new season. Her destination was Chicago with stops scheduled for Milwaukee, Racine, and Kenosha. Departure was at noon from Johnston's pier. Captain John Morris was in command.

A news item and a small ad in the *Milwaukee Sentinel* on the morning of April 8, 1868, announced that the side-wheel steamer *Seabird*, Captain John Morris, would leave at 7:00 P.M. for Chicago inaugurating a new service for the season of 1868. The fare was $1.00, which was less than by railway, and there was no charge for staterooms.

Everything went well on that first trip until *Seabird* was off Waukegan, a little after 6:00 A.M. on the morning of April 9. The night had been cold and the large stove in the main cabin had been kept going all night to provide some warmth and comfort for the passengers. As daylight came, the porter cleaned the fire in the cabin stove and then stepped to the rail to throw the still hot ashes over the side. Unfortunately he emptied his

S.S. ORION — This is a stern-view of the *Orion* at Manitowoc.

container into the wind and the hot ashes, fanned by the brisk northwesterly wind, blew back aboard and into the cargo stowed on the main deck. Some highly varnished tubs, packed in excelsior, were quickly ignited and the dread cry of "Fire!" swept the ship! As the flames made their way topside and into the cabin area they were fed by the newly painted woodwork and the entire steamer was soon engulfed in a mass of flame. There was no place for the terrified passengers and crew to go except over the side into the numbing cold waters of Lake Michigan. Survival in the 36-degree water lasted only a few minutes for most.

The first intimation of the disaster was received in Manitowoc late in the afternoon of April 9 in a telegram from Captain Goodrich to his brother J. M. Goodrich, who conducted a store on York Street near the west end of the present Hotel Manitowoc.

The telegraph office, which was located in Shepard's jewelry store on York Street, was in a small one-story building and was besieged for several days with relatives and friends of those who took passage on the *Seabird* from Manitowoc, anxiously awaiting news. Mr. Shepard, who ran the jewelry store, was also telegraph operator.

Only two passengers were saved. They were A. C. Chamberlain and Edwin Henneberry, both from Sheboygan.

The schooner *Cornelia*, with Captain Yates in command, and bound for Chicago, sighted the burning steamer when she was about eight miles northeast of Waukegan. He bore down on her immediately and put a yawl over the side. On arrival at the burning ship they discovered Chamberlain lashed to the stem. Henneberry was located on a plank at the stern.

After searching, without success, for additional survivors or bodies, *Cornelia* then squared away for Chicago, arriving there at 4:30 P.M.

Northeast winds blew the wreck towards Rockland Station where it sank about one mile from shore. Both survivors suffered from scorched and frozen hands. Captain Goodrich gave each survivor a lifetime pass on the Goodrich line. In 1898, Mr. Chamberlain and his wife were aboard the *Georgia* en route to Mackinac Island. Captain Edward Carus was in command. It was during this trip that he told the following story to Captain Carus:

"On that April morning, about half past six, I was out on deck when I saw the porter come out of the cabin with a scuttle of ashes and live wood coals which he threw overboard on the

S.S. NORTHWEST — This ship was launched in 1867 and sold the following year. She was considered the most palatial steamboat on the Great Lakes. Here she is shown docked in Chicago.

Courtesy: Chicago Historical Society

GOODRICH ADVERTISEMENT OF 1863

windward side. Some of the contents blew back on board, falling on the freight on the lower deck.

"In about fifteen minutes there was a cry of 'fire' and flames were issuing from the main deck. Immediately there was great confusion. The wind was aft of us and soon the fire spread to the forward end which made it impossible to get to the lifeboats. I had heard it said among the sailors in Sheboygan that the stem of a vessel is the last thing to burn on account of it being constructed of heavy oak timbers.

"With this in mind, I made my way forward. I found a piece of rope and climbed over the bow to the anchor stock, passed the rope through the anchor ring and lashed myself to the stem where I had a clear view and observed everything that was going on. Most men jumped overboard and were drowned, but the women and children were burned to death. I think there were six or seven families aboard, and the cries of the women and children and even the men powerless to help either themselves or those dependent on them, were heart-rending. It was the next thing to the horrors of death to have heard and seen what I saw. The roaring fire, the crashing timbers, and the escaping steam made a terrifying sound and a terrible sight."

Many of the 102 persons lost aboard the *Seabird* were from Manitowoc. The entire town went into mourning and a deputation committee was sent to the area to search for bodies and to arrange to return them to Manitowoc for burial.

The *Seabird* disaster was the tenth most serious Lake disaster caused by fire. Coming, as it did, just five years after the loss of *Sunbeam* on Lake Superior, it struck Goodrich's Steamboat Line another severe blow. For some unexplicable reason, *Seabird* carried no insurance and this fact added greatly to the seriousness of the financial loss involved.

As an aftermath to the *Seabird* disaster and its ensuing claims and law suits, the Goodrich Transportation Company sought limitation of liability action in the United States Circuit Court at Chicago on June 19, 1873.

The plea was heard by Judge Blodgett who refused, at that time, to pass on the amount of liability. As provided for under the terms of the Limitation of Liability Act of 1851, the Judge appointed appraisers to determine the amount.

Then the Goodrich Transportation Company petitioned the court to limit its liabilities in Circuit Court at Chicago, on July 30, 1873. The court then handed down a ruling limiting Goodrich's liability to the value of the vessel at the time of the tragedy which amounted to $22,000.

About this time the need for larger steamers with much better and more comfortable passenger accommodations began

Courtesy: Yates Collection, Muskegon County Museum

FREIGHT HOUSE AT MUSKEGON — A shore-side view of the Goodrich
docks at Muskegon.

to make itself felt. Always alert to the whims of the traveling
public, Captain Goodrich began to cast about for a larger steamer,
one that would incorporate the more elegant public rooms and
generally provide an improvement in passenger comfort. This
was quite a contrast to the thinking that prevailed when the
staunch little *Huron* was built but still a far cry from the inter-
pretation of the term "passenger comfort" as built into Goodrich
steamers in the years to come.

Again Captain E. B. Ward was his salvation. In June of
1863 the steamship *Planet* was purchased from Captain Ward
and Mr. Owen Patten for $38,000. Rated at 994 tons burden,
Planet was a leviathan for her time and was nearly twice as large
as any previous steamer used by Captain Goodrich. The press of
the west-shore ports was loud in its praise of Captain Goodrich
when he announced that *Planet* would be assigned to those routes.

Planet had been built in the Ward Yard at Newport in 1855
and was considered to be one of the finest steamers afloat. A
side-wheeler, she was fast, easily handled, and actually ideally
situated for the west-shore and Lake Superior routes. *Planet* gave
a good account of herself during her life as a Goodrich boat. In
1866 Captain Goodrich decided that she had outlived her usefulness and she was dismantled in June of that year. Her engines
and some of the machinery and fittings went into the new steamer

THE GOODRICH MUSKEGON DOCK—Built by A. W. Goodrich in 1895, this site was later known as "The Mart." Today it is used by the *Milwaukee Clipper.*

Northwest. Her hull was converted into a tow barge at the same time.

The years 1860 to 1865 were trying years for those engaged in the steamboat business on the Lakes. In addition to the tragedies that befell the Lake steamers and that slowed patronage seriously, public unrest over the question of slavery swept the nation. First the threat of Civil War and then the War itself hung over the country like a vast storm cloud. Business suffered and investors were reluctant to start new ventures.

Shipping fell off at an alarming rate and the steamship operators suffered accordingly. Many of the smaller lines and single-ship operators had to curtail operations and some had to quit altogether. During these trying times Captain Goodrich was forced to give up any ideas of future ship acquisitions and to concentrate all his time and effort in finding a sufficient volume of traffic to keep his existing fleet in operation. It was not until 1865 that the economic situation improved enough for Captain Goodrich to turn his thoughts again to further expansion and additional ship acquisitions.

In glancing back over his progress from the founding of Goodrich's Steamboat Line in 1856 to the beginning of the year 1865, the captain certainly must have found his accomplishments most reassuring. Counting the scrapping of *Ogontz* in favor of

Union, the total number of steamers flying the Goodrich flag was eight. Both of the west-shore routes and the cross-lake route were, by this time, firmly established. Manitowoc, the hailing port, was rapidly becoming the base of operations, maintenance and ship repair. Even at this early date, some of the steamers were placed in winter storage in the river. By any standards, Goodrich's Steamboat Line had made remarkable progress in the first seven years of its existence.

Steamer acquisition was resumed with the purchase of *May Queen* in May, 1865. This wooden side-wheeler was built at Trenton, Michigan, in 1853 by Captain Ward. Her cost to Goodrich was $34,000 in cash and the *Lady Franklin* in trade. *May Queen* did not last long with her new owner. On September 17 of the same year she was wrecked off Sheboygan. There was no loss of life, and after the accident she was pumped out and towed to Milwaukee for repairs. On January 13, 1866, while tied up at a shipyard on Jones Island, Milwaukee, she caught fire and burned to the water's edge. Declared to be junk, her engine was removed and later used to power the new steamer *Manitowoc.* The burned-out hull was then sold to Galen Eastman for use as a barge for the sum of $600.

Following his usual pattern, Captain Goodrich then purchased the wooden side-wheeler *Michigan* on July 17, 1865, at a cost of $6,000. This older steamer was built in Detroit in 1847. Bought expressly for her good engine, she was immediately scrapped and her power plant used in the new steamer *Orion.* The hull of the *Michigan* was converted into a tow barge and sold.

Orion was a wooden side-wheeler of 495 tons. She was launched at Manitowoc during the winter of 1865-1866. All outfitting was completed at Manitowoc and the new vessel delivered to Captain Goodrich in late March of 1866. Built at a cost of $68,000, *Orion* was a fine, dependable steamer and a welcome addition to the growing Goodrich fleet.

The first master assigned to the new *Orion* was Captain John Richardson. Prior to coming to the Goodrich company, he had spent twelve years with the Northern Transportation Company. His last command for that line had been on the steamer *Odgensburg.* Captain Goodrich considered himself most fortunate to have attracted such a well-known and experienced master for the new ship.

Originally it had been announced that Captain Thomas Butlin would sail the *Orion.* Captain Goodrich later decided to have Captain Butlin take full charge of the task of transferring the engine, boilers, and machinery from the burned-out *May Queen* to the new steamer *Manitowoc.*

On October 16, 1870, *Orion* was crossing Lake Michigan

when she was overtaken by a storm of full gale proportions. In trying to gain the harbor entrance at Grand Haven, she stranded on a bar and was completely wrecked. There was a total of sixty-one persons aboard and fortunately all were saved.

Her cargo, valued at $20,000, was a complete loss. The total loss of cargo and vessel was placed at $50,000. Her fine engines and machinery were salvaged and used to power the new side-wheeler *Muskegon*. The total insurance claim paid to Goodrich amounted to $24,000.

Shortly after the Civil War the Bates interests at Manitowoc were taken over by Greenleaf S. Rand. The former Bates Yard continued to be the source of some of the finest vessels built on the Great Lakes, under the name G. S. Rand Shipyard. Regardless of the change in name and management a very fine relationship between Captain Goodrich and this yard was continued over the years.

In the spring of 1867 the new side-wheeler *Northwest* was launched at Manitowoc. Built by G. S. Rand, this elegant steamer cost Captain Goodrich $117,000 and she was conceded to be the finest steamboat on the Great Lakes by all shipping men. Of 1110 tons burden, she was very large and no expense had been spared on her passenger accommodations and public rooms. Strangely enough, this largest and finest steamer Captain Goodrich had ever built or acquired up to that time was destined to be in his fleet for only one year.

In 1868, the *Morning Star* of the Detroit & Cleveland Steam Navigation Company was lost in Lake Erie following a collision with a sailing vessel. The *Morning Star* and the *R. N. Rice* had been running opposite each other on the Detroit-Cleveland route. The loss of *Morning Star* was a serious blow to the D & C Line and an immediate replacement was a most urgent matter.

The officials of D & C made a hurried trip to Chicago where they made an appeal for assistance to Captain Goodrich. This meeting resulted in the sale of *Northwest,* his pride and flagship, to the D & C Line for $115,000. For the next eighteen years *Northwest* ran between Cleveland and Detroit. In 1885 she was sold to the White Star Line, given another engine, and renamed *Greyhound*. She continued to sail under the Star Line flag until she was scrapped in 1902. This was a truly fine record for a steamer that was a real tribute to her builders and the lines that operated her for thirty-five years.

By now the reader must begin to recognize in Captain Goodrich a man that had unusual knowledge of fine steam engines and their potential worth. Time after time, as this narrative unfolds, it will be noted that Goodrich often purchased steamers merely to acquire their good engines and sundry machinery. This equipment would then be placed in new vessels and render reliable and dependable service for many years to come. It is a known fact that if a reciprocating steam engine is given proper maintenance and care its life span is almost indefinite because worn parts can be replaced as the need occurs.

One of the very early pioneers to settle in the Muskegon area was Martin Ryerson. Born on a farm near Patterson, New Jersey, on January 6, 1818, he migrated to Michigan in 1834. His first stop in the Wolverine State was in Detroit where he sought employment to bolster his depleted finances. He finally reached Grand Rapids in September of 1834. He remained there until 1836 and then journeyed to Muskegon. There he engaged in trading with the Indians. Later he married an Indian wife.

By 1843 he owned a large boarding house which was the scene of the first Protestant church service in that part of the state. In 1845 Ryerson and Knickerbocker became sawmill owners by buying out T. Newell.

He was among the earliest people to commence the steamboat passenger business and owned two steamers, the *G. J. Truesdell* and the *Ottawa*. These two wooden propellers were used as

Courtesy: C. P. Labadie

S.S. TRUESDELL — A rare photo of the former Reyerson steamer before she was sold to Goodrich in 1867.

combination lumber and passenger boats and operated in competition to Goodrich between Muskegon and Chicago.

In March of 1867 Martin Ryerson sold his steamboat business to Captain Goodrich. The *Truesdell* was sold for $50,000 and *Ottawa* for $20,000. His firm, at this point, was known as Ryerson & Morris.

Truesdell was built in Chicago in 1864. She was rated at 498 tons burden and considered to be a fine steamer in every way. During the winter of 1867-1868 she was extensively remodeled at the Rand Yard at Manitowoc.

The purpose of the remodeling was to convert *Truesdell* into a very comfortable night boat. Up to now the passenger comfort of the overnight traveler had been badly neglected by steamship operators. After her overhaul and remodeling the 158-foot steamer was placed in overnight service on the west-shore routes as an experiment to find out the public reaction to her new accommodations.

Ottawa had been built at Cleveland, Ohio, in 1854. Rated at 578 tons, she was slightly larger than *Truesdell*. Although ten years older than *Truesdell*, she, too, was in fine condition and considered a very sturdy and capable steamer.

Right after her acquisition she, too, was sent to the Rand Yard and given similar treatment to that accorded *Truesdell*. When the work on these two propellers was completed they were considered as having the most comfortable overnight accommodations of any steamers on the Lakes.

After the complete overhaul and rebuilding, *Ottawa* also was placed in overnight service on the west-shore routes. The acceptance of both steamers in their new overnight service was closely watched by Captain Goodrich. He was strongly convinced that the traveling public had a need and a desire for more such service. He was certain that the improved cabins and general accommodations of these two small propellers would vastly increase the patronage of night travelers. Just how accurate his assumptions were and just how much of an impact this experiment had on the traveling public and future policies of the Goodrich line is revealed as we move through the story of the Red-Stack line.

The first dock used in 1859 at Muskegon was the Mill Dock of Chauncey Davis on East Western Avenue at the foot of Cedar Street. Other passenger steamers used the Mill Dock of Ryerson, Hill, on Western Avenue at Pine Street.

In May of 1863, Captain Goodrich notified the city of Muskegon that his steamers had discontinued departures from that city for Grand Haven and Chicago, because the water depth at the entrance to Muskegon Lake from Lake Michigan was too shallow. This condition was caused by sand bars.

S.S. ALPENA — This artist's conception of the loss of the *Alpena* appeared in the *Muskegon Chronicle* in October, 1890.

Other steamers began to avoid Muskegon for the same reason. A group of local businessmen organized a company to improve Muskegon harbor. Slabs were obtained from local lumber mills and used to construct two piers that extended into Lake Michigan. The sand bars that caused the difficulty were then dredged and the entrance to Muskegon harbor was again available to all steamers regardless of their draft.

In 1865 Goodrich moved its operation to a dock known as Central Wharf. Its ships continued to use Central Wharf until 1894. During that year A. W. Goodrich purchased the former Blodgett & Byrne fill property on the Lake front near the Amazon Knitting Mill, on a street subsequently named Goodrich Street. On this new location Mr. Goodrich erected a new warehouse and office. The new docks were formally opened on June 25, 1895. This site served as the Muskegon headquarters for Goodrich for the rest of its history. After that the site became known as the "Mart" and today this same dock serves the *Milwaukee Clipper* engaged in cross-lake service from Muskegon to Milwaukee.

The next steamer to be acquired by Captain Goodrich was *Alpena*. A wooden side-wheeler of 653 tons burden, she was built by Ward at Marine City in 1866. Goodrich purchased her from Gardner, Ward & Gardner, on April 10, 1868, for $80,000. The tragic loss of *Alpena* on October 15, 1880, is told in detail in a later chapter of our story.

The last newcomer to the Goodrich flag, in 1868, was the wooden side-wheeler *Manitowoc*. Built during the winter of 1867-1868, by G. S. Rand, she cost $78,000. She was rated at 570 tons burden, was 212 feet in length, had a beam of 29 feet with 52 feet over the guards and a depth of 14 feet. Powered by the low-pressure vertical-beam engine that had been removed from *May Queen*, she was considered an elegant steamer in every respect.

Manitowoc was commissioned on April 10, 1868, and commanded by Captain B. Sweeney. Considered quite fast the new ship was placed on the Chicago-Milwaukee route. On April 24, 1868, she made the southbound run from Milwaukee to Chicago in six hours and thirty minutes. Two days later she clipped thirty minutes from this running time, making the same trip in exactly six hours. Her fastest running time on this route was made on July 2, 1868, when she made the southbound trip in five hours and forty-five minutes. This record stood for many years until the advent of the larger and more modern steamships.

S.S. ALPENA — En route from Grand Haven to Chicago, the *Alpena* was caught in a bad storm and was lost with all eighty-six lives on board.

Courtesy: Dowling Collection

As time went on, it was found that *Manitowoc* was not a good seaboat. The basic fault was the ratio between her beam and her length. She was too narrow for her length and this made it hard to handle her in any kind of sea. Her masters also complained that she was unpredictable and hard to manage in tight places. In an attempt to correct this fault she was widened with a bustle in 1869. This extra width, being above the water line, did not help her much and she retained her reputation as a poor seaboat.

On May 9, 1868, *Manitowoc* made her first call at Kewaunee, on a special trip with a full load of new settlers taken aboard at Chicago. The spring and summer of this particular year were noted for the large number of Bohemian immigrants the Goodrich line handled from Chicago to Manitowoc, Two Rivers, and Kewaunee.

In 1873 there was a bad fire aboard *Manitowoc*. Her interior and topsides were badly damaged and it was decided not to repair the cranky side-wheeler. In 1874 she was ordered dismantled. Her boilers and the reliable vertical-beam engine, rebuilt by Fletcher in 1874, were transferred to the *Chicago*, then being built by Rand at Manitowoc.

After dismantling, the hull of *Manitowoc* was converted into a barge by the same name. It was then sold for $18,000.

This chapter brings us to the conclusion of the first twelve years in the history of Goodrich's Steamboat Line. Except for his brief partnership with George C. Drew, Captain A. E. Goodrich was the sole operator during this period. The progress he made is nothing short of amazing. His record of steamers purchased, constructed, and traded, to say nothing of the routes and volume of both freight and passenger traffic developed in this relatively short span of time, speaks clearly of his tireless effort and sheer genius. By this time Captain Goodrich was looked upon by all in the steamboat business on the Lakes as a respected and fearless competitor.

MILWAUKEE RIVER SCENE — An artist's conception of the steamer *Sheboygan* near the Goodrich dock at the foot of Michigan Street in 1870.

Courtesy: Marine Collection, Milwaukee Public Library

Chapter Four

THE FOUNDING OF THE
GOODRICH TRANSPORTATION COMPANY

T HE YEAR 1864 WAS AN IMPORTANT ONE IN THE LIFE
of Captain Goodrich. In the previous year he had met and since
then courted a very beautiful and lovely young lady from Milwaukee by the name of Rosamond Frances Whaling. During the
late summer of this significant year Rosamond gave her consent
and the couple announced their engagement. The beautiful wedding, a social highlight in Milwaukee, took place in the Episcopal
Church on November 30, 1864.

After the honeymoon, Captain Goodrich took his charming
bride to Chicago to live. He carried her over the threshold at
1474 Michigan Avenue, and this address remained the captain's
home as long as he lived.

A total of three children were born to this very happy
marriage. The first, a daughter named Grace, was born in 1865.
The second daughter, Gertrude, was born in 1867. The year 1867
proved to be a sad and tragic year for the captain and Rosamond,
for in that year their daughter Grace was taken ill and passed
away at the tender age of two years. This sad event was quickly
followed by the death of their second daughter at the age of only
two months. This tragic turn of events was a severe blow to the
vivacious Rosamond and her illustrious husband.

In the early part of 1867, Captain Goodrich purchased a
yard and some docks at Manitowoc. By this action the Goodrich
Yards, which for so many years were the shore base of opera-

tions and maintenance work for the Goodrich steamers, were established. Repair shops were built on the same site in 1896.

During the winter of 1867-1868 Captain Goodrich took time to reflect on his progress and to contemplate the problem that lay ahead. Up to this point he had operated alone and had built up Goodrich's Steamboat Line to a very secure position in the Lake Michigan trade. While the total number of steamers actually in operation was eight, he had purchased, constructed, sold and scrapped the amazing total of sixteen steamships in the past twelve years!

His steamboat line had survived the recession of 1857, the slump in passenger travel following the loss of the *Lady Elgin* in 1860, the ravages of the War between the States and the sinkings of *Sunbeam* and *Seabird* with their combined loss of well over one hundred lives. In spite of these many and serious setbacks, Goodrich's Steamboat Line was, in 1867, in a good financial position.

Business throughout the country was good. Travel and shipping on the Lakes was booming after the Civil War. Lake steamers were now being built larger, more palatial and of course more expensively.

In addition to the very successful operation of his steamboat line, Captain Goodrich had also been fortunate in some of his other investments and ventures. He had, for example, done quite well in real estate in fast-developing western Michigan. Numbered among his holdings was some very desirable improved land in the vicinity of Grand Haven and Muskegon. He also owned land in the St. Joseph area.

As the volume of business grew, it became increasingly apparent to Captain Goodrich that he would have to provide a more formidable organization to handle the operation of his company. This was especially true if he were to have any time at all for his other interests.

After considering all the angles, Captain Goodrich reached the conclusion that the formation of a formal corporation would be the most logical way to secure stable management and to give his loyal staff an opportunity of sharing in some of the profits as shareholders.

No doubt the decision to incorporate was influenced by the fact that the state of Wisconsin on January 23, 1868, had passed the Wisconsin Incorporation Bill.

Captain Goodrich carefully planned and engineered the formation of a new corporation known as the Goodrich Transportation Company. In the course of organizing the new company, Captain Goodrich was most fortunate in being able to interest his Ward Line friend, Captain Thomas G. Butlin. After listening carefully to Goodrich's plans and ideas for the development of the new company, he decided to purchase a block of stock for himself and continue as an employee. This was the beginning of a long and very close relationship between these two great Lake captains.

Goodrich Transportation Company was organized under the laws of the state of Wisconsin with authorized capital of $500,000. The charter was issued on April 18, 1868, and the first officers of the new corporation were as follows:

Captain Albert E. Goodrich, President
Joseph M. Goodrich, Vice President
W. H. Wright, Secretary and Treasurer
Captain T. G. Butlin, Superintendent

The corporate offices were designated as Chicago and the port-of-hail was officially registered with the Federal Government as Manitowoc, Wisconsin. At the time of incorporation the Goodrich Transportation Company fleet consisted of the steamships *Alpena, Comet, G. J. Truesdell, Manitowoc, Northwest,* and *Ottawa.*

The house flag then adopted consisted of a pure-white dovetail pennant with the initials "G.T.Co." shown in the same bright red used on the stacks of the proud steamers. It was also decided at this time that the standard ship colors were to be a black hull to the main deck and white above, including white cabins and topsides. The stack was to be bright red with a large black band at the very top.

In addition to the founding of the Goodrich Transportation Company on April 18, another very important and happy event took place in the year 1868. On November 24 Rosamond Goodrich delivered a bouncing baby boy to the proud captain. This only son was named Albert Whaling Goodrich. He was destined to play a long and important role in the future history of the Goodrich line.

The arrival of Albert did much to help ease the painful loss of the couple's two daughters the year before. Albert W. Goodrich was the last child born to Rosamond and the captain. Like all fathers, Goodrich was delighted beyond description that he now had a son that could carry on the Goodrich name and some day take over the helm and the destinies of the Red-Stack fleet. From this point forward much of the captain's planning and thinking was directed toward that day when his son and heir would take over.

In March of 1869, the wooden propeller *St. Joseph* was purchased from Irving Pearce for the sum of $26,000. This ship had been built by Hitchcock & Gibson at Buffalo, New York, in 1867. She was a small steamer, being rated at 474 tons burden. Appar-

Courtesy: H. H. Bennett Studios

S.S. SHEBOYGAN — This photo was taken shortly after her launching in 1869. Notice the deer antlers between her stacks.

ently she was originally purchased for her machinery but evidently this feature of the little steamer did not come up to expectations because she was merely retained by Goodrich in her original condition. Her record with Goodrich was quite uneventful and the ship was sold to Charles Chamberlin and others, from Detroit, on April 22, 1873. The selling price was $30,000 and this was one more instance when a Goodrich steamer was sold for more than had been paid for her.

All was not always peaceful and tranquil on the early steamers. On April 4, 1873, Louisa Fairman instituted an action of trespass suit against the Goodrich Transportation Company to the amount of $10,000.

The complaint alleged that while a passenger aboard the Goodrich steamer *St. Joseph,* en route from Milwaukee to St. Joseph, Michigan, she was the sole occupant of a stateroom. An unknown person, or persons, entered the stateroom and violently assaulted and seriously injured Miss Fairman. A total of $500 was stolen from her and her doctor bills amounted to $400. Evidently this suit was settled out of court as no statement of a verdict in the matter appears in the records.

The second ship acquired in 1869 was the new *Sheboygan.* Built at Manitowoc by Rand, she was a splendid, large side-wheeler rated at 625 tons burden. The new steamer was 220 feet in length and had two tall stacks mounted side by side. After launching, she was towed to Detroit for installation of her engine, boilers, machinery, and cabins. Her boilers and engine had been salvaged from *Garden City*, a former D & C steamer that foundered on Martin's Reef at the top of Lake Huron. The cost of completing the ship was $93,000 and she was widely acclaimed to be the finest side-wheeler of her day.

Sheboygan had a long and very successful career as a Goodrich steamer. Used almost entirely on the west-shore routes, she was a familiar and welcome sight in such Lake ports as Racine, Milwaukee, Port Washington, Sheboygan, Manitowoc, and Two Rivers. Some time during her colorful career, a large Indian head was mounted on her hurricane deck. The motion of the walking beam activated a large tomahawk held by the ferocious-looking Indian. This feature attracted amused attention wherever she went.

Typical of the local service provided by the steamers to the townspeople of the ports they served was a news item that appeared in the *Manitowoc Herald* in 1870. This article described the fact that the officers of the steamers *Sheboygan* and *Manitowoc* had been bringing in the Milwaukee papers as an extra service. The article went on to give public thanks to these men because by their effort the Milwaukee newspapers were available in Manitowoc twelve hours ahead of the best delivery service by mail.

Sheboygan was not only a good money-maker for Goodrich

S.S. *SHEBOYGAN* — This photo shows the ship after the all-black color scheme for the hull was adopted in 1890.

Courtesy: Henry Barkhausen

but a very lucky steamer as well. Throughout her entire career she was never involved in a really serious accident or one involving loss of life to either her crew or passengers. One of her more serious mishaps occurred in 1898 when she went aground south of the entrance to the Sturgeon Bay canal in a dense fog. When she was finally hauled off, it was found necessary to send her to dry dock at Manitowoc for repairing her extensive hull damage.

Near the end of her career, July 17, 1913, to be exact, the reliable old side-wheeler was approaching the entrance to the Chicago River when she became involved in a collision with her sister ship *Iowa*. A dense fog was the cause and while the *Iowa* eventually sank at her dock, *Sheboygan* sustained relatively light damage to her bow.

Winter after winter *Sheboygan* was laid up at Manitowoc. Summer after summer the gallant side-wheeler moved in and out of the port with clocklike regularity until she became a very definite part of the community life.

In 1912 she was taken out of regular passenger service and was used for freight and as a stand-by steamer. For much of the next two years she remained moored in the river at Manitowoc. On July 10, 1914, the old steamer was turned over to the Manitowoc Metal Company for dismantling. Her engines, boilers, paddle wheels and everything else of value were removed from her

S.S. SHEBOYGAN — Here the proud steamer is entering the harbor of Sheboygan, the city for which she was named, in tow of the tug *Peter Reiss*, in 1907.

Courtesy: Marine Collection, Milwaukee Public Library

S.S. SHEBOYGAN — Scene of the fiery end of the staunch old steamer as the torch was applied to her on September 24, 1914, after having served the Goodrich company for forty-five years.

hull. It was then decided to burn the hull and what remained of her topsides. On Thursday, September 24, 1914, the proud old side-wheeler *Sheboygan* was "buried."

The tug *Arctic*, under command of Captain B. N. Sniffin, took *Sheboygan* in tow as she had so many times when the steamer was active. As the tug towed the old ship out of the harbor for the last time, factory whistles, locomotives and craft in the river bid farewell by blowing the Great Lakes salute of three long and two short blasts. To this sincere salute the *Arctic* dutifully replied. An air of mourning settled over the city of Manitowoc as the former queen of Lake Michigan was towed to a point two miles north of Manitowoc harbor, beached, and then set afire.

The details of applying the torch were handled by Mr. William Schroeder, foreman of the carpenter shop, under the direction of Captain D. M. Cochrane, operating superintendent of the Goodrich line.

Set afire at 4:25 P.M. the flames raged for most of the night. Captains of the car ferries that arrived from Ludington and Frankfort reported the flames could be seen in the sky from fifty miles away.

A. W. Goodrich, accompanied by Harry W. Thorp, then general superintendent, headed a party of Goodrich officials who made the trip from Chicago to witness the demise of one of the best steamers ever to serve the line.

The building of the wooden side-wheeler *Corona* by Rand, at Manitowoc early in 1870, was a significant milestone in Goodrich history. *Corona* was the first Goodrich ship built specifically for service to the east shore of Lake Michigan. Her first assignment was to the Milwaukee-St. Joseph route and marked the captain's return to the scene of his earlier activity as a master for the Ward Line.

Built at a cost of $42,000 this very handsome, single-stack steamer was equipped with a vertical-beam engine. She was 172 feet long, had a beam of 44 feet 6 inches over the guards and was rated at 470 tons burden. Her engine was from the steamer *Comet*. At the time *Comet* was built this engine was already second hand, and had been bought by Captain Goodrich from a source on the east coast!

Corona continued on the Milwaukee-St. Joseph route until 1876. She was then leased to the Flint & Pere Marquette Railway. The F. & P.M. used her in cross-lake traffic and this was the forerunner of the present Chesapeake & Ohio fleet of car ferries that operate from Ludington and Milwaukee, Manitowoc and Kewaunee today.

When the charter to the railway company expired, *Corona* was returned to the Goodrich company. She was then placed on the west-shore route and remained there until the close of the season in 1891. On January 30, 1892, she was sold to John W. Ward of Chicago for $7,500.

In 1893, under the ownership of John Ward, *Corona* carried thousands of sightseers from downtown Chicago to Jackson Park, the scene of the Columbian Exposition. After her tour of service as a World's Fair steamer, she was sold for service out of Buffalo, New York. She was used as an excursion steamer on Lake Erie with some success. The gallant old side-wheeler caught fire while at her dock in Tonwanda, New York, in 1898. The fire had a head start before being discovered and as a result *Corona* was a total loss.

No new steamer had a shorter career with Goodrich than the fine-looking *Navarino*. Launched at Manitowoc just one year after *Corona*, she was a wooden propeller built by Rand at a cost of $60,104. Construction took place during the winter of 1870-1871. Rated at 761 tons burden, the *Navarino* was 184 feet in length, had a 35-foot beam and a draft of 12 feet 6 inches. Somewhat larger than most propellers before her, she was the forerunner of the larger and more comfortable class of screw ships that were to follow. She was placed in active service on April 8, 1871. Her first assignment was to the west-shore route and Captain Alexander Clark was her first commander.

Sunday evening, October 8, 1871, was unusually warm for the time of year. Chicago, like most of the Midwest, was tinder dry, the result of a prolonged summer drought.

Courtesy: Beeson's Marine Directory

GOODRICH ADVERTISEMENT — This advertisement appeared in the *Marine Directory* of 1888.

About 8:30 P.M. fire broke out in the small barn of an Irish family by the name of O'Leary. The O'Learys lived at 137 DeKoven Street in the Bohemian quarter of the sprawling wooden city. This location is, today, just east of Taylor and Halsted Streets.

Fanned by a strong southwest wind that grew in velocity as the fire spread, the wall of destruction moved from the southwest section of the city in a northeasterly direction. When the fire reached, and then finally leaped across, the Chicago River, it took with it the bridges and ignited the ships in the river itself.

The harbor tugs did brave and yeoman service in towing all shipping free of the river and out into the safety of Lake Michigan. After the bridges failed, the tugs served as ferry boats to transport panic-stricken persons to the north bank of the river, as they fled ahead of the inferno.

As the fire moved eastward, toward morning on Monday, Captain Goodrich became concerned about the company records and the families of his Chicago staff. There were two Goodrich steamers in the river at the Goodrich dock as the rising sun dimly made its appearance through a wall of smoke, highlighted by large, flying, burning embers. One was *Navarino*, under the command of Captain Clark, and the other vessel was *Skylark*.

S.S. CORONA — Here she is seen approaching the Manitowoc harbor. Note the lumber-laden schooners in the background.

Courtesy: Henry Barkhausen

Courtesy: Henry Barkhausen

S.S. CORONA—This ship was built especially for the Milwaukee-St. Joseph route. She was a very dependable and fine steamer.

The harbor tug *Magnolia*, under command of twenty-five-year-old Captain Joseph Gilson, had worked like a beaver through the long night of holocaust and terror. As the fire threatened Elevators A and B on the south bank of the river just east of the Michigan Central Depot, the tug and her fearless captain had succeeded in towing two freighters from their berths in the slips at the elevators and out into the Lake.

Magnolia then proceeded to the *Navarino* who was now in the direct path of the flames. A line was passed to her, and the tow downstream to the Lake was begun. In trying to tow *Navarino* as rapidly as possible, she ran aground on the north side of the channel, directly in front of Rathbone's Stove Works, which was the next structure east of Kirk's Soap Factory. Try as he might, Captain Gilson could not dislodge *Navarino*. Later she was scuttled to prevent her from floating free and becoming a blazing torch as the current carried her toward the Lake. Shortly thereafter she caught fire and burned at the water's edge.

Captain Goodrich ordered all the company records, the families of his staff, office furniture, and many unscheduled passengers

Courtesy: Father Edward J. Dowling, S.J.

S.S. NAVARINO — This is a reproduction of a painting of the ship by Father Edward Dowling, S.J. The ship was lost in the Chicago Fire.

aboard *Skylark*. Captain Gilson and his somewhat charred *Magnolia* then managed to tow her safely into the open Lake.

The Michigan Central Depot, Elevator A, the Goodrich wooden office building, the freight sheds, and the docks were all consumed by the flames. Only a small part of the loss of the office, sheds, and docks was covered by insurance. The insurance claim on the loss of *Navarino* amounted to $16,112.

Like so many Chicagoans that were faced with the complete destruction of their property and the loss of their businesses that had gone up in smoke and flame, Captain Goodrich refused to be discouraged by his losses. Compared with many firms in Chicago, he felt that the Goodrich company was not too bad off.

The office and freight sheds were soon rebuilt from the shipload after shipload of Michigan pine that poured into the stricken city. The boilers, engine and machinery from the burned and sunken *Navarino* were salvaged. The hull was raised and sold for use as a barge. The salvaged equipment was used to power a new propeller, *Menominee*, built at Manitowoc the following year.

THE GREAT CHICAGO FIRE — This is a reproduction of a painting of the great fire. The artist made a mistake in the direction of the wind. The flames actually swept toward, rather than away from, the Lake.

On February 1, 1871, the small propeller *Skylark* was purchased from Thomas L. Parker for the sum of $6,000. Rated at only 91 gross tons and already quite old when purchased, having been built in 1857, the only purpose of acquiring her was for using her machinery in a new steamer.

During the season of 1871 *Skylark* was used between Chicago, Kenosha, Racine, and Milwaukee. Considering the yeoman service rendered the Goodrich interests by *Skylark* during the Chicago fire, her purchase price of only $6,000 turned out to be a prudent investment!

The performance of *Skylark* during the season of 1871 convinced Captain Goodrich that her engine was all he had anticipated. At the close of the season she was laid up at Manitowoc. On November 26, 1871, she was ordered dismantled.

Her engine, fittings and some machinery went into a new hull being built by Rand during the winter of 1871-1872. This new steamer was 142 feet in length, had a beam of 28 feet and a draft of 9 feet 6 inches. Her cost was $42,204 and upon launching she was christened *Oconto*. Rated at 535 tons burden, she was somewhat smaller than *Navarino* and *Menominee*.

Courtesy: H. H. Bennett Studios

S.S. OCONTO — Here the *Oconto* is seen at the Goodrich dock in the Milwaukee River.

She was placed in service in April, 1872, and assigned to the west-shore route where she proved to be a big asset in the Goodrich bid for the Lake Michigan tourist trade.

On September 20, 1880, *Oconto* was under the command of Captain F. W. Spafford. Raymond Flint was chief engineer and Edward Carus wheelsman. *Oconto* was making a scheduled stop at the city of Green Bay. As she made her way to her dock, she passed through the Cherry Street bridge. Right then fire broke out in the Astor Planing Mill. Fanned by a gale from the southeast the flames quickly spread and were soon raging out of control. A strip two blocks wide extending from the Fox River to the East River and containing over seventy buildings was completely consumed. The toll included fifty-nine homes, a school, churches, stores, a bank, and a vinegar factory!

The population of Green Bay was up in arms as sparks from the stack of *Oconto* were blamed for starting the conflagration. Lawsuits were filed and the litigation lasted for nearly six years with the Goodrich Transportation Company the victor.

In 1878 *Oconto* blew a cylinder head while on the Lake. The engineer cut a replacement from a gang plank and fitted it sufficiently tight for the ship to proceed to the next port. A fine example of how resourceful the early Lake sailors had to be to keep their steamers underway.

There were few times during the life of *Oconto* that she drew notice for anything but steady, faithful and dependable service. Testimony to her seaworthiness was the fact that she was on the Lake the night that the *Alpena* was lost. A few bouts with Lake Michigan ice gained her mention in the press but for the most part, like *Sheboygan,* she just became an institution and a household word among the west-shore ports that she served so many years.

S.S. OCONTO—An old photograph of the *Oconto* taking passengers aboard.

Courtesy: Father Edward J. Dowling, S.J.

S.S. MUSKEGON — An early photo of the unfortunate steamer before her bustle was added.

Oconto finally outlived her usefulness. On August 15, 1883, she was sold for $13,500 to a gentleman by the name of Caldwell.

The next ship to be constructed for Goodrich was the side-wheeler *Muskegon*. Powered with the engine from *Orion*, she was 193 feet long and measured 46 feet over the guards. Her depth was 12 feet and she was rated at 620 gross tons. Her cost to Goodrich was $69,460. As she had a single tall stack, and the familiar walking beam on her hurricane deck, she was almost identical in size and general appearance to *Corona*. She was launched at Manitowoc during the early spring of 1871 and began her active service that same year.

Muskegon was commanded by Captain Edward Carus from 1892 to 1896. During the World's Fair at Chicago she was assigned to the Chicago-Manitowoc route and did a huge business. On one of her northbound trips she departed from Chicago with a full load of passengers and freight. When off Evanston, Illinois, the forward end of her walking beam broke, which rendered her dead in the water.

After some delay she was towed back to Chicago where her passengers and freight were transferred to another Goodrich steamer. The *Muskegon* was laid up over three weeks for repairs at the very peak of the season. The beam was very definitely the weakest part of this type of engine, and incidents, such as the one just described, were not unusual with steamers so equipped. This happened to *Muskegon* on three different occasions during her service with Goodrich.

On her last trip of the season of 1893, while en route from Milwaukee to Manitowoc, it was necessary to stop the ship three times to permit the crew to chop the accumulated ice from the paddle-wheel boxes! This is an example of one of the many problems presented by early-winter navigation.

September 22, 1896, found *Muskegon* in dry dock at the yard of the Milwaukee Dry Dock Company located on the Milwaukee River. For some unexplainable reason some of the bracing gave way and the sturdy side-wheeler slid off the keel blocks and broke in two at the forward gangway. Sufficient repairs were made to enable her to be towed to Manitowoc. On arrival there careful examination disclosed her so badly damaged that further repair was deemed useless. She was then laid up in the river and a lawsuit was filed against the Milwaukee Dry Dock Company.

Litigation followed and the case was in the Milwaukee courts for quite some time. Milwaukee Dry Dock Company finally lost the suit to Goodrich. The *Muskegon* has the questionable distinction of being the only Goodrich steamer lost while completely out of her element, the water. After the lawsuit was settled she was dismantled.

THE MANITOWOC INNER HARBOR — Winter lay-up scene with the Goodrich steamers *Sheboygan, Corona,* and *Chicago* clearly shown.

Courtesy: Marine Collection, Milwaukee Public Library

As a replacement for the burned *Navarino,* Captain Goodrich ordered another wooden propeller of 796 tons burden. Named *Menominee,* she was built at Manitowoc in the winter of 1872-1873 and cost Goodrich $60,600. She was powered by the machinery from the unfortunate *Navarino* and was almost identical in size and appearance to her, having only a thirty-ton greater burden rating. Both vessels had a single stack located well aft. Each carried a tall single mast forward with the familiar gaff boom. Both steamers had arched trusses that added strength to the hull.

Upon launching, *Menominee* was used as a freighter to the Lake Superior ports for the summer of 1873. During the following winter she was laid up at Manitowoc where a passenger cabin was built on her.

On May 1, 1874, she made her first trip to Muskegon from Chicago. She replaced the *Alpena* that season and remained on the cross-lake route until the close of the season of 1876. She was then used on the west-shore route until 1882 when she again returned to the Muskegon-Grand Haven-Chicago route running opposite *De Pere.*

Menominee was much more fortunate than *Navarino* in that she served Goodrich very dependably for fourteen years. In 1896 she was dismantled and her hull and machinery were used in the construction of the famous, but ill-fated *Iowa* of which the reader will learn a great deal more later in our story.

By 1872 the experiment with the *Truesdell* and *Ottawa* had been in effect long enough for the results to be carefully evaluated. The popularity and good earnings of these two small propellers left no doubt as to the wisdom of Captain Goodrich's decision to build steamers that catered to the comfort and convenience of the overnight passenger. This policy of offering an overnight service on a year-around basis wherever the traffic justified was maintained until the very end of the company's existence.

De Pere, a wooden propeller of 736 tons, followed *Menominee* just a year later. Built at a cost of $57,200 by Rand, she was almost identical in size and appearance to both *Navarino* and *Menominee.* Upon completion she was placed on the west-shore routes.

Operating as much as possible on a year-around schedule, *De Pere* was a real pioneer in winter operation. At the time she was built special emphasis was placed on her bow and hull construction to combat the ice. During her career she proved to be a most capable winter steamer. Her regular schedule included ports north of Manitowoc and she became a very familiar sight in the Green Bay area.

When *De Pere* would find a harbor frozen solid, as she often did on her winter travels, she would approach as close as possible and then discharge her cargo into horse-drawn sleighs that would come out from shore. A large wood-burning stove heated the main cabin but many parts of the sturdy little steamer were without heat of any kind. Life aboard the early steamers engaged in winter service was certainly not for the timid or the weak.

On the night of December 3, 1881, *De Pere* was caught in a fierce southwest gale. The wild snowstorm and blizzard reduced visibility to an absolute zero. At the height of the storm the ship was driven ashore on Lone Pine Tree Point, near Two Rivers. All efforts to free her were to no avail so Captain Goodrich decided to let her remain where she was until the next spring. Two men were placed aboard to live there and act as watchmen. Their means of transportation to and from the beach was a medium-sized dory.

On the night of December 11, 1881, the wind velocity began to increase rapidly from the southeast. By daylight the beached vessel was pounded unmercifully by heavy seas while a heavy snowstorm blew in off the Lake.

The two watchmen became alarmed when the *De Pere* began to buck and pound heavily. They discovered to their dismay that the heavy seas had staved in their boat and they now had no means of getting ashore.

They managed to make their plight known to those on shore and word was then relayed to the keeper of the Lifesaving Station at Two Rivers, about one mile away.

The station was closed for the winter but the keeper was able to muster the crew quickly.

The snow was so deep that a sleigh had to be used to get the surfboat down to where the grounded steamer was being pounded. Huge blocks of ice presented a difficult obstacle to the launching of the surfboat as well as to its landing on the return trip.

Operations got underway about 10 A.M. and by noon the two watchmen were safely ashore. Their situation had been grave indeed because it seemed certain the steamer would break up from the punishment inflicted by the storm.

The survivors were deeply grateful for the prompt rescue and the local press paid proper homage to the fearless men of the U. S. Lifesaving Service.

The rest of the winter passed uneventfully for the stranded *De Pere*. On April 19, 1882, the Goodrich tug *Arctic* arrived at the scene to begin the task of freeing the grounded steamer. After several days of effort the husky tug managed to haul *De Pere* off the beach and into deep water. Then she took the steamer in tow and set a course for Manitowoc.

Courtesy: Historical Collection, Milwaukee Public Library

S.S. DE PERE — Used in year-around service, she proved to be a sturdy and reliable ship. She is shown here entering the Manitowoc harbor.

There, *De Pere* was placed in dry dock where she underwent a close inspection. No severe damage was discovered and after minor repairs the sturdy little steamer was returned to service. This time she was assigned to the cross-lake route to Muskegon and Grand Haven.

De Pere was always a very popular steamer at Milwaukee and for a very particular reason. During the summer months, Goodrich offered a moonlight excursion on Lake Michigan on Thursday and Saturday nights. This excursion was a highlight in the summer recreational life of the younger Milwaukee set. Moonlight dances and a bar were provided on these trips and they were very well attended.

On December 31, 1891, *De Pere* was sold to S. B. Grummond, of Detroit, for $9,000. Later in her career she was owned by the Barry Line. In October of 1901 she was finally lost in Lake Michigan, just off White Lake. A piston rod broke and pierced her hull. She sank slowly, and as the weather was calm, all aboard were able to leave in her lifeboats so no lives were lost.

In the spring of 1874 another wooden-hull side-wheeler was ready for launching at the Rand Yard in Manitowoc. This was the *Chicago*, built at a cost of $85,000 and rated at 746 tons.

Courtesy: Marine Collection, Milwaukee Public Library

S.S. DE PERE — Unloading cargo on the ice in 1885, just off the Manitowoc harbor entrance.

Chicago was slightly larger than *Sheboygan* but the two were almost identical in general appearance. Both steamers had ornate pilothouses, side-by-side twin stacks, arched longitudinal arches on their hurricane decks, and the familiar walking beams.

After *Chicago* was launched the *Manitowoc* was moored alongside and her engines, boilers, and machinery were laboriously transferred to the new ship. This was a slow process in 1874. Heavy-duty hoists and gantry cranes were still unheard of and the job had to be accomplished with ordinary screw jacks and lots of blocking.

The low-pressure beam engine came originally from the *May Queen* built by Captain Ward in 1853, after having served on the *Manitowoc* first.

This same fine engine served *Chicago* until her career ended in 1921. In all, the engine was used in three fine steamers, giving a total of sixty-eight years of continuous and trouble-free duty! Quite a record, even by today's standards of mechanical perfection!

Upon completion *Chicago* was placed under the command of Captain Barney Sweeney and he remained her master for a long period of her career. Her first assignment was on the Chicago-Manitowoc route where she ran opposite *Sheboygan*. She remained on this run for many years. Throughout her long life *Chicago* was always a dependable, safe ship. She suffered no major accident in her long life and made excellent earnings for her owners.

By 1915, *Chicago* was nearing the end of her career. In that year she was operated as a freight boat and then only for the months of July and August. In 1916 she was dismantled. The following year Manitowoc Shipbuilding & Dry Dock purchased her from the Goodrich company and refitted her for use as a floating hotel. Lack of housing in the city of Manitowoc made this action necessary to accommodate the large crew employed by the yard.

Chicago was equipped with two large dining rooms and a smoking room, a bakery, kitchen, shower baths and lunch counters on the main deck.

On the upper deck were staterooms to accommodate 110 men, another dining room for office employees, pool tables and a reading room. All facilities were either new or completely overhauled and the new accommodations met with instant and enthusiastic approval by the men of the shipyard.

With the exception of the iron *City of Milwaukee,* built in 1883, *Chicago* was the last of the side-wheelers to be built for the Goodrich company. After the *Chicago* the rate of acquiring new steamers slowed down.

In October of 1880 disaster struck again!

The weather on October 15 was very warm, with temperatures ranging as high as 72° during the bright sunny day. The evening was warm and pleasant when the steamer *Alpena* departed from Muskegon for Chicago with her usual stop at Grand Haven en route.

It was exactly 9:00 P.M. when Captain Nelson Napier gave the signal to "let go" at the dock at Grand Haven and the overnight cross-lake trip to Chicago was begun. Chief Engineer Robert Johnston was at the controls in the engine room as the ship worked her way clear of the dock and headed down the river to Lake Michigan. The night was still warm and the wind calm.

Apparently all went well for the early part of the night crossing. Just before midnight the wind began to make up from the southwest and as the wind increased it began to get colder. In a relatively short time the temperature plunged to 30° and a full gale began to pound *Alpena*. This storm has always been referred to by Lake Michigan sailors as "the big windstorm." Evidently this freak storm contained winds of near tornadic force.

Just exactly what took place aboard the brave little *Alpena* in the next few hours will never be known. Other captains reported seeing her far off her normal course and having a bad time with the huge seas.

Captain Ludwig, of the schooner *Challenger,* was apparently the last person to sight her. He reported later that *Alpena* was then approximately thirty miles east of Kenosha, wallowing badly in the troughs of mountainous seas and blowing distress signals. *Challenger* herself was then under bare poles and fighting for her own life and was powerless to aid the stricken steamer.

Arrival time came and passed at Chicago with no word as to the whereabouts of *Alpena*. *Oconto* was also on the Lake that night and she, too, was long overdue at Manitowoc. Telegraphic inquiries to other Lake ports brought only negative replies as to the whereabouts of the missing steamers.

On the morning of October 17, 1880, the Chicago newspapers carried the following news item:

> Nothing has been heard from the Goodrich Transportation Company steamer ALPENA. The ship departed Muskegon at her scheduled time and made her regular call at Grand Haven on the evening of October 15th. The ship departed Grand Haven at her usual time with a moderately heavy load of freight. While the exact number of persons aboard is not known it is believed that total passengers and crew is about eighty.

A follow-up story appeared in the Chicago papers on October 18 and read as follows:

> The fate of the Goodrich Line Steamer ALPENA which has been reported missing since the severe wind storms of three days ago is still cloaked in mystery. No word has been received at any lake port and all indications now point to the steamer's loss with all on board. Several vessels have reported sighting ALPENA far off its normal course but none can shed any definite light on the probable fate of the Goodrich steamer.

The press of Holland, Michigan, carried the following sad solution to the mystery:

> The steamer ALPENA of the Goodrich Line, reported missing since the severe wind storm that swept Lake Michigan a few days ago, has certainly gone down. Debris from the ship is floating near this Harbor. At Saugatuck one of ALPENA's lifeboats and the ship piano, together with some life preservers bearing her name, were found on the shore.

At the same time the Chicago newspapers carried the final story on the subject:

> Goodrich Line Officials remained at their offices throughout the day and at evening they announced they had given up all hope for the safety of the steamer ALPENA and its passengers and crew, believed to number about eighty persons.

In the pre-dawn early hours of the seventeenth, the *Oconto* limped into Manitowoc. The ship and her crew had taken a terrific beating and all considered themselves fortunate to have remained afloat. Her topsides had suffered damage and two of her lifeboats were missing.

This freakish storm wrecked or badly damaged 94 vessels and 118 lives were lost that wild night. Only a small number of bodies were ever recovered.

Piecing together fragments of information and talking to masters of vessels having sighted *Alpena*, Captain Goodrich came to the conclusion that she foundered about twenty-five miles east of Kenosha. Like with so many ships that "sail away," there were no survivors and therefore no eyewitness as to what actually caused her to founder. Her previous record with Goodrich had been good. Only two years old when acquired, she had been completely overhauled in 1876. The loss of *Alpena,* judged to be the greatest Lake disaster of 1880, was the first one with loss of life to befall the line since it had been incorporated as Goodrich Transportation Company in 1868.

One of those lost on *Alpena* was the editor of the *Grand Haven Herald*. After this tragedy Goodrich withdrew their service from the Grand Haven-Chicago route. It was not restored until the spring of 1882.

Courtesy: Henry Barkhausen

S.S. CHICAGO

As previously pointed out, one of the most bothersome aspects of winter service were harbors that became frozen solid and thus prevented the steamers from getting to their docks to discharge freight and passengers. One of the most persistent offenders in this regard was Milwaukee harbor. Being a very important port on the west-shore route, steps were taken to make Milwaukee more accessible to the steamers of the Red-Stack line during the winter season.

To accomplish this, Captain Goodrich placed an order with Rand & Burger for a wooden tug of unusually heavy and sturdy construction. When launched in 1881 the new tug was named *Arctic*. Built at a cost of $16,015, she had the following dimensions: length, 65 feet; beam, 18 feet; draft, 9 feet; gross tonnage, 53 tons; net tonnage, 42 tons; propulsion, single screw; engine, high pressure, noncondensing, 16 x 18; horsepower, 225; revolutions per minute, 115.

Designed, as she was, for ice-breaking, special attention was given to her bow and hull construction. The *Milwaukee Sentinel* had the following to say about *Arctic* on November 16, 1881:

Courtesy: Chicago Historical Society

CHICAGO RIVER SCENE IN 1884 — The steamer *Chicago* is seen here at the Goodrich dock. This photo was taken from the Rush Street bridge.

An attempt will be made to keep navigation open at this port all winter for the regular line propeller ships. The tug ARCTIC owned by Goodrich Transportation Company will arrive this port about December 12th from Manitowoc where she has been engaged in towing. The ARCTIC was built last season by Rand & Burger for the Goodrich Company, who intended her especially for the breaking of ice and assisting any boats of the line which might become disabled. The ARCTIC was built for strength and no doubt she has it. She has extra heavy frames with heavy outside oak planking. For several feet back of her stem she is built of solid oak so that the ice will not stave her in. She is heavily ironed from stem to stern, but, as yet, she has not had a test of heavy ice, but it is claimed that she can make her way through eighteen inch ice. Steam will be maintained and the crew kept under pay. She will be kept near the mouth of the harbor so that a moment's notice she can start to the assistance of any of the Company's boats outside.

During the summer months *Arctic* was kept busy as a harbor tug at Manitowoc with an occasional Lake towing job. When the winter ice began to be a menace, she was transferred to Milwaukee to remain there until the following spring. *Arctic* lived up to all the predictions made of her in very fine style. In addition to the assistance rendered to the Goodrich steamers, her name frequently appears as the tug that aided this or that vessel in

Courtesy: Henry Barkhausen

THE TUG *ARCTIC*

Courtesy: Henry Barkhausen

S.S. CITY OF LUDINGTON — This photo was taken a few days after her completion in 1881.

the upper half of Lake Michigan. On several occasions she went to the aid of the car ferries of the Ann Arbor Line.

To enable her to do her rugged job in the ice better and to improve her ability in a sea, *Arctic* was returned to Manitowoc Shipyard during the winter of 1898-1899 and lengthened twelve feet. During this lay-up she was given a complete overhaul.

In 1919 *Arctic* was again returned to the shipyard at Manitowoc. This time she underwent a complete rebuilding at a cost of $21,000. This was $5,000 more than her original cost when new.

From 1923 to 1925 *Arctic* was stationed in Chicago. The historic old tug was finally abandoned in 1930. Testimony to her sturdiness and usefulness is the fact that she served the Goodrich line for forty-nine years. This was the longest continuous service record of any ship that sailed under the Goodrich flag.

A contract to build another wooden propeller was awarded to Rand & Burger during the winter of 1880-1881. She was completed and delivered to Goodrich in early spring of 1881. Christened *City of Ludington*, this 842-ton steamer cost $60,000 and was destined to be one of the most dependable ships of her size ever built by Goodrich. She was 180 feet long, had a beam of 35 feet 6 inches and a draft of 12 feet.

Designed especially for use on the year-around cross-lake route between Ludington and Milwaukee, she was given a heavily re-enforced bow and a sturdy stiff hull. Forty-four passenger cabins were constructed on the promenade deck and her public rooms were made spacious and given elegant decoration in keeping with the best decor of the day. The arched trusses, to add longitudinal strength to the hull and so typical of the ships of this era, appeared on her hurricane deck. Incidentally, *City of Ludington* was the last steamer built by Goodrich to use these arched trusses.

In addition to her extra hull strength, *City of Ludington* had one other unusual feature and that was the engine used to power her. Captain Goodrich, always interested in experimentation and especially so with engines and methods of propulsion, had tried unsuccessfully to use a new system of propulsion as far back as *Sunbeam* in 1861. This failure did not deter him from trying a wholly new concept of marine engine in *City of Ludington*.

The source of propulsion power he used in the *City of Ludington* was a Reynolds-Corliss high-pressure marine engine. It had a 24-inch bore and a 36-inch stroke. It was produced in the plant of Edward P. Allis of Milwaukee. Later this plant became part of what is now known as the Allis Chalmers Company of that same city.

Seemingly the production of marine engines did not fit well into the scheme of things for Mr. Allis because the Reynolds-Corliss marine engine for the *Ludington* was the only one ever built under the Corliss name. This is probably regrettable because that engine had a fine record during the time it powered this steamer.

Captain Goodrich specifically built *Ludington* for the cross-lake route to handle package freight for the Flint & Pere Marquette Railroad from their western terminal at Ludington to Milwaukee and other Wisconsin ports. It was for this reason that she was named in honor of Ludington, Michigan.

The first winter *Ludington* was in service proved to be a most severe one. By all standards of comparison the winter of 1881-1882 was a tough one and the ability of the new steamer to withstand the crushing ice of Lake Michigan was put to many tests. On one occasion, while on an eastbound crossing, *Ludington* became entrapped in a huge ice floe as she approached the Michigan shore. Unable to work free she had no choice but to move up and down Lake Michigan in the relentless grip of the huge floe. After a week the sturdy steamer found herself at the southern end of the Lake just off St. Joseph one morning and a few days later the next recognizable bearing found her off Manistee. In that length of time she had traveled over a hundred and fifty miles without her shaft turning a single revolution!

At one point in her long imprisonment of over a month, some of her crew actually made their way ashore to make contact with Goodrich officials and pick up badly needed supplies. Finally a warming spell and a sudden shift in wind caused the floe to break up and release its unwilling prisoner. Examination revealed no hull damage from this long and trying experience and *City of Ludington* returned to her regular run. One can imagine the anxiety this delay caused the shippers and receivers of the freight and the ship's owners, to say nothing of the concern of the families of those on board.

In 1883 the F. & P.M.R.R. terminated the contracts with Goodrich in favor of railroad-owned steamers, the first of which was *F. & P.M. No. 1*. This was quickly followed by *F. & P.M. No. 2*. The *City of Ludington* was now assigned to the regular Goodrich routes.

This colorful steamer continued to have many bouts with Lake Michigan ice over the next few years. In February of 1885 she was locked in the ice off Big Point Sauble. This ordeal was not a record-breaker like the experience of 1882, but it did last long enough for some of the crew to make their way ashore and report their whereabouts to the crew of the Big Point Sauble Lifesaving Station.

In the same year *Ludington* rendered assistance to the *Oneida*, ice-bound in a huge field just off Grand Haven. Food, supplies, and some fuel were given to the hapless *Oneida*, who was to spend twenty-three days in the ice before being able to work free.

S.S. GEORGIA — This photo shows the handsome ship at Mackinac Island in 1898.

Courtesy : Murdick Collection

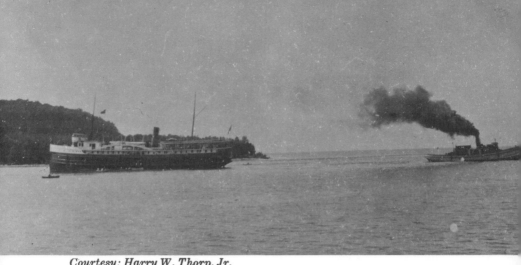

S.S. GEORGIA — Here she is seen grounded at Fish Creek, Wisconsin, with the tug *Peter Reiss* attempting to free her.

Records show that she was aground on a bar, just off Manistee, in January of 1886. With the aid of the Lifesaving Service crew from Manistee, she managed to free herself without hull damage and continue across Lake Michigan with her cargo of barreled salt.

A heavy fog in November of 1889 caused her again to go aground, this time at Peninsular Point just off Escanaba, Michigan. A tug managed to pull her free without severe damage.

Within that same month and on Thanksgiving Day, she was again in trouble. While seeking shelter behind Horseshoe Island, she parted her lines in a storm of gale force. Then she drifted past Eagle Harbor and ended up on a large flat rock in Shanty Bay on the west shore of Eagle Harbor. After the storm, the Goodrich steamer *De Pere* went to her assistance. *De Pere* removed the cargo in an attempt to lighten her draft. This was to no more avail than the combined effort of three tugs. The *Ludington* was in a sheltered spot, so Captain Butlin decided to let her remain where she was until spring when conditions would be more favorable for her removal. A shanty was built on the beach and one man kept lonely vigil on her all winter.

In the spring of 1890, efforts to free *Ludington* were renewed. By the use of heavy hydraulic jacks and the services of the tugs *Arctic* and *Monarch* the steamer was finally inched into deep water. The tugs then towed her to Manitowoc where she arrived on May 15, 1890.

There she was immediately placed in dry dock where inspection revealed that she had sustained severe hull damage. Mr. Goodrich decided not only to repair her hull damage but he authorized the expenditure of another $10,000 for general improvements to the ship. When work was completed she was returned to the regular Goodrich routes during the summer of 1890.

Ludington was often used by Goodrich to assist other of their steamers that were in difficulty. In 1896 she went to the aid of the *Lansing* that was badly aground off Two Rivers, Wisconsin. In 1897 she spent several days searching for the *Iowa* which had not been heard from in over a week. The *Iowa* was located in mid-lake, firmly locked in the grasp of a huge ice field. The *Ludington* succeeded in cutting the ship free and escorted her to Milwaukee.

One of the first steamers on the Lakes to be lighted by electricity was *Ludington*. She was also the first Goodrich steamer equipped with an electric searchlight. This old carbon-arc affair, while not entirely reliable, was a real innovation in the steamboat business.

Captain Henry E. Stines was master of the *Ludington* in 1895. His brother, Captain Edward G. Stines, was master of the ill-fated *Chicora* of the Graham & Morton Line. When the *Chicora* came up missing on January 21, 1895, Captain Henry Stines on the *Ludington* spent two full days seeking the lost steamer. *Chicora* was lost in a freak storm and no trace of those aboard her was ever found.

In the spring of 1898 *Ludington* was again back in the yard of Burger & Burger at Manitowoc. This time she was cut in two and lengthened thirty feet. This increased her tonnage rating to 950 gross tons. After eighteen years of trouble-free service, the Corliss engine was removed in favor of a new and larger power plant. The new engine was built at the Dry Dock Engineering Company at Detroit. During the course of the rebuilding the public rooms and the sleeping accommodations were completely done over and much improved. When the work was all completed her name was changed to *Georgia*. On her return to regular service *Georgia* was assigned to the Chicago-Mackinac

S.S. GEORGIA — The tug *Arctic* is standing by to assist the sunken ship in the Manitowoc inner harbor after the ice pulled the caulking from her planking, February 29, 1920.

Courtesy: Harry W. Thorp, Jr.

Island route. On this run she departed from Chicago every Monday afternoon at 2:00 P.M. En route to Mackinac she stopped at Milwaukee and other west-shore ports. Her return to Chicago was on Friday afternoon and that same night she departed for White Lake. The final return from White Lake was on Sunday night with arrival in Chicago early Monday morning to give the commuters the opportunity to get to the office on time to begin a new week.

For the most part, *Georgia* had a very uneventful existence. One exception was the foggy night of June 6, 1903. Under the command of Captain Edward Carus, she was groping her way in the zero visibility and shortly after midnight fetched up on Dunlop Reef. Unable to free herself, she remained there until daylight at which time aid came in the form of two tugs. Superintendent Cochrane supervised the refloating of the stranded steamer. When *Georgia* was finally pulled free she was sent to Manitowoc for inspection. Found to have sustained some hull damage, she was then laid up for repairs. At the company investigation of the accident it was ruled that her master was at fault and Captain Carus was dismissed from duty with Goodrich.

Georgia was equipped with a very fine and powerful steam fire pump. One mid-winter day a bad fire broke out in the Mears Block, near the 8th Street bridge in Manitowoc. At the height of the blaze a fire engine broke down, causing a very serious situation.

The fire chief noted that *Georgia* was moored at the Goodrich outer dock so he immediately appealed to her master for assistance. As a result *Georgia* was immediately moved to a spot close to the 8th Street bridge and the fire hoses from the disabled engine were connected to the outlets aboard the steamer. The chief engineer of the *Georgia* asked the fire chief how much pressure he wanted applied to the fire hose. "All you've got," was the quick reply as the fire appeared to be getting out of hand. The engineer complied to the request and to the dismay of the fire chief the hoses promptly burst!

In 1914 *Georgia* again went to the yard for an extensive overhaul. This time she received new Scotch boilers but retained the engine that was installed new in 1898. All decayed or faulty hull planking was replaced and the ship given a general refurbishing. After this overhaul, *Georgia* was no longer used in winter service and as a result she was laid up each winter at Manitowoc. During her lay-up in the winter of 1919-1920 she had her last and most unique misfortune.

Georgia was moored in the Manitowoc River at the Goodrich dock under the bluff in the upper harbor. Her starboard side was to the dock and she was made secure with the usual extra

Courtesy: Harry W. Thorp, Jr.

S.S. GEORGIA — Here she is shown resting on the bottom after her unusual accident while in winter lay-up at the Goodrich dock in the Manitowoc inner harbor in 1920.

lines and a wire cable. During the night of February 19, 1920, the ice in the river began to move and pulled the caulking from her hull planking. As a result water poured into the steamer and she filled and sank. The next morning *Georgia* presented a sad and forlorn sight as she rested on the river bottom with a sharp list to her port side. Shortly after this strange accident she was pumped out, raised, and taken to dry dock for new hull caulking. After a thorough interior cleaning she was ready again to resume her role as a popular Goodrich summer boat.

During the summer of 1920, Goodrich sold *Georgia* to the Crosby Line for the sum of $75,000. Her new owners placed her on the cross-lake route for which Captain A. E. Goodrich had originally built her. *Georgia* gave excellent service as a Crosby Line and later a Pere Marquette Line steamer. She was finally declared obsolete and unfit for further service in 1927. She was then laid up at Manistee, Michigan.

Captain John Roen purchased *Georgia* at Manistee and towed the proud old steamer to Sturgeon Bay for dismantling. After removal of her machinery and most of her topsides and interior, the bare hull was sold to a group that was developing a new stone quarry on Summer Island, located just north of famous Washington Island. On arrival at Summer Island, *Georgia* was filled with stone and sunk to help form a loading dock for the new quarry. So ended the career of one of the most successful and dependable steamers ever to sail the inland seas for Goodrich.

From the time of the incorporation of the Goodrich Transportation Company in 1868 until 1881, the port-of-hail for all Goodrich steamers was Manitowoc. In January of 1882, the city of Manitowoc enacted some new tax laws. These new laws directly affected the tax rate of the Goodrich company since Manitowoc was its home port.

The higher taxes displeased Captain Goodrich· very much. To avoid them he changed the port-of-hail for the Goodrich line from Manitowoc to Kenosha, Wisconsin. This city remained the Goodrich port-of-hail until the incorporation of the Goodrich Transit Company in 1906. At that time the port-of-hail was changed to Duluth and this remained so for the rest of the life of the company.

THE CHICAGO RIVER IN 1884 — Reproduction of a drawing of the Chicago River viewed from Lake Michigan. The Goodrich steamer *Chicago* is shown outbound in the foreground.

Courtesy: Chicago Historical Society

Chapter Five

THE PASSING OF A GREAT LEADER

THE WESTERN TERMINUS OF THE OLD FLINT & PERE
Marquette Railroad was established at Ludington, Michigan.
Freight destined for places across Lake Michigan was removed from the freight cars on arrival at Ludington and then
loaded aboard the steamers for the trip across the Lake. In Milwaukee the freight was removed from the ship and again loaded
into railway freight cars for movement to its ultimate destinations.

From 1876 until 1883, all of this break-bulk package freight
was shipped across the Lake on Goodrich Transportation Company steamers. This traffic was on a year-around basis and was
most profitable for the Goodrich company.

About this time the Detroit, Grand Haven and Milwaukee
Railway Company established their western railhead at Grand
Haven, Michigan. The break-bulk handling of the freight here
was the same as at Ludington and again Goodrich enjoyed the
cross-lake haul of the package freight to Milwaukee.

To handle this very lucrative business, Captain Goodrich
first built the *City of Ludington* in 1880. As described in the
previous chapter, she was one of the most successful Goodrich
steamers ever built, and no small amount of her fine money-earn-
ing record was due to this cross-lake railroad traffic.

As time went on, the volume of railroad traffic offered Goodrich at both Ludington and Grand Haven grew at a rapid rate.
To handle this growing volume of business new contracts were

negotiated with the railroad management. In order to provide the increased service specified in the new agreements it was necessary for the Goodrich company to build new vessels at once.

Captain Goodrich engaged the famous naval architect Frank E. Kirby to design three new steamers. Two of these were to be identical iron propellers, capable of year-around service, and the third was to be an iron side-wheeler. All three were to be elaborately equipped for the comfortable handling of overnight passengers in addition to generous cargo capacity. These were to be the first metal ships ever owned by the Goodrich line.

The three new ships designed by Mr. Kirby were built by the Detroit Dry Dock Company at Wyandotte, Michigan. At the time the Burger Yard at Manitowoc was not equipped to build metal-hulled vessels. These were the first new Goodrich steamers not to be constructed at Manitowoc in many years and it was with some regret that Captain Goodrich found it necessary to turn to another source for these, the most palatial and expensive **red-stackers ever built.**

Courtesy: Father Edward J. Dowling, S.J.

S.S. MICHIGAN — Reproduction of a painting by Father Dowling.

First of the three to be completed was the side-wheeler. Christened *City of Milwaukee* upon launching, she slid down the ways at Wyandotte on February 11, 1881. Rated at 1149 tons, her cost to Goodrich was the staggering sum of $179,000! No expense had been spared to outfit the *City of Milwaukee* with the most elegant interior of any ship on the Lakes. In addition to her luxurious and very spectacular public rooms, she had elaborate passenger sleeping accommodations on the galley deck. She was quickly dubbed "Queen of the Lakes" by the press and the title was richly deserved. *Milwaukee* was a truly palatial steamboat in every way.

The second steamer to be launched was the *Michigan*. Amid elaborate ceremonies she entered the water at Wyandotte on August 20, 1881, and from there was taken to Milwaukee to be fitted out.

The *Wisconsin* followed her twin down the ways at Wyandotte on October 11, 1881. Like the *Michigan*, she, too, was taken to Milwaukee for fitting out and completion. Both new steamers were finished and in regular service by the end of the year.

Both propellers were rated at 1183 tons and both were 215 feet in length. They had a beam of 34 feet and their depth of hold was 14 feet. Each cost the identical sum of $159,212. They were especially designed for cross-lake winter service and had

Courtesy: Detroit Dry Dock Company

S.S. WISCONSIN — This picture was taken a year after the ship was built. Note the steadying sail at the foremast.

heavy ice-breaking qualities incorporated in their construction. Each had the rounded forefoot and full entrance found on our modern car ferries of today. This feature permits the ship to rise up on the ice, crushing it with its sheer weight. The twins were also equipped with double iron bottoms and the main deck was fashioned of the same material. The new ships excited much comment in the press and many articles about their safety and unusual qualities appeared in Midwestern newspapers and marine publications.

Strangely enough, these three new palatial additions to the fleet ran only for about two years for the Goodrich line! In 1882 the first two railroad-owned ships arrived in Ludington. They were *Flint & Pere Marquette No. 1* and *Flint & Pere Marquette No. 2.* With the purchase of these two new steamers it was apparent that the railway company intended to go into the Lake steamboat business for itself.

Slowly business was taken away from the Goodrich steamers. On April 1, 1883, Captain Goodrich lost the most important of the railroad contracts and that meant that the Ludington-Milwaukee route would have to be abandoned for lack of traffic. This was a serious blow to the Goodrich Transportation Company. A huge portion of its capital and funds borrowed from the banks had been invested in the new steamers and the development of the new service. The termination, after really less than two years' earnings from the new service, meant insufficient return on the cash outlay. To avoid a financial crisis within his company, Captain Goodrich wisely decided to sell his three new steamers to satisfy his creditors and obligations. On May 1, 1883, the three

S.S. CITY OF MILWAUKEE

Courtesy: Mariners Museum, Norfolk, Virginia

fine ships were sold to the Detroit, Grand Haven & Milwaukee Railway Company. The railroad paid $180,000 for the *City of Milwaukee* and $160,000 each for the twin propellers *Michigan* and *Wisconsin*. Thus, by regaining the initial cost a financial crisis was averted. The service the three ships provided was the forerunner of the present Grand Trunk Line operating between Muskegon and Milwaukee.

The winter of 1884-1885 was most severe. While searching for the steamer *Oneida*, missing for some time on the ice-choked Lake, *Michigan* became locked in the relentless grip of a huge ice floe just off Grand Haven. After a four-week unsuccessful struggle to free her, the ice began to run and she suffered hull damage. In spite of heroic efforts on the part of her officers and crew to save her, she sank on March 22, 1885.

The tug *Arctic*, stationed at Grand Haven that winter, put

The Banner Summer Route

—TO AND FROM THE WEST IS VIA THE—

GRAND HAVEN ROUTE,

And the Elegant Steamer

"CITY OF MILWAUKEE"

The Finest Steamer on Inland Waters.

Time, Distance and Money Saved

TO MILWAUKEE

And all Points in WISCONSIN, MINNESOTA, DAKOTA, and the Northwest, during the Summer Months.

The Elegant Steamer "CITY OF MILWAUKEE" and Steamer "WISCONSIN" are placed in Service on the Route about May 1st, and afford

A Delightful Ride Across Lake Michigan.

During the Summer Season

Low Rate Tourist and Excursion Tickets

Are made to all

Northern Michigan Resorts and the Northwest.

ELEGANT DAY COACHES AND PARLOR CARS

On Day Trains, and Sleepers on Night Trains, between

Detroit and Grand Haven.

Courtesy: Dowling Collection

An advertisement of 1866 calling attention to the service offered by the Detroit, Grand Haven, and Milwaukee Railway.

out to pick up the crew from the *Michigan* off the ice. *Arctic* was caught by the same running ice and was lifted clear out of the water. For a while it appeared that she would suffer the same fate as *Michigan* and that she, too, would be lost. Fortunately, the pressure passed and the sturdy tug settled back in the water, unharmed, permitting her to complete the rescue of the unfortunate crew from *Michigan,* many of whom were the victims of severe frostbite to their hands and feet.

Caught in the same ice field, *Wisconsin* had a struggle to avoid the same fate as her sister ship suffered. Her crew carried the heavy oak fenders into the hold and used them to provide extra bracing for the sides of the hull. In spite of everything that was done, *Wisconsin* suffered major hull damage. When she was finally released, she went directly to the shipyard for extensive repairs. After considerable repair work, costing upwards of $40,-000, she was returned to the cross-lake route and went on to a long and spectacular career. Her detailed life story is told in Chapter Twelve.

The *City of Milwaukee,* being a side-wheeler, was operated by the Detroit, Grand Haven & Milwaukee Railway Company only on a summer schedule. In 1876 she was sold to the Graham & Morton Line of Chicago. They used her on their cross-lake routes to west Michigan ports at the southern end of Lake Michigan.

In 1906 Graham & Morton changed her name to *Holland,* but this change did nothing to change her bad luck, and she continued to be plagued with all sorts of misfortune and unusual accidents. By 1915 she was looked upon with fear by her owners. As a result they decided that it was imperative that the elaborate old side-wheeler be sold. Finding a willing buyer for the hard-luck steamer was not easy. Her reputation was such that it was generally believed throughout the Lake region that *Holland* was a jinxed steamer. In spite of this, however, a sale was finally made to the Crosby Line in 1916.

In another attempt to divert the traveling public's attention, her name was again changed, this time in early 1919 to *Muskegon.* Nothing seemed to help, however. On the stormy night of October 28, 1919, the *Muskegon* was attempting to make her way into the harbor at Muskegon, Michigan. The seas were running heavy and fast as the old iron side-wheeler approached the pier heads that marked the entrance to safety. Just as the steamer was abeam the south pier head a huge sea swung her bow directly into the South Pier with a crushing blow. The impact was so great that the ship literally exploded and in minutes the harbor channel was choked with wreckage and debris. Twenty-nine lives were lost in the final and fatal mishap to the luckless steamer that had once been labeled "Queen of the Lakes."

MANITOWOC HARBOR, 1890 — Shown in the ice in the inner harbor are the steamers *City of Racine, De Pere,* and *Menominee.* Note the fine derby hats some of the skaters are wearing.

Just prior to the railroad fiasco of 1883, the health of Captain Goodrich began to fail. The cold winter days and long, windy winter nights spent in unheated pilot houses and cold cabins began to take their toll. The captain had been a victim of frequent attacks of neuralgia for quite some time. As time went on, these attacks became more frequent and more severe. The Lake winds seemed to affect him the most in fall and spring. In 1884 this situation became so serious that he rode from his residence on Michigan Avenue to his office in a closed carriage to avoid exposure to the chill winds that blew in from the Lake.

Due to the condition of his health he had, for quite some time, ceased to take an active part in the actual operation problems of the Goodrich line. This huge responsibility was entrusted to the very capable Captain Butlin, who continued to function in the capacity of general superintendent of the Goodrich Transportation Company.

The outside interests of Captain Goodrich also required some of his time. In 1879 he had purchased the Gardner House on Michigan Avenue in Chicago. This fine hotel was later known as the LeLand Hotel. This did not prove to be a profitable investment and he availed himself of the first opportunity to sell out.

Captain Goodrich had been quite successful in his other ventures besides the steamship line. His holdings now included mining interests and improved lands in Michigan, Indiana, Illinois, and Iowa. At this point in his life he had "amassed a large fortune," to quote the Chicago press at the time of his passing.

On Thursday, August 29, 1885, Captain Goodrich attended the funeral services of an old friend in Chicago. While there he was overtaken with a chill and was immediately taken home. This incident was followed by the most violent attack of neuralgia in his long bout with the malady. Typhoid symptoms soon developed and the famous captain was indeed seriously ill.

On Saturday, September 12, the attending physician expressed the opinion that Captain Goodrich was somewhat improved. The very next day he suffered a relapse and became steadily worse through that night. On Monday morning, September 14, 1885, at 9:25 A.M., the beloved Captain Albert Edgar Goodrich passed away. He was survived by his wife Rosamond and his only son Albert Whaling Goodrich, who was then nineteen years of age. Albert W. Goodrich was attending school in Germany when his father passed away.

Courtesy: Marine Historical Collection, Milwaukee Public Library

THE GOODRICH DOCK AT MILWAUKEE — Before dismantling, these docks on Michigan Street were Milwaukee's oldest industrial buildings.

Courtesy: C. P. Labadie

MANITOWOC—A typical scene at the Goodrich Transportation Company's repair yard and docks during the winter of 1900-1901.

Said the Chicago press of his passing:

Flags were flying at half mast throughout the harbor yesterday as a mark of respect to the memory of Captain A. E. Goodrich who died at his residence, number 1474 Michigan Avenue, yesterday morning after many years of patient suffering. Captain Goodrich was one of the pioneer steamboat men of Lake Michigan having been prominently identified with the Lake Marine for nearly forty years. He founded what was known as the Goodrich Transportation Company and was its first President from time of incorporation until he died. There are few men who have done as much toward building up Lake Marine as Captain Goodrich and his death will be regretted throughout the lake region. Captain Goodrich was born in the western part of New York State and at an early age removed to the little town of New Buffalo, Michigan which was founded by his father and uncle, at a time Captain Goodrich used to say when Michigan was shaking from one end to the other with fever and ague.

Another long tribute in the Chicago press closed its article as follows:

He leaves a wife and one son Albert W. Goodrich, who is now in school in Germany. By his express wish the Company will continue as at present organized under the management of T. G.

Butlin. The deceased was very much esteemed by all who knew him and his loss will be deeply felt.

The funeral for Captain Goodrich was conducted in the home at 1474 Michigan Avenue. Simple services were read by the Reverend L. O. Osborne of the Episcopal Church of Chicago. Burial was in Rosehill Cemetery.

The Goodrich will was published in the Chicago press on September 20, 1885, and the article read as follows:

> The will of Albert E. Goodrich, the wealthy steamboat operator was probated yesterday. It is very brief. Each of his three sisters, Cordelia Grannis, Cornelia Knapp and Catherine Bristol, receives a legacy of $5,000 and everything else goes to the widow, Rosamond F. Goodrich in equal shares. Letters testamentary were granted to Mrs. Goodrich and John S. Cowan. The will was executed on September 5th, 1855, only nine days before testator's death. The estate consists of personal property estimated at $485,000 and realty worth $75,000. The executors gave their bond in the penalty of $1,120,000.

Not only were all those connected with the Goodrich Transportation Company saddened by his death but all Lake shipping mourned his passing. He had been a tough competitor but admired by all who knew him for his fairness and tremendous foresight in matters pertaining to Lake shipping. He had, during his lifetime, put together the largest and most prosperous steamship line in the history of the Great Lakes. So, at the age of 59, ended the outstanding career of the greatest steamboat man in the history of navigation on the inland seas.

MANITOWOC — An excellent view of Manitowoc harbor as it was in 1898. The Goodrich docks can be plainly seen near the entrance to the river from Lake Michigan.

Courtesy: Henry Barkhausen

Chapter Six

NEW HANDS ON THE HELM

U NQUESTIONABLY ONE OF THE UNSUNG HEROES OF
the Goodrich story is Captain Thomas G. Butlin. Born near London, England, in 1824, he and Captain Goodrich were very nearly
the same age.

When ten years of age, Thomas Butlin migrated to America
with his parents. His father was a farmer by trade and on arrival
in this country they settled in St. Clair, Michigan, in 1834, when
the state was still a territory of undeveloped land and resources.

The education of Tom Butlin was such as was afforded by
the common schools in the neighborhood of his father's farm,
and several terms in the village school at St. Clair. An avid
reader and of an inquisitive nature, he soon developed his mind
beyond the educational opportunities available.

In 1842, when just eighteen years of age, Tom Butlin left
home and made his way to Chicago. There he gained employment
as cabin boy on the Ward Line and sailed between Chicago and
St. Joseph, Michigan. His keen interest in what was going on
around him soon earned him a promotion to wheelsman. By
1845 he was running on the steamers that carried supplies to
Sault Ste. Marie.

Promotion came rapidly for the energetic Butlin. In 1846 he
was promoted to first mate on the *Detroit*. In the fall of 1847
he became master. The very next spring the *Detroit* was running
from New Buffalo to Chicago. It was during this time that he
and Captain A. E. Goodrich first became friends.

105

Courtesy: Henry Barkhausen

S.S. CITY OF RACINE — Here she is shown leaving Manitowoc for her trials in June of 1889.

The spring of 1849 found Captain Butlin on his way to Detroit, where he brought out the new steamer *Canada*. He remained master of this ship for two seasons and then, in 1851, transferred his flag to the new steamer *Arctic*. He remained on *Arctic* until the Michigan Central entered Chicago in 1853, except for the later part of 1852 when he was commander of the *E. K. Collins* for a short time. He returned to *Arctic* at the outset of the 1853 season.

During early 1852, Captain Butlin purchased a financial interest in the Ward Line. When Captain E. B. Ward sold the line in 1854, Butlin sold his interest at the same time. He decided to leave the Lakes and became interested in the booming lumber business at Forestville, Michigan.

This new venture proved to be very profitable and he remained there until the spring of 1857. Later that year he sailed as master on the steamer *Planet* from Chicago to Milwaukee.

The call of the Lakes was strong and in 1858 we find him again associated with the Ward Line. For a while he sailed in the ore trade on Lake Superior. In 1859 he was again back on Lake Michigan and in command of the *Gazelle*.

On July 22, 1859, the steamer *Gazelle* was chartered by a group of leading citizens of the village of Manitowoc to make a good-will trip to Pere Marquette, Michigan (now Ludington), for the purpose of encouraging the management of the Flint & Pere Marquette Railway to begin a boat service to Manitowoc.

The detailed report of this trip across Lake Michigan is most interesting. It reveals, for example, how little was known about the east shore of Lake Michigan by those living on the west shore, less than a hundred miles away! Here follows a report of the committee on an excursion from Manitowoc to Pere Marquette, now called Ludington, in 1859 on the steamer *Gazelle*, Captain Thos. G. Butlin:

"The citizens of Manitowoc feeling a deep interest in the construction of the Flint and Pere Marquette Railroad of Michigan, to the number of about 150 persons, on the 15th instant, made an excursion to Pere Marquette, aboard the Ward Line Steamer *Gazelle*, Captain Thomas G. Butlin, leaving in the night, and returning on the evening of the following day.

Courtesy: Dowling Collection

S.S. *CITY OF RACINE* — This is what she looked like before becoming the *Arizona*.

"At a meeting held on board the steamer, the undersigned were appointed a committee to prepare a report of such facts, connected with the objects of the excursion, as they might deem useful for publication.

"The Michigan shore was neared at about 4:00 o'clock on the following morning. For the company the excursion had much of the interest of a voyage of discovery and adventure; for no person, not even the Captain, had ever seen Pere Marquette, or was acquainted with the Michigan shore at this part of Lake Michigan, which at first appeared to be an unbroken and uninhabited wilderness.

"For some time the steamer wandered on its course, following here and there the remote and doubtful signs of man's habitation and improvement. But our approach to the shore, with the aid of the Captain's glass, gradually revealed thin settlements and clearings scattered for miles on the coast, and a rising column of smoke and steam, sent up from a distant steam-mill, as if to signal us, told that we were not far from the desired land. A considerable village now disclosed itself a few miles to the north with a large pier extending into the lake, which was reached about 6:00 o'clock A.M. As the pier was neared it seemed very much like approaching an unknown country and people, and we were obliged, somewhat after the fashion of Virgill's wandering hero in the A Enead, to hold a parly with the population of the village who had rushed to the pier to greet us.

S.S. ARIZONA — Here she is shown southbound from the Soo in the St. Mary's River.

Courtesy: A. E. Young

" 'Is this Pere Marquette?' Answer 'no.' 'What place is this?'
Answer 'Little Sable.' 'Where is Pere Marquette?' Answer 'About
three miles to the South.' 'How much water is there at your
pier?' Answer 'Plenty for you — eleven feet.' The steamer was
soon made fast and this was the first vessel of its character that
had ever visited this part of the Michigan shore. So at least, said
the inhabitants, who were overjoyed at our arrival, and some of
whom responded to the music of the band, by dancing upon the
pier and in various other modes.

"The village of Little Sable is mainly the results of the
enterprise of Messrs. Mears, wealthy lumber merchants, who
manufacture lumber largely for the Chicago market at this place,
also a few miles to the north, at Big Sable Point, where there
is a large lake pier, and also three miles south at Pere Marquette.
The population is between two and three hundred. The village
is handsomely situated at the mouth of the Little Sable River
directly upon the lake, from ten to fifty feet above it, and with
its neat painted buildings presented a cheerful sight, in striking
contrast to the dense forests which surround it.

"A steam pile driver was at work. Messrs. Mears now being
engaged in extending one of the piers, using slabs for filling.
This is a very cheap system of pier building, where slabs can be
easily obtained, and suggests an easy mode of improving many
of our lake harbors.

"After a two hour stay at Little Sable village, the steamer
was put on her course for Pere Marquette. There being no pier
at this place, we anchored off the cut, a party of ten or twelve
was taken ashore in a small boat, to make observations. The
main settlement at Pere Marquette consists of a steam saw mill
and six or seven other small buildings, situated at the northern
extremity of Pere Marquette Lake, which is formed by a river
of the same name just at the entrance to Lake Michigan.

"This lake is about three and one half miles long, and aver-
ages about a mile in width. For about half of its length it lies
parallel to Lake Michigan, and is separated from it by a narrow
sand wall or ridge, from ten to eighty feet in height, and about
two hundred feet through at the base. The entrance from Lake
Michigan into Pere Marquette Lake is by a narrow channel cut
through the sand about fifty feet wide and one hundred fifty
feet through, it has a depth of five or six feet as we saw it, a
current of about five miles an hour. The lake then being entered
is then seen in all its parts entirely surrounded by hills or highlands, and a perfect lock up against storms from every point
of the compass, it had a general depth of from twenty to fifty
feet, with deep water close to its shores, and, by cutting off a
small sand bar in Lake Michigan, may easily be converted into

one of the best harbors we have ever seen. Pere Marquette River is about forty miles long. Logs are floated down it for about thirty miles. There are upon it several settlements, and we were informed that about two thirds of the neighboring country is valuable for farming lands and the balance for pine.

"The people of Manitowoc and Central Wisconsin, as also Minnesota, will naturally look with great interest for the completion of the Michigan Railroad to this point, which we are assured is now in rapid progress, and will be finished as far as Saginaw this present year. The Manitowoc and Mississippi Railroad being now almost graded as far as Menasha, will, when completed, be a natural link in the great Railroad Chain, from the east, via Pere Marquette and Manitowoc, direct to St. Paul.

"Manitowoc is nearly opposite Pere Marquette; at this point Lake Michigan is but sixty miles wide, and the Pere Marquette and the Manitowoc Highlands were both plainly visible to the naked eye from the middle of the lake, for a space of about twenty minutes.

Jacob Leups
Jarvis E. Platt
Alex W. Buel

Committee
Manitowoc, July 18th, 1859."

In 1863, Captain Butlin built the popular steamer *Antelope.* He sailed her for two years and then sold her. For the second time in his career, he turned his back on the magic call of the saltless seas and once more entered the lumber business. In this venture he developed large pine properties along the east shore of Lake Michigan. The great pine lumber boom was then just beginning to gather momentum. These holdings were profitably sold in 1868.

During the season of 1867 Captain Butlin sailed steamers for Captain Goodrich and their association was a most pleasant one.

When Goodrich decided to incorporate his steamboat line as the Goodrich Transportation Company in 1868, Captain Butlin purchased a block of stock in the new company, and was appointed superintendent. When Joseph Goodrich passed away, Captain Goodrich appointed Butlin to the post of vice-president and general superintendent. He retained these titles until Goodrich's death in 1885.

Prior to his death, Captain Goodrich had made it quite clear that he wished that the presidency of the company be passed on to Butlin until the time his son, Albert Whaling Goodrich, would become of age and have the opportunity to gain experience in the management of company affairs.

With all his outside interests besides his activity in procuring steamers, maintaining good public relations with city officials at the various Goodrich ports and proper relations with other steamboat operators on the Lakes, Captain Goodrich had to have reliable management to keep a close watch on the actual operation of the steamers. During the last six or seven years of his life, Captain Goodrich was hardly able to leave his home at times, due to his very poor health. The result of this was that a great deal of responsibility was entrusted to Captain Butlin. The fine progress made by the line during this period was mute testimony to Captain Butlin's ability to carry on.

In September, 1885, Captain Butlin faced a new task. The chief under whom he had served so long was gone and now he faced the dual role of general superintendent and president of the Goodrich Transportation Company. Certainly no individual in the organization was better equipped to undertake the job.

Rosamond Goodrich, the captain's widow, wisely agreed that Butlin should be immediately elected president and serve in that capacity until Albert would become of age. Meanwhile her son could gain experience before assuming the title of president in accordance with his father's wishes. This arrangement was entirely agreeable to Captain Butlin who, after all, was also getting along in years.

S.S. ARIZONA — When her career with the construction firm was finished, she was permitted slowly to rot away in the Maumee River.

Courtesy: William A. McDonald

Courtesy : Marine Historical Collection, Milwaukee Public Library

S.S. INDIANA — This photo shows her in the stocks at Manitowoc when her boilers were being cribbed aboard.

Some of the losses incurred from the railroad contracts of 1883 were still on the books and in the opinion of Captain Butlin no new steamers or further expansion of the routes were in order at this time. When Captain Butlin took over the presidency the fleet roster of the Goodrich line listed the following ships: *Chicago, Corona, City of Ludington, De Pere, Menominee, Muskegon, Sheboygan,* and the tug *Arctic.*

1886 and 1887 were good years on the Lakes and they were especially good for Goodrich from the standpoint of earnings. Traffic volume was very good and no accidents or serious losses occurred to delay the continued financial improvement. At the end of 1887, Captain Butlin felt that his astute program should be continued for still another year.

Upon the death of his father, Albert left school in Germany and came back to Chicago to be with his mother and to participate actively in the management of the Goodrich company. Knowing full well that he was destined some day to assume the job of president, he was anxious to have a maximum exposure to the company affairs, especially while his father's old friend was there to teach him the ways of the Lake steamboat business.

As a result of Captain Butlin's determination to restore the strong financial position of the Goodrich Transportation Company, no new steamers were acquired from 1885 until the late fall of 1888.

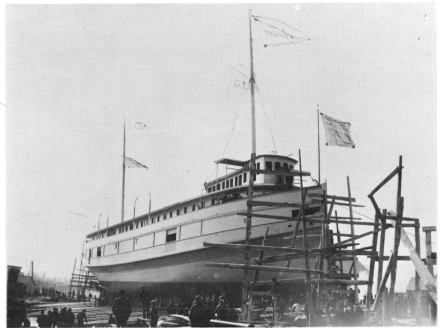

Courtesy: Henry Barkhausen

S.S. INDIANA — Here she is poised on the ways, ready for her launching.

All of the steamers that made up the Goodrich fleet in 1885 were proven to be thoroughly dependable and economical by virtue of years of service under the Goodrich flag. The one undeniable fact that remained was that some of them were getting old and were too small to serve the available traffic volume on their routes efficiently. During their long service they had made many friends among the traveling public and had done much to establish the fine reputation Goodrich was enjoying. The fact did remain, however, that if the reputation of the Goodrich line was to be maintained, some of the older steamers would have to be replaced.

The year-around service was now an established fact. Shippers of freight and passengers alike had now gained confidence in the winter service. In spite of the ice and severe winters, the advertised schedules were, with few exceptions, well maintained. By now the Goodrich routes were well established and could be divided into two kinds. One was the cross-lake service centering around Muskegon and Grand Haven and the other the service along the west shore as far north as Mackinac Island and the Soo. Basically, the routes in effect in 1888 remained unchanged throughout most of the history of the Goodrich line.

The route from Chicago to Muskegon and Grand Haven was doing extremely well. Discovery of certain mineral qualities in the spring water at Grand Haven and Spring Lake was being widely publicized. This attracted many thousands who wished to try the "baths" as a possible remedy for various ailments. The famous spas, hotels and watering places were rapidly built and quickly filled to capacity.

A popular way to reach these health and relaxation centers was to use the Goodrich "night boat" from Chicago to Muskegon or Grand Haven. The "cars" could then be used to reach Fruitport or various other places located on the shores of Spring Lake. Boat service to the same places was offered from Grand Haven. Other communities on the west Michigan shore made various "discoveries" of mineral qualities in their water but none reached the high stage of development found in the Grand Haven-Spring Lake spas.

The Cutler House at Grand Haven and the Spring Lake House at Fruitport were fine examples of the luxurious accommodations provided by these fine hotels. The Spring Lake House had superb accommodations for two hundred and fifty persons and enjoyed a national reputation for its fine facilities and tasty cuisine. The very plush nature of this traffic demanded keeping the best steamers possible on this route.

Courtesy: Henry Barkhausen

S.S. INDIANA — She enters her element with an impressive splash!

The communities served by the west-shore route were also booming and the freight and passenger volume in this area was heavy. Cities like Racine, Kenosha, and Milwaukee were enjoying rapid growth and their business was brisk. The ports on Green Bay, especially in Door County, were doing well. Door County was rapidly being recognized as a most desirable summer resort area and the summer routes of Goodrich offered the ideal way to get there from Chicago and Milwaukee. The opening of the Sturgeon Bay canal in 1882 had done much to stimulate commercial traffic by boat.

On May 15, 1888, the *Chicago Graphic News* had the following to say about the passenger service offered to the public by the Goodrich Transportation Company. The same seven steamers that were in the fleet when Captain Butlin took over command in September of 1885 were still in service.

S.S. INDIANA — Underway and in her prime as a Goodrich steamer.

Courtesy: Historical Collection, Milwaukee Public Library

Courtesy: Marine Historical Collection, Milwaukee Public Library

S.S. INDIANA — Here she is shown tied up in the St. Mary's River where she served the Connelly Contracting Co. as a floating hotel and powerhouse.

The palatial steamboats run by the Goodrich Line from Chicago to all points north on the west shore of the lake are running on regular time. This company operates the finest and best equipped boats leaving Chicago ports. Illustration on this page gives an idea of the company's large and elegant steamers at their docks at the foot of Michigan Avenue. For the Chicago and Milwaukee and West Shore Line the elegant sidewheel boats SHEBOYGAN, CHICAGO and MUSKEGON, and for the Grand Haven and Muskegon Line are the beautiful steamers MENOMINEE and CITY OF LUDINGTON; for the Green Bay, Escanaba, and Manistique West Shore Lines the palatial CORONA and DEPERE.

The Goodrich Line have seven of the most elegant equipped side wheel and propeller passenger boats that travel the great lakes. They have every improvement that can add to the comfort of the traveler or tourist. They traverse the west shore of Lake Michigan, touching all important points between Chicago and Manistique. The steamers CORONA and DEPERE make regular trips between these and all important points on Green Bay, the "tourists Paradise". The picturesque scenery along the shores of Green Bay are not surpassed. Each succeeding year, when the first bright freshness of the spring foliage gives place to the dust and dryness of the June sunshine, and the spring showers are superseded by the sprinkling cart and garden hose and the spring overcoat for the linen duster, when the business man begins to hug the shady side of the street, on his daily trips to and from his office, a large portion of the City people turn their thoughts toward the country and make plans for the summer vacation, which has now become an indispensable element in these days of rapid money-getting and high pressure living. A more delightful and enchanting place for the pleasure seeker, or those wanting a short respite from business, cannot be found than the points on Green Bay touched by the Goodrich Line. It is not only the paradise of the fashionable world but the angler's mecca of inexhaustible resources, the huntsman's bonanza, the invalid's acme of sanitary perfection; in short, the complete utopia of the tourist and pleasure seeker.

Those who wish to make a shorter trip between Racine, Milwaukee, Sheboygan, Manitowoc, Kewaunee, Sturgeon Bay, Menominee, Escanaba, and in short, a trip any desired time can be taken by this line. John J. Singleton, General Passenger Agent for the Goodrich Line, cheerfully furnishes those contemplating a trip with all information.

By 1888 the financial stability of the Goodrich company was fully restored. The program of economy had paid off and the line was now completely out of debt. With business booming on all routes and the volume of traffic at an assuring high level, Captain Butlin now permitted his thoughts to turn to the replacement of the older steamers. If Goodrich was going to remain competitive, more comfortable and luxurious ships were badly needed.

The Goodrich management was, by this time, convinced that all new steamers built for their service should be of the propeller type. The side-wheelers had served the line well but the propeller-driven ships were, by far, the most popular with the public. Also, they were far more adaptable for the year-around routes so often confronted with ice floes and ice-bound harbors.

G. S. Rand, of the Rand Shipyard in Manitowoc, had passed away in 1885 and his name had now completely disappeared from the yard founded by Stephen Bates. Henry Burger, an experienced shipwright from Germany, had joined forces with Rand and for a while the yard was known as Rand & Burger. Later Henry Burger was joined by his nephew George Burger. With the passing of Rand the firm then became known as Burger & Burger.

Late in the year 1888, a contract for a new wooden propeller of 1041 tons was awarded to Burger & Burger by the Goodrich company. Her specifications were to be as follows: hull, wood; length, 220 feet; beam, 38 feet; draft, 13 feet; propulsion, single screw; engine, triple expansion; gross tons, 1041.02; net tons, 802; speed, 14 mph.

Work progressed according to schedule and the new steamer was launched on April 18, 1889. She was christened *City of Racine* in honor of Wisconsin's second largest city. Fitting out continued at Manitowoc and she was ready for service approximately three months later. Her total cost was $125,000.

In spite of his many years ashore at the company's general office in Chicago, Captain Tom, as he was so affectionately referred to by the Goodrich staff, longed for the feel of a ship under his feet. When the new *City of Racine* made her maiden voyage, Captain Butlin was listed as her master. He remained this until the "bugs" were all out of the new steamer.

The *City of Racine* was a splendid example of the ship styling of her day. The single stack was just a little aft of center. Her two masts were nicely raked and carried a gaff boom on each mast as was so typical of all Goodrich steamers. The arched trusses, so prominent on previous Goodrich steamers, were missing. Her stem was relatively high and all in all she was a handsome ship. Captain Butlin had taken a keen interest in her building and when the new steamer made her maiden voyage along the west shore, he was delighted to be on her bridge and in command!

The new steamer had overnight accommodations for two hundred fifty passengers. No expense had been spared or any detail overlooked to make her attractive to the night traveler. Her public rooms were very ornate and done in the best taste of the times. Her beauty excited much favorable comment in the press and thousands passed through the steamer when she was placed on public display in Milwaukee, Racine, and Chicago. Her arrival at the Goodrich dock in Racine was a gala event. The city officials presented the new ship with a beautiful flag and a set of silver service. After her successful trials and public showing the *City of Racine* was placed on the Chicago-Milwaukee route in night service. She was scheduled to make a stop at Racine in each direction.

The *City of Racine* became a very popular steamer. As time went on she was used on almost all of the routes at one time or another. During the period from her launching in 1889 until 1912, she had an accident-free record and earned a good profit for her owners.

In 1912, the ship was sent to the yard at Manitowoc for a complete rebuilding. In the process she was repowered and given new boilers. Her overnight capacity was increased by the addition of new cabins and her entire interior was completely refurbished. Upon the completion of this extensive work she was renamed *S. S. Arizona* and returned to general service.

In 1925, *Arizona* was retired from regular service and placed on an extra or stand-by duty. As such she was used in charter service for a few seasons and then, eventually, she was

Courtesy: Dowling Collection

S.S. ATLANTA — This photo shows her at the Muskegon dock.

permanently laid up at Manitowoc. In the early thirties, *Arizona* was purchased by a marine contracting firm and used as a power plant during the improvement project of the Livingstone Channel in the Detroit River.

After the completion of this project the contracting firm had no immediate use for her and she was laid up in the Maumee River near Toledo. Eventually the proud old steamer was stripped to the water line and left to rot. Her bones still lie there in the river for all to see.

On December 1, 1889, Albert W. Goodrich was installed as President of the Goodrich Transportation Company. Captain Butlin agreed to continue to function as general superintendent for a while longer. From that knowledgeable position he could give the young new president the benefit of his many years of experience in the steamboat business. Young Albert had been a good student of the affairs of the company since his father's death, and very little time elapsed before all those around him were convinced that he would make a fine and capable replacement for Captain Goodrich. The years that followed certainly justified this conviction.

Just 13 days less than a year from the launching of *City of Racine* another new Goodrich steamer slid down the ways at the Burger & Burger Yard in Manitowoc. This new steamer was launched on April 5, 1890, and was christened *Indiana*. In size and general appearance she was almost identical to her predecessor. Constructed at a cost of $135,000 her principal dimensions were: hull, wood; length, 220 feet; beam, 40 feet; depth, 24 feet; draft, 14 feet; gross tonnage, 1178; net tonnage, 962; propulsion, single screw; engine, fore and aft compound, 26 x 50 x 36; horsepower, 775; revolutions per minute, 92; service speed, 14.5 mph; fuel, coal.

In the planning of *Indiana,* a great deal of thought was given to accommodations for overnight passengers. As a result she could sleep two hundred persons in her staterooms and parlor suites. Her spacious cargo holds provided capacity for over one thousand tons of freight.

After her fitting out at Manitowoc, *Indiana* was assigned to the Chicago-Racine-Milwaukee route as a night boat running opposite the *City of Racine*. Her acceptance by the public was immediate and she retained that popularity throughout her life as a Goodrich ship.

In 1895 *Indiana* was assigned to the cross-lake route serving Chicago, Muskegon and Grand Haven. She remained on this route until replaced by the *Alabama* in 1910.

In 1916 *Indiana* was returned to Manitowoc to the yard of the Manitowoc Shipbuilding Company for a major overhaul. She

was cut in two and twenty-two feet were added amidships. Steel
bulkheads were installed and eight deluxe parlor suites were
added to her sleeping accommodations. Some of her public room
space was improved and new boilers were installed. A careful
overhaul of her wooden hull completed the work and *Indiana* went
back into service looking like a brand-new steamer, even to her
changed silhouette! The changes made in her hull length during
this rebuilding increased her gross tonnage rating to 1979.

Indiana was now placed on the west-shore route to Washington Island. During her life with Goodrich, this dependable and
popular steamer served on all routes including the plush Grand
Haven and Muskegon route. Always a lucky ship, she avoided
many serious accidents and groundings. One or two incidents of
trouble in her career must be mentioned.

The winter of 1916-1917 was very bitter. On January 14,
1917, *Indiana* was making her difficult way through the ice as
she entered Chicago harbor. As is so often the case with ice in
the Lake, steam and vapor were rising from the water, greatly
reducing the visibility from the bridge of the ship. At a point due
east from Navy Pier, there was an extension of the Chicago Outer
Breakwater that was submerged. Captain Richardson, who was
in command, well knew of the existence of the submerged portion
of the pier but the presence of so much steam and fog made him
unsure of his exact position. As a result *Indiana* struck the obstruction a solid blow. Due to conditions, she was running only
"slow ahead" but the impact was enough to shatter some of her
hull planking. Her pumps were able to control the water that
rushed into her hull and she made her way to Manitowoc, for
repairs, under her own power.

On January 30, 1918, *Indiana* was a prisoner of the ice off
the harbor entrance at Racine, Wisconsin. In spite of yeomen efforts by Captain Richardson and his crew to cut a channel in
the heavy Lake ice, the steamer was unable to move. Windrows
and floe ice fifteen feet high at her stem made it impossible to
back the ship.

All perishable freight was removed and rushed ashore. Her
heavy cargo of general merchandise remained aboard until a
change in wind and weather, several days later, made it possible
to work the sturdy propeller into Racine harbor.

In the summer of 1922 *Indiana* again met with trouble in
Chicago harbor. While approaching the harbor entrance in an
early-morning, dense summer fog, she collided, bow on, with the
Carter H. Harrison water-intake crib. The force of the collision
severely damaged her bow section. Again her pumps were equal
to the task of controlling the inrushing Lake Michigan water and
she proceeded to her dock. After discharging her passengers and

freight a canvas collision cloth was rigged over her damaged
bows and she proceeded under her own power to Manitowoc for
repairs. The second accident resulted in the permanent revocation
of Captain Redner's master's license by the United States Steamboat Inspectors. Examination had revealed that the captain's
eyesight had become badly impaired.

In 1928 the reliable old steamer was retired from regular
service and laid up at Manitowoc. Purchased by the Connelly Contracting Company of Minneapolis in 1930, for $16,200, she was
taken to the St. Mary's River where she served as a powerhouse
and housing unit for the men working on the West Neebish
Channel cut.

The project of deepening the West Neebish Channel in the
St. Mary's River required the building of two dams besides the
dredging. A work force of 120 men was needed for several
months. No housing was available, so the *Indiana* was anchored
near the job to provide a floating hotel.

With 148 staterooms, each equipped with hot and cold running water, a luxurious dining room, lounging rooms, a barber
shop and eleven shower baths, the workers really enjoyed their
stay aboard the former luxurious Lake steamer. The construction
superintendent set up his office in the captain's quarters.

TUG *TESSLER* — The heroic efforts of the captain and crew of this fish
tug saved all but one of those aboard the fire-stricken *Atlanta*.

Courtesy: Edwin Wilson Collection

Courtesy: Marine Historical Collection, Milwaukee Public Library

S.S. VIRGINIA — This is what she looked like shortly after her delivery to Goodrich.

When the work on the west cut was completed the same firm took a contract to construct the Livingstone Channel improvement project just below Detroit in the Detroit River. *Indiana* was moved to the new location and performed the same duties. There she was joined by her former sister ship the *Arizona* (formerly *City of Racine*) who was being utilized for the same purpose.

Upon completion of the Livingstone Channel work in 1935, the *Indiana,* now partially dismantled, was moved to Monroe, Michigan. Later she was moved to Toledo, Ohio, where she was allowed to rot away. Her ribs still protrude above the Maumee River when the water is low.

The third new wooden propeller, built to replace the older steamers, was *Atlanta*. Constructed by the Cleveland Dry Dock Company, she was launched at Cleveland, Ohio, on April 25, 1891. Her launching was a significant event in that this was the first wooden-hulled steamer built for Goodrich that had not been built at Manitowoc since the construction of *Union* there, in 1861, thirty years before!

Atlanta, like *Indiana,* was very similar in size and general appearance to *City of Racine.* Her general specifications were as follows: hull, wood; length, 200 feet; beam, 32 feet; draft, 13 feet 6 inches; gross tonnage, 1129; net tonnage, 958; propulsion, single screw; engine, fore and aft compound, 24 x 44 x 36; revolutions per minute, 106; service speed, 14.5; fuel, coal.

Built at a cost of $108,678 she, like *Indiana,* had been planned with the overnight passenger in mind. She had sleeping accommodations for about 175 persons and her cargo capacity was 950 tons. Upon completion she was assigned to service on the cross-lake route to Grand Haven and Muskegon. Her first trip from Chicago to Muskegon was made on June 21, 1891. On arrival at Central Wharf she was put on display and thousands viewed the new steamer. Unlike her two predecessors, she was not destined for the same long life under the Goodrich banner as *City of Racine* and *Indiana.*

S.S. VIRGINIA — This photo shows her with her pilothouse moved forward and added cabins topsides.

Courtesy: Marine Historical Collection, Milwaukee Public Library

By 1906 *Atlanta* had been replaced on the cross-lake route by *Virginia* and was being used on the west-shore route. This is the story of her last trip as told to the author by Captain D. J. McGarity, who was her wheelsman on the fateful morning she was lost in Lake Michigan:

"The steamer *Atlanta* was on the run from Manitowoc to Chicago. On this route she would stop at Sheboygan and Milwaukee and then go on to Chicago. On the morning of March 18, 1906, *Atlanta* departed from Manitowoc at 4:00 A.M. She arrived at Sheboygan about 6:30 A.M. and immediately began to load her southbound cargo as she was due to depart from Sheboygan, for Milwaukee, at 10:00 A.M.

"All went as scheduled and *Atlanta* got underway for Milwaukee about 10:15 A.M. The weather was clear and quite cold and the wind was gusty. In the aft hold there was a quantity of furniture and other inflammable cargo. At 11:30 A.M., when the steamer was about fourteen miles south of Sheboygan, fire was discovered in the aft hold. Due to the inflammable nature of the cargo in this hold, the fire gained headway very rapidly. Soon it burned its way into the firehold and then the engine room, driving all personnel topside. With the conflagration centered around the boilers and engine room the firemen could no longer stoke the boilers and *Atlanta* ran out of steam. This made the fire pumps inoperative and the flames raged out of control.

"The crew made a desperate attempt to save the steamer. Whenever it appeared that they were gaining against the flames, the fire would break out anew in another part of the ship. Finally the order to abandon was given by Captain McCauley. The passengers and crew, totaling sixty-five, prepared to take to the lifeboats still undamaged by the fire.

"The fishing tug *Tessler*, working out of Port Washington under the command of Captain G. H. Smith, noted that the *Atlanta* was acting strangely and appeared to be in distress. Captain Smith ordered the work stopped and the *Tessler* proceeded with all possible haste to the *Atlanta*. It was not until the tug was well alongside that Captain Smith realized that the steamer was afire. It was then that he discovered that those lifeboats not damaged by the fire were swung out and ready to be lowered. The boats were badly overcrowded and some people were trapped on the hurricane deck close to the bow.

"Quickly lines were passed from the tug to the hurricane deck of the burning steamer. Those trapped there immediately slid or partly fell down these lines to the deck of the *Tessler*. Some were injured in the process but all of those huddled on the port bow were saved by the gallant action of Captain Smith and the staunch *Tessler*.

"As the lifeboats were hastily pulling away from the scorched sides of the ill-fated *Atlanta* a scream of terror was heard and the face of the Negro cook appeared at a port hole and begged to be taken off. Two sailors scaled the side of the ship and cut a hole through the side of the deckhouse, thereby releasing him from the pantry in which he was trapped.

"There was only one life lost in the whole incident. A seaman, Mike Hickey, was lost, but not by fire. He made a misstep trying to board and take his place in Lifeboat Number One and plunged into Lake Michigan. He drowned before aid could reach him.

"As the survivors were taken aboard the little *Tessler*, Captain Smith sent those with wet or scant clothing to his engine room to keep from freezing. After all survivors in sight were taken aboard, a roll call was held and Captain McCauley was convinced that all that had been aboard the *Atlanta* were now safe aboard *Tessler* with the exception of the drowned seaman Hickey.

"There were now over seventy persons crowded aboard the little tug and she was badly overloaded. Captain Smith decided to

S.S. VIRGINIA — Here she is shown at the Muskegon dock. Note the changes in her silhouette due to the addition of cabins topsides and her wheelhouse having been moved forward.

Courtesy: Marine Historical Collection, Milwaukee Public Library

make a run for the safety of Port Washington. Just as they were nicely underway the northbound *Georgia* of the Goodrich line hove into view. She had departed from Milwaukee at 11:00 A.M.

"The *Georgia* was signaled and she immediately stopped and took all the survivors aboard. She then proceeded to Sheboygan where the injured were hospitalized and additional clothing was secured for those who lost their possessions in the fire."

In this act of fine seamanship, bravery, and excellent ship handling, Captain Smith and the crew of the *Tessler* upheld every tradition of the sea and wrote a brilliant page in Great Lakes history. The next day they received proper acclaim for their brave act in the press of the nation.

Captain Con. McCauley, master of *Atlanta*, went on for many years as a Goodrich captain. George Stines, first mate on *Atlanta* on that fateful day, later became a master in the Goodrich service as did Wheelsman Daniel J. McGarity, whose life story is told in a later chapter.

One very interesting sidelight on the *Atlanta* fire had to do with the then new Milwaukee fire boat known as *M.F.D. No. 15.* Shortly after noon on the day of the fire the chief of the Lifesaving Service on Jones Island, Captain Ingar Olsen, phoned Chief Clancy of the Milwaukee Fire Department and told him of the report he had just received to the effect that the *Atlanta* was afire five miles off Port Washington.

In just twenty minutes *M.F.D. No. 15* picked up Captain Olsen, some of his men and their gear and started north up the Lake in search of the burning vessel.

When abeam of Port Washington, about 3:00 P.M., there was no sign of a burning steamer, no smoke or even wreckage, so the search was abandoned and *M.F.D. No. 15* returned to Milwaukee. Only then did they learn that the burning steamer was some twelve miles north of the point at which the search was abandoned.

After delivering the *Atlanta* survivors to the *Georgia*, the *Tessler* went back to the burning hull and finally managed to beach it, fourteen miles south of Sheboygan. The total value of *Atlanta* at the time of the fire was placed at $150,000. The insurance claim netted $82,680 to the Goodrich company. Later the hull was purchased by D. O. Smith of Port Washington.

Just seven days after the launching of *Atlanta* at Cleveland, another Goodrich steamer was christened as she started down the ways at the shipyard of the Globe Iron Works. This first steel, twin-screw steamer ever built for the line was launched on May 2, 1891, and named *Virginia*.

The selection of design and an agreement on all details pertaining to the new steel steamer were the result of many long discussions and a great deal of planning among the members of the staff at Goodrich. Mr. A. W. Goodrich had now been president long enough to have some very definite ideas of his own. As a youth, he had crossed the Atlantic to Europe and he had a strong feeling that at least one of the several new ships being planned for building should be built of steel, should have twin screws and be fast like the liners he had crossed the ocean on and had observed in the world ports he had visited. He also hoped that in general appearance the new steel steamer could look more like an ocean-going craft than the new wooden propellers like *Indiana*, etc. did. The Lehigh Railroad had a new package freighter, the *Cuyuga*, that he cited as an example. To bolster his reasoning that an unusual steamer was necessary at this time, he quoted the fact that the word was out regarding the proposed construction of the world's first whaleback passenger vessel, *Christopher Columbus*. With the World's Fair in the offing, it seemed important to Albert Goodrich that the Goodrich line also have something equally as large and as fast if the prestige of the Red-Stack line was to be maintained.

A contract to build Goodrich's first all-steel, twin-screw steamship was awarded to the Globe Shipbuilding Company of Cleveland, Ohio, at a cost of $301,163.89. This cost made her the most expensive steamer ever built for the Goodrich line by over $100,000.

Launched on May 2, 1891, the beautiful steamship was christened *Virginia* and immediately designated as the flagship of the Goodrich fleet. *Virginia* had two steel pole masts and one stack located amidship. All three were sharply raked and gave a very sleek look to the new boat. Finished in the standard Goodrich colors of black hull, white cabins, topped with the bright red stack, she was a truly beautiful steamer. There are many who claim that *Virginia* was the most handsome ship in all Goodrich history. With her red funnel, there was a marked similarity to the liners operated by the Cunard Line of England on their trans-Atlantic routes.

The general dimensions of *Virginia* were as follows: hull, steel; length O.A., 285 feet; beam, 38 feet; draft, 14 feet; molded depth, 22 feet; gross tonnage, 1,985; net tonnage, 1,186; propulsion, twin screw; horsepower, 2,600 shaft hp; engines, two triple expansion, 20-32-50 x 36 in. stroke; shaft speed, 105 rpm; service speed, 18 mph; maximum speed, 20 mph; cargo capacity, 1500 tons.

Virginia was equipped with two large double-end boilers. This gave the big ship two fireholds and as a result she carried an unusually large firehold crew or "black gang" as it was called in those days. Because of her large boiler capacity, she was a heavy consumer of coal when running at her full, normal, service speed.

Virginia had exceptionally broad decks and very spacious

public rooms. Her parlors, cabins, and suites were as ornate and fine as any ocean-going vessel of the time. Her main dining room, seating 125 and located in the bow on the lower deck, was a thing of beauty, as were her main saloon and lounges. As Goodrich moved her from one Lake Michigan port to another, in order that the public could view this newest and most outstanding steamer, she created considerable interest and the press was generous in its praise. *Marine Review* of the day described the new ship as "the most elegantly appointed passenger vessel that flies the American flag."

Samuel Ward Stanton, America's most famous illustrator of ships who lost his life in the sinking of the *Titanic* at the age of forty-two, included an accurate and beautiful engraving of *Virginia* in his now priceless book *American Steam Vessels*. The same engraving is currently included in the book *Great Lakes Ships* now published by Mr. Stanton's family. An adaptation of this engraving appeared for many years as a part of the label and trademark of the Lakeside Packing Company of Manitowoc, Wisconsin. Many of our readers undoubtedly remember this label on cans of peas, corn, and tomatoes.

Equipped with the melodious chimed whistle that was a trademark of all Goodrich steamers, she was indeed a spectacular ad-

Courtesy: Chicago Historical Society

S.S. VIRGINIA — View of the main saloon, looking forward.

Courtesy: Chicago Historical Society
S.S. VIRGINIA — View of the main dining room.

dition to the fleet and ready to meet the challenge of any steamship
on the Great Lakes.

On arrival at Chicago the new steamer was made available
for public showing for the final time before being placed in regular
service. The press of Chicago had given much space and acclaim
to *Virginia* and as a result thousands upon thousands made their
way to the dock at the foot of Michigan Avenue to admire the
great ship and her elegant interior.

After the public showing, which had to be held over extra
time to accommodate the thousands that waited in long lines at the
dock to get aboard, *Virginia* was placed on the Chicago-Milwaukee
route on a day-and-night schedule. The new steamer met with
instant success.

At the close of the Columbian Exposition in Chicago, the
Hurson Line purchased the *Columbus* and placed her on the
Milwaukee route in competition with Goodrich. The *Columbus,* as
an excursion boat, made a round trip each day. In order to meet
this competition, Goodrich placed the flagship *Virginia* on the
identical schedule. With both ships leaving Chicago at the same
time, the passengers were often treated to the added attraction of
a daily race between these two giants of the Lakes. On July 20,
1894, *Virginia* and *Columbus* raced on the northbound trip. These

Courtesy: Chicago Historical Society

S.S. VIRGINIA — View of the aft lounge

two greyhounds of Lake Michigan covered the eighty-five miles from Chicago to Milwaukee in four hours and twenty-seven minutes with an average of nineteen miles per hour.

Virginia was an extremely good seaboat. Invariably, when there was a good sea running, she would be the victor in the unofficial race. On calm days *Columbus* would usually be declared the winner. These races caused much excitement, not only with the paying guests, but among the respective crews who would often wager heavily on the outcome. During one of these exciting contests, a boiler exploded on *Virginia*. This caused death and serious injury to some of the firehold crew and near-panic among the passengers, none of whom received any injury. After this unfortunate incident the racing between the two steamers was stopped.

In 1894, Albert Goodrich employed a well-known Chicago news writer to take the daylight trip from Chicago to Milwaukee and then write the story of the trip and his impressions of the beautiful steamship. Upon completion of his story, it was published as a paperback booklet with the name VIRGINIA emblazed across the pure white cover in gold, old-English lettering. The contents of this interesting booklet read as follows:

ITINERARY

It is nine o'clock in the morning on one of those perfect days
when all nature seems glad, that we find ourselves cosily seated
in one of the observation cabins on the topmost deck aft of the
Texas or wheel house of the superb steamship "VIRGINIA" of the
Goodrich Transportation Company line at their dock at Rush
Street bridge. We are going to visit several northern resorts and
chose this charming route to reach Milwaukee. The sharp whistle
is sounded, the signal for the lines to be cast off, and with an
almost imperceptible motion the steamship glides from her dock,
and past the bustling, busy, smoking, screeching tugs in the harbor, steamers and vessels of all descriptions, the coal piles, lumber
yards and the grand old lighthouse, we are out in Lake Michigan,
now placid, calm, serene.

Behind us we have left the heat and dust of our great metrop-
olis. Its lofty buildings are fast receding from view, and the
scenery is being replaced with that of nature. The steamship
plows through the water at the rate of 19 miles per hour, but not
one throb or pulsation of her powerful machinery is noticeable.
Closely following the coast line, well in to shore, we have a plain
view, without the aid of glasses, of the charming coast line
scenery. The beautiful north shore, lined with the mansions of
the rich, first comes to view; then Lincoln Park, emerald tinted,
with its heroic monument to General Grant; the pretty suburban
towns nestling amid nature's grand and lofty groves pass as in a
panorama before us; Evanston, with its church spires, University
buildings and green lawns sweeping down to the glimmering
waters of the lake; Lake Forest, amid ravines and nature's groves;
Kenosha, a charming city, and Racine, located on a high bluff
and alive with manufactories.

It is the dinner hour, and what a refreshing feeling that cool,
invigorating and always fresh and pure air of the lake has given
us. It has acted as a tonic, and we are ready to do justice to the
menu that the able chef has provided. We reach the dining room
by a solid mahogany staircase. It is 55 feet in length, and has an
average width of 24 feet, with a 14 foot ceiling. It will seat 110
persons. The hand of the decorative artist is here displayed. The
ceiling is divided into panels, each filled with Lincrusta-Walton,
from the center of which an electric light is pendent. From three
grand electroilers hung from the central beam are nests of electric lights. Daylight and fresh air are admitted to the saloon
through twenty large brass "deadlights" each of which is con-
cealed from view by a screen of stained glass. An electric light
placed behind these screens gives the effect of the most brilliant
sunlight passing through. A portion of the saloon is finished in
Moorish fretwork, worked out of rich mahogany, and backed at a
distance by mahogany panel work. With the exception of the
mahogany the entire saloon is finished in the tasteful and fashionable style of decoration known as "ivory and gold". The

ventilation is perfect. Altogether it is unique and original in
design and decoration is unexcelled in convenience and comfort.
We enjoyed a repast such as is served but by few of the great
hotels of the City, and excelled by none. Our appetites being
whetted by the lake breeze, we did justice to the excellent cuisine.
After our repast we had occasion to inspect the steamship. We
learned that she was constructed by the Globe Iron Works of
Cleveland. To use nautical terms, her dimensions are as follows:
278 feet overall, 260 feet keel, 38 feet beam and 25 feet depth of
hold. An important feature in her construction is the system of
transverse frames of the bulkheads, which give the main deck a
high degree of stiffness and stability, the result being the elimination of that disagreeable vibration and jarring movement
experienced on most steamers, that induces wakefulness. The hull
has six water-tight bulkheads in addition to the collision and
stuffing box bulkheads, so that if the boat should be cut squarely
in two, both ends would float. We found the boiler room with its
grimy firemen, interesting. Here are two mammoth double end
boilers, 13 feet in diameter by 21 feet in length, having 12 furnaces and being equal to four 13 foot boilers. Ascending to the
engine room, we were astonished at its neatness, brightly polished
steel and brasswork everywhere. The cylinder heads on the powerful engines shone like mirrors. These great motors are known as
"triple expansion engines", the cylinders being 20, 30, and 52
inches, with a 36 inch stroke. They turn screws, make 150 R.P.M.
and drive the boat at the rate of 19 M.P.H. In the engine room
are eight auxiliary engines which run the two dynamos, the air
pumps, pumping machinery, steering gear, etc. But it was the
main cabin that for artistic beauty and originality of design
caught our attention.

It extends nearly the whole length of the steamship and is finished in solid mahogany and treated in ivory and gold, richly
carpeted, with a profusion of costly easy chairs, berths hung with
curtains similar to those on Pullman sleepers, but more expensive
and tasteful, a grand piano harmonizing with the whole; and
with 800 incandescent lights shining from every nook it presents
a scene of oriental splendor. Each stateroom has four berths, two
of which can be drawn into the cabin. There are eight double and
four single family staterooms, with all the comforts of a home
boudoir. We found here four ladies' waiting maids to attend to
the wants of the ladies and children, and every comfort that home
could supply. The steamship has cabin accommodations for 300
passengers. Above the cabin is the topmost deck, on which two
observation cabins — ladies' and gentlemen's. When we had finished our inspection of this model steamship we were entering
Milwaukee Bay and viewing that architecturally beautiful city —
the Cream City — sitting on a commanding position 90 feet above
the lake.

We were loth to leave the boat, and on the dock took one last
look, for the present, at her yacht-like lines and sylph-like mold,

Courtesy: Chicago Historical Society

S.S. VIRGINIA — View of main stairway to main saloon.

and pronounced her, as did the Marine Review, the standard authority in marine architecture "the trimmest, neatest, handsomest and most elegantly appointed passenger steamship built, but more than that, the finest ship that flies the American flag." The VIRGINIA affords the residents of both cities opportunity to breathe the pure air of Lake Michigan at an insignificant cost compared with railroad travel and its discomforts.

It will be noted that in the closing lines of this vivid description of a trip on the *Virginia,* Goodrich could not resist the opportunity to take still another dig at the high cost of smoky, dirty rail travel.

In 1898 the *Columbus* came under the control of the Goodrich interests and *Virginia* was returned to the day-and-night service between Chicago and Milwaukee.

At the beginning of the season of 1908 *Indiana* and *Iowa* were running opposite each other on the Muskegon-Grand Haven-Chicago route. The *Virginia* made her first trip from Chicago to Muskegon on July 18, 1908. She then replaced *Iowa* on the run and remained in this service until 1917. Following the addition of *Virginia* to the east-shore run *Iowa* returned to the west-shore routes. Business on the cross-lake route had been on the increase and the peak was not reached until the years 1912 to 1916. In 1912

Goodrich carried approximately 200,000 passengers between Chicago and Grand Haven.

During her career as a Goodrich steamship, *Virginia* made several trips to the shipyard at Manitowoc for overhaul and some remodeling in the form of additional cabins topside. In 1911, an upper pilothouse was built on her bridge and a third cabin was added. This made a definite change in her silhouette.

Virginia, except for the boiler explosion previously mentioned, had a remarkably accident-free record for the twenty-six years she served on the Goodrich line. In 1917 she was requisitioned by the United States Navy for use on the Atlantic Ocean. The Navy ordered her to be sent to Boston Navy Yard for conversion to a troop transport ship.

In order to permit her passage through the St. Lawrence River locks, twenty-eight feet of her bow was removed and stowed on her main deck. This permitted her collision bulkhead to be open to the sea so it was heavily shored to strengthen it for the long journey. Some twenty feet of her stern overhang was also removed and stowed aboard. The bow and stern were replaced on arrival at Montreal. On arrival at Boston she was renamed *U.S.S. Blue Ridge.* Actually the *Blue Ridge* never saw active service with the Navy and in 1920 she was declared surplus to the need of the Government.

Courtesy: Chicago Historical Society

S.S. VIRGINIA — View of the "Gentlemen's Lavatory."

In that same year she was purchased by Mr. William Wrigley, of chewing-gum fame. This caused a rumor in the press to the effect that Mr. Wrigley intended to convert her to a private yacht for his personal use. Such was definitely not the case. She had been purchased for use between San Pedro, California, and Catalina Island, a recent purchase by her new owner.

The announcement of the acquisition of the *Blue Ridge* by Mr. Wrigley set off rumors in California that the newly purchased steamer was really the ill-fated *Eastland*. To offset this bad publicity, Mr. Wrigley wrote to Mr. A. W. Goodrich and secured the complete story and photographs of *Virginia*. This material was the basis of several articles on the steamer that appeared in California newspapers. As a result of this action, the rumor finally died.

Immediately after the sale, the former Goodrich Queen began her long trek to California via the Panama Canal, which she completed without incident.

In California, *Virginia,* or more properly, *Blue Ridge,* was sent to the shipyard to be made ready for the Catalina Island service. Her topside cabins were removed and replaced by a large sun deck. When all work was completed her silhouette was almost the same as when she was first launched in Cleveland. In her new role as a steamer for the Catalina Navigation Company, she was painted all white with a yellow stack. On the yellow stack was a navy-blue flag with the letter "W" in the middle, the trademark of her new owners. She was renamed *Avalon* and began the new service in 1921.

For the next thirty-odd years very few people made the popular trip from the mainland to Catalina Island without traveling in one direction or the other on the *S. S. Avalon.* She soon became one of the best-known vessels on the West Coast. Her chimed whistle's melodious note thrilled California travelers as it used to do her host of admirers on Lake Michigan.

Alas, all things must come to an end, even the life of a former queen of Lake Michigan. *Avalon* was taken from active service early in the 1950's and not too long after that she was scrapped, having been a real beauty and a fine ship to the very end.

S.S. VIRGINIA — This is an interesting bow view of the magnificent ship at her Muskegon dock.

Courtesy : Robert Radunz Collection

Chapter Seven

THE GAY NINETIES

IN THE EARLY 1890's THE RAILROADS BEGAN TO MAKE a serious play for some of the lucrative passenger traffic enjoyed by the Lake steamship lines. Chicago was, by this time, already a great railroad center and certain schedules and rates were slanted to favor some of the destinations from Chicago that were normally served by the Goodrich line.

While the railroads, during this era, were themselves the victims of many terrible rail wrecks across the nation, they did not hesitate to make thinly veiled references in their publicity and advertising copy to the fact that the Lake steamers had been involved in some serious fires, wrecks, and founderings. They even went so far as to indicate to the public that a journey in a railway passenger car was far safer than the same trip by a Lake steamer.

Never a company to shy away from the press as a means of conveying a message to the traveling public, a lot of interesting views of the interior of the new steel steamer *Virginia* were supplied to the *Chicago Graphic News*, a highly illustrated weekly publication. In Volume VII, Number 5, dated July 30, 1892, a long and well-illustrated article on Lake steamer travel appeared. The following extract from this lengthy story is most interesting. The reader will note that no holds are barred in the frank answer to the railroad intimidation regarding the questionable safety of travel on the Goodrich line boats.

True there have been accidents to lake steamers by which lives have been lost, but a comparison of the statistics upon the subject shows a far larger percentage of loss of life by railway transportation than either by ocean or lake steamers. One can hardly pick up a newspaper which does not detail the horrors of some railway wreck, and so frequently are they that they hardly excite any comment. The Government called attention to the appalling loss of life by this means in the form of the President's last annual message in which it was stated that the percentage of disasters had largely increased of late years. While the percentage of total risks has seemed to increase in travel by rail, the same percentage has largely diminished in travel by water, and especially upon the Great Lakes owing to the adaption of new machinery and the observation of precautions that were formerly neglected. The late Captain Albert E. Goodrich·may well be considered the father of the lake passenger traffic, for he was the first to establish a perfectly equipped line of steamers to lake ports, which have kept abreast of every movement of the times, until now the famed Goodrich boats will rival the great ocean steamships in point of beauty, speed and safety. Mr. A. W. Goodrich was elected President of the Company when but twenty one years old, and under his direction, as under that of his father, it has been the aim of the Goodrich Steamer Company not only to make their boats the swiftest and safest upon the lakes, but the most beautiful as well and to achieve this result they have spared neither money nor effort.

The very blunt statements made in the above article will give the reader an insight into the bitter "war-on-paper" that was being waged between the Lake steamship operators and the railroads for the passengers' patronage. It is interesting to note that the issue of the *Chicago Graphic News* that carried the above story also carried railway advertisements but none, in that issue at least, for the Lake steamboat lines. This is certainly an indication that the editorial policy of the publication was not unduly influenced by the advertising department!

Almost four years to the day after assuming the presidency of the Goodrich Transportation Company, another very important event in the life of Albert W. Goodrich took place. On November 30, 1893, Albert was wed to the very beautiful Elizabeth McKay, daughter of a socially prominent Chicago family.

To this very happy marriage three children were born. The first was a daughter, Rosamond, born on February 3, 1895. Three years later another lovely daughter arrived, on November 5, 1898, and was named Elizabeth. Nearly nine years passed before the couple were blessed with their third child, a son. Albert Edgar Goodrich was born on February 11, 1907, and he was named after his famous grandfather, Captain Goodrich.

Courtesy: Muskegon County Museum

S.S. MENOMINEE — This ship ran for many seasons on the cross-lake route, serving Muskegon, Grand Haven, and Chicago.

For much of their married life the Albert W. Goodriches made their home at 942 Lake Shore Drive in Chicago.

After four years at the helm of the Goodrich line, Albert W. Goodrich had demonstrated, to everyone's complete satisfaction, that he possessed many of the qualities of leadership so capably demonstrated by his father. Like his father, he was keenly interested in all aspects of the Goodrich company and its operation. In addition, he had a very definite flair for the publicity and public relations department of the steamboat business. He even found the time to take an interest, and later an active, behind-the-scenes part, in Chicago politics.

In 1890, Chicago was selected as the site for the great World's Fair, the Columbian Exposition. Originally scheduled for 1892, it was to mark the four-hundredth anniversary of the discovery of America by Christopher Columbus. Actually the completion of the fairgrounds and the fabulous buildings was delayed and the fair did not open until 1893. A site on the Lake shore, south of downtown Chicago, and known as Jackson Park, was selected. The architects Burnham and Root were chosen to supervise the design and complete layout of the huge project. Early in the work Mr.

Root was taken ill and died. Daniel Burnham, for whom Burnham Harbor on Chicago's Lake front is now named, carried on alone and did a masterful job of bringing that great work to completion.

The fairgrounds covered 666 acres, laced with canals and lagoons. Among the many firsts seen at the exposition was the world's first Ferris wheel. The fair boasted of a greater power consumption than all of that used in the city of Chicago.

Erection of the fair buildings also brought a great real estate boom to the city. Chicago expanded to the south and there was a big increase in population. Many new hotels and restaurants were built. John R. Thompson arrived from downstate Illinois in 1892 and opened his first lunchroom on Madison Street, just east of La-Salle Street. Similar new ventures, many of whom are still in business in Chicago, sprang up all over the city.

The fair opened May 1, 1893, and closed November 1 of the same year. During this period a total of 27,539,041 persons were admitted to the grounds and the total cost exceeded forty million dollars. All of this stimulated much travel and proved to be a great boon to the Lake steamboat business. Again that shrewd Goodrich judgment was in evidence. All four of the new Goodrich propeller steamers were completed and in service before the opening of the exposition. Even had it opened as scheduled, in 1892, they would have all been ready for the heavy influx in passenger traffic.

In 1893, a great depression began to sweep the country. This was the worst, up to that time, ever to befall our great nation. The huge influx in business in Chicago, brought about by the World's Fair, kept hard times away from Chicago that year but by 1894 the depression caught up with the city in all its devastating force. The Goodrich line, being in very good shape financially by this time, was able to take the big slump in business in its stride.

With the arrival of the three new wooden propellers, *City of Racine, Indiana,* and *Atlanta* and the new steel flagship of the line, *Virginia,* it was now possible to retire some of the older ships. One of these was the *Menominee,* which had been built new in 1872 for Goodrich. In 1896 *Menominee* was sent to the yard at Manitowoc for scrapping. After stripping her of her cabins and fittings it was found that the hull was not only sound but in a fine state of preservation. Upon learning of this, Mr. Goodrich decided to build a new steamer on the old hull. This was done at a cost of $145,000 and upon completion the new steamer was named *Iowa.*

While rebuilding her, the old hull was covered with sheet iron as a precaution against ice damage. This protective covering extended about six feet above her water line. Extra sheets were carried aboard to replace those the ice might tear off. These iron sheets were fastened to the hull with extra long iron nails. When a sheet needed replacing, it was necessary for the crew to cut one to size and make the installation at the dock or sometimes even out on the ice.

Iowa had a rather blunt bow. At the time of the rebuilding, this had been heavily reinforced from the inside, to enable her to smash her way through the ice fields more easily. This blunt bow gave her a tendency to be somewhat cranky and she seemed to roll heavily on the slightest pretext. However, this easy roll made her a good boat in the ice. By throwing her wheel from hard-over to hard-over, she would roll heavily and as a result would not easily stick in the ice.

When *Iowa* was completed she was placed in regular service on the cross-lake route where she ran opposite *Indiana* on the Muskegon-Grand Haven run. With *Iowa's* capacity for over two hundred overnight passengers, she was ideally suited for use on this popular route.

It seems that in every fleet of ships there is one that has the tendency to get into more trouble than any of the others. This was particularly true of *Iowa*. It did not take her very long after she was built to earn the title of "jinx steamer" of the Goodrich Transportation Company. As a result of this well-deserved title, Goodrich captains avoided duty on her whenever they possibly could. It got so that assignment to *Iowa* was akin to being discriminated against. Her troubles began very shortly after she was placed in regular service.

In the severe winter of 1897, *Iowa* became ice-bound in a a huge mid-lake field and was unable to work herself free of the

S.S. IOWA — The *Iowa* and her sister ship *Sheboygan* docked at the Manitowoc outer harbor dock.

Courtesy: William A. McDonald Collection

firm grip of the ice. After several days with no word from *Iowa*, the Goodrich management became deeply concerned over her safety. The *City of Ludington*, under command of Captain Edwin Carus, was dispatched to conduct a search for the missing steamer. *Ludington* finally located her, and after a tremendous effort *Iowa* was cut free of the ice. The two vessels then made their way to the nearest port, which was Milwaukee. Being trapped in the ice in mid-winter was not an unusual experience in those days and this incident did nothing to label *Iowa* a "jinx" steamer.

At 3:45 A.M. on the morning of November 2, 1905, *Iowa* went ashore one-half mile north of Milwaukee's North Point. Captain John C. Raleigh was in command on this voyage from Chicago to Sheboygan, Wisconsin.

Weather conditions at the time the *Iowa* struck were good. The wind was very light and from the south. The Lake was calm and visibility was hazy. A freighter, towing a coal barge, had gone aground almost on the same spot and it is believed that her presence there confused those on the bridge of the *Iowa*.

After the steamer came to a screeching, grinding halt, the captain ordered a quick inspection of the bilges to determine, if possible, the extent of hull damage and to learn how rapidly she was taking water in.

Inspection indicated no immediate danger of sinking, so a lifeboat was sent ashore and the superintendent of the line, Captain D. M. Cochrane, was notified of the accident. Captain Coch-

S.S. IOWA — Here she is shown after she sank at the Goodrich dock on the north side of the Chicago River following her collision with the *Sheboygan*.

Courtesy: Harry W. Thorp. Jr.

rane just happened to be at the Goodrich office in Milwaukee when the call was received.

The tug *Welcome* and a lighter immediately put out from Milwaukee for North Point. Captain Cochrane accompanied them. They arrived at the *Iowa* at 8:45 A.M. By this time the wind had freshened from the southeast and a good sea was building up.

A small amount of cargo from the stern was placed aboard the lighter and the tug *Welcome* was then able to pull the stranded steamer into deep water. *Iowa* was now able to proceed to Milwaukee under her own power, arriving there at noon on November 2.

After discharging her passengers and cargo the ship proceeded to the Milwaukee Dry Dock Company, West Yard, where she underwent major repairs to her hull. Discharged on January 10, she proceeded to Manitowoc. Additional work was done at the Goodrich yard and she was finally returned to service on February 24, 1906. As a result of this incident her master was relieved of duty with the Goodrich line.

During the early spring of 1906, *Iowa* was downbound in the Milwaukee River under command of Captain McCauley. The rains had been heavy and the river was high and running strong. As the temperamental *Iowa* approached the Detroit Street dock the current in the river suddenly took over and the ship headed straight for the dock. With a grinding crunch of timbers and planking she moved forty feet into the structure before fetching up solid.

After Captain McCauley made a hasty inspection and it was determined that there were no injuries and no damage to the *Iowa*, a tug was summoned and the cranky steamer was soon pulled free. She resumed her trip down the river to Lake Michigan with only a few scratches on her hull but the Detroit Street dock had to be completely rebuilt.

November of 1907 found *Iowa* again in difficulty. Under the command of Captain Edward Dorsey, she stranded on Hill's Point in Sturgeon Bay. She had fetched up very firmly aground and it took the services of two tugs to free her. Superintendent Cochrane supervised the efforts to refloat her. In the opinion of the Goodrich management, Captain Dorsey was at fault and he, too, was dismissed from further duty with the Goodrich line. When the sturdy steamer was once more refloated, she made another trip to Manitowoc for repairs. With this incident, causing the second captain to lose his job, the name "jinx" was now firmly attached to *Iowa*.

After the grounding in Sturgeon Bay, all went well with the Goodrich jinx steamer until April 23, 1910. At 2:53 A.M., while en route from Chicago to Milwaukee, with a stop at Racine,

Courtesy: Harry W. Thorp, Jr.

S.S. IOWA — A close-up view of the damage the *Iowa* sustained after her collision with the *Sheboygan*.

the cranky *Iowa* went ashore five and a half miles north of Kenosha, Wisconsin. Captain William Plummer was in command. When the *Iowa* ground to a sudden halt, a boat was lowered to inspect the situation which then made its way to shore to notify the Goodrich office of another mishap to the luckless *Iowa!* Once more Captain Cochrane made his way to the scene to supervise her release personally.

The tugs *Welcome* and *T. T. Morford*, with lighters in tow, were dispatched from Milwaukee to the scene. On their arrival a large part of the cargo was transferred to the lighters. With her draft lightened, the two tugs were able to pull her into deep water at 2:45 P.M. on April 26.

The *Iowa* was then towed into Racine where the balance of her cargo was unloaded. She arrived at Racine at 5:30 P.M. At 9:05 P.M. on the same evening the tugs *Welcome* and *T. T. Morford* took the damaged steamer in tow and started for Milwaukee. They arrived there at 1:38 A.M. the following day.

Iowa entered dry dock at the West Yard of the Milwaukee Dry Dock Company for major repairs. The work on her was completed promptly and she returned to regular service on May 24, 1910. Total cost of wrecking and repairs was $13,162.36.

An investigation placed the blame for her grounding on Captain Plummer and he was released from further employment with the Goodrich line. The jinx that seemed to be hanging over *Iowa* was now causing her to be a ship to be feared by the masters of the line.

On the very foggy morning of July 17, 1913, the *Iowa,* with Captain J. C. Cook in command, arrived in Chicago harbor on her regular run from Milwaukee and Racine. Nothing can be thicker or more dense than a mid-summer fog on Lake Michigan. Under these conditions Captain Cook, very carefully and with great skill, brought *Iowa* safely to the main Goodrich dock on the south side of the Chicago River, at the foot of Michigan Avenue. It was 5:52 A.M. when a short toot on her big chimed whistle indicated that she was tied up and "all was secure."

All but two passengers disembarked at that early hour. The freight handlers then hurriedly put off the baggage, express and fast freight. To discharge the balance of her cargo it was customary to cast off from the main dock on the south side of the river and proceed to the outer harbor where the ship would be turned. She would then make her way back up the river to the Goodrich dock on the north bank of the river, near where the present *Chicago Tribune* dock is located. By this procedure, she would lay at the dock, head-up, to facilitate cargo handling.

At 7:00 A.M. the urgent cargo was all off and the signal to make the move to the other dock was given to the bridge. In spite of the heavy fog, Captain Cook elected to follow the usual routine of going to the outer harbor to turn the ship instead of winding her at the main dock.

Another Goodrich steamer, the *Sheboygan,* running a little late because of the zero visibility, was groping her way toward the Chicago harbor entrance. The old side-wheeler was inbound from Milwaukee. As the two steamers neared each other in the outer harbor, there was an exchange of whistle signals. A few minutes later there was another exchange of signals but apparently a misunderstanding took place. Those on the bridge of the *Iowa* were horrified to see the bow of the *Sheboygan* suddenly loom out of the fog on the port bow. Before anything could be done to prevent a collision, *Sheboygan* struck *Iowa* a severe blow hard on the port bow, cutting a fifteen-foot-long gash that reached down to within three feet of her keelson.

In spite of the fact that *Iowa* began to fill rapidly, Captain Cook was able to bring her to her regular berth at the North Dock and stop the steamer exactly on her gangway markings. Thereupon *Iowa* settled to the bottom of the Chicago River with a list to the port side.

Once more Captain Cochrane took charge of restoring his problem steamer to her turn in regular service. Temporary repairs were made to the huge gash in her bow and the ship was pumped out and raised. This work took nine days and at 6:00 P.M., on Sunday, July 27, 1913, *Iowa,* under escort of the tug *Starke,* departed Chicago for the dry dock of the Manitowoc Shipbuilding & Dry Dock Company at Manitowoc, Wisconsin.

There the jinx steamer was given a complete overhaul and was returned to regular service in October of 1913.

The collision at Chicago resulted in damage and lost cargo amounting to $81,891.96. The steamboat inspectors held *Sheboygan* at fault for the actual collision. As a result of this action a total of $55,390.95 was collected in cargo salvage and insurance. This left a net loss to the Goodrich company of $26,501.01.

In the opinion of Mr. A. W. Goodrich, Captain Cook had used poor judgment in going outside the river to turn *Iowa* and he was dismissed. Captain Andrew Voight, master of *Sheboygan,* had his license revoked for a period of time by the inspectors and he, too, was dismissed from service with the Goodrich line. The *Iowa* was now placed under the command of Captain D. J. McGarity.

On November 10, 1913, came the "big storm" as it is referred to by Great Lakes sailors. It is to the credit of *Iowa* that she lived through the terrible two days and nights of this wild storm that sank sixteen or seventeen fine Lake steamers. The story of this storm is related in detail in the life story of Captain McGarity in Chapter Ten.

In September of 1914, *Iowa,* under the command of Captain G. E. Stufflebeam, was upbound in the Milwaukee River. As she approached the Walker Point bridge, the usual three long blasts on her chimed whistle failed to produce the desired results as the bridge was stuck and could not open to let her through. To avoid striking the bridge, Captain Stufflebeam rang for "full astern" on the engine-room telegraph. As the *Iowa* lost way, the current caught her stern and the temperamental old gal swung broadside toward a nearby dock. A small harbor tug, moored to the dock, was crushed like an egg shell and sank immediately. Fortunately, none of the crew were aboard so no lives were lost in the accident. No wonder Goodrich captains began to dread assignment to *Iowa.*

The winter of 1914-1915 was very severe. Long periods of zero or below-zero temperatures caused heavy ice fields to form in Lake Michigan. On the night of February 3, *Iowa* departed

from Milwaukee, bound for Chicago with her regular stop at
Racine. She departed from Racine at 11:45 P.M. The entry in
her log indicated wind south-southeast and fresh. Visibility was
recorded as being hazy, a common condition on the Lake in
winter time.

All went well and no ice was encountered until *Iowa* was
abreast of Grosse Point Light at 4:15 A.M. Then a large and
heavy ice field, extending well out into the Lake from shore,
was observed dead ahead. Upon sighting the ice field, the course
was ordered changed and *Iowa* hauled southeast for fifteen minutes, running along the outside edge of the ice field. Then Captain
Stufflebeam ordered her engines stopped and the steamer drifted
in open water, awaiting the arrival of daylight.

Just after daylight the *Iowa* was joined by the steamer
Racine, of the Chicago, Racine and Milwaukee Line. *Racine* was
also bound down for Chicago and, like the *Iowa*, was seeking a
path through the ice field. The two steamers ran close together
as they sought passage through the fourteen-inch-thick ice that
lay between them and the entrance to the Chicago River.

Earlier that morning the *Alabama* had cut her way through
the same heavy ice. The lane left by her passage was frozen over
sufficiently heavy to keep the heavier ice on either side from
blowing together. The *Racine* located this lane and began breaking her way through, closely followed by *Iowa*.

Using his wireless, Captain Stufflebeam kept the Goodrich
office at Chicago fully informed on the progress and problems
of both steamers. At 7:45 A.M. he sent the following message:
"*Iowa* and *Racine* abreast of Carter Harrison Crib. In open water.
Looking for opening."

The next message received from *Iowa*, at 8:50 A.M., said:
"South track abreast of Carter Harrison Crib. Making good
progress."

Iowa maintained a distance of about 150 to 200 feet between
her and *Racine*, and while progress was slow it did appear that
all was going well. The wind began to increase with the coming
of daylight and by 10:00 A.M. it was blowing very strong.

Suddenly and with no warning the ice began to "run" and
the lane ahead of *Iowa* closed with a grinding crunch as hundreds
of tons of ice began to pile up ahead of the steamer. *Iowa* came
to a jarring halt as she found herself completely locked in the
huge ice floe. Ahead the Racine also came to a halt.

As the ice piled up forward of the starboard gangway it
actually began to pry the upper decks loose from the hull! Now
Captain Stufflebeam sent the following and last wireless message,
recorded at 10:10 A.M.: "Send tug at once. Fast in ice. Ice run-

ning. Starboard forward gangway planking struck loose. Leaking badly. *Racine* stuck ahead."

Captain Stufflebeam then stepped out on the ice to inspect his vessel's condition. He found that the ice had already lifted the main deck two feet and the hull was rapidly filling with water. He ordered Otto Grimm, first mate, to abandon ship.

The crew and the lone passenger had time to don warm clothing and in most instances to fill their suit cases before stepping out on the ice. The only woman aboard was Miss Elizabeth Smith, a stewardess, and the one passenger was Edward H. Hoover of Milwaukee. All aboard reached the ice safely except Frank Lowery, a fireman. He suffered a broken collarbone when he slipped on the ice as he scrambled from the doomed steamer.

The seventy members of the crew and the lone passenger then stood on the ice and watched in horror as the hull, rent by the pressure of untold tons of moving ice, keeled over and sank at approximately 11:00 A.M.

Parts of the hurricane deck and the pilothouse remained on the ice after the hull sank from sight. The survivors of the lost ship now made their way, with occasional leaps over open

S.S. IOWA — The "jinx" among the Goodrich steamers outbound from Grand Haven.

Courtesy: Henry Barkhausen

water, to shore and safety. The point of sinking was a little less than two miles northeast by north from the government pier near the mouth of the Chicago River.

The *Racine*, having a steel hull built for winter service, managed to free herself and dock safely at Chicago.

The sunken *Iowa* presented a menace to navigation as she lay in relatively shallow water. Great Lakes Dredge and Dock Company were given a contract for her removal. The hull was partly refloated and some of the cargo and machinery were salvaged. Dynamite was used to destroy what was left.

After the total loss of *Iowa*, Captain Stufflebeam was reduced in rank to first mate. He continued with Goodrich, however, and later his rank of captain was restored. Before resigning from Goodrich to manage the state of Michigan ferries at the Straits of Mackinac, he commanded both the *Alabama* and *Nevada*.

This brings to a close the story of the "famous" and temperamental *Iowa*, the most persistent "jinx" steamer in all of Goodrich history. It is significant to note that while this unlucky steamer cost several captains their jobs with Goodrich, and the company itself a lot of money, not a single life was lost in any of her escapades or accidents.

S.S. CHRISTOPHER COLUMBUS—This photo was taken during her trial run at Superior City, Wisconsin. At that time her hull was white and her stack cream-colored.

Courtesy: A. E. Young

Chapter Eight

TURN OF A CENTURY

IN THE YEAR 1898, MR. A. W. GOODRICH TOOK STEPS
to remove a big competitor, big, that is, because the great whaleback steamer *Christopher Columbus* was 362 feet long!

At the close of the Columbian Exposition the big ship had
been sold and her new owners had placed her on the Chicago-
Milwaukee route in competition with Goodrich. To meet this
excursion competition meant placing *Virginia*, the finest steamer
in the Goodrich fleet, on an identical day-excursion schedule. All
of this seemed a waste of ship tonnage to Mr. Goodrich, and
he made plans to do something about it. Just how this was accomplished is an interesting part of the story of one of the most
exciting steamers ever to ply the Great Lakes.

The whaleback-type vessel was conceived, designed, and built
under patents granted to a former Great Lakes skipper, Captain
Alexander McDougall.

Captain McDougall was born in Scotland and as a small boy
he emigrated with his parents to Canada. In 1864 he began his
career as a sailor and eventually became a master. One of his
outstanding commands was the steamer *Japan*. The *Japan* was
one of the Anchor Line's original "Lake Triplets" that over the
years became very famous on the Lakes.

In 1872 Captain McDougall conceived the idea of the moni-
tor-type ship, later known as the whaleback. From then on he
spent all his time in the development and sales promotion of this

type of ship. By very hard work and persistent effort Captain McDougall succeeded in constructing the first whaleback tow barge in the year 1888. This barge, known only as "Hull Number 101," was launched in Duluth, Minnesota, on June 23 of that year.

Barge Number 101 was most successful and she was rapidly followed by other hulls of the monitor type. In all a total of forty-three whaleback vessels were constructed, thirty-nine of which were built at the head of Lake Superior. The last one built was christened *Alexander McDougall,* in honor of the man who invented them. She was launched in July of 1898 and was in active service on the Lakes for over fifty years! *Alexander McDougall* differed from the other whalebacks by having a regulation-type bow instead of the blunt pig-snout type used on all the others. As a result she was referred to as a "straightback." It was the snout-like bow that gave the whalebacks the nickname "pig boat."

Of all forty-three whalebacks built, only one was a passenger ship and she was destined to become a very famous and well-known steamer in the forty years she sailed Lake Michigan. Hull Number 128 was a steel excursion ship built at Superior, Wisconsin, by the American Steel Barge Company for the World's Fair Steamship Company of Chicago.

Her keel was laid in September of 1892 and work was rushed to make certain that she would be completed in time for the World's Fair traffic in the spring of 1893. It took only eighty-seven days to complete work on her hull; and upon launching at Superior, on December 3, 1892, she was christened *Christopher Columbus,* in honor of the Columbian Exposition. Her fitting-out work continued at a brisk pace and in the spring of 1893 the huge new ship was delivered to her owners exactly on schedule.

Christopher Columbus was 362 feet long, had a beam of 42 feet and a loaded draft of nearly 17 feet. Gross tonnage was 1,500 tons and her 72 - 56 - 36 x 48 triple expansion steam engines developed over 4,000 horsepower and were built by S. F. Hodge & Company of Detroit. Single screw, she carried an eighteen-foot propeller which developed the amazingly fast cruising speed of twenty miles per hour.

Seven steel turrets projected upward from her hull to the first deck giving an appearance similar to that of the battleships of her era. Designed primarily as a day boat, much thought was given to expedient handling of vast hordes of passengers. It was not uncommon for her to handle as many as five thousand passengers in a single trip. It is said that she could completely discharge a full load of that many passengers in as little as five minutes!

The combination of her gleaming white hull, pink-colored stack and unusual design features made her a most spectacular and much discussed vessel. She received mention in the press of the entire nation and was immediately one of the secondary highlights of the World's Fair.

On delivery at Chicago, she was placed in service from a dock at the foot of Randolph Street to Jackson Park, along the shore of Lake Michigan. Travel to and from the fair from downtown Chicago by boat was very convenient and popular. It is estimated that the *Christopher Columbus* carried over two million passengers in that first year of her existence. All of these gay, holiday-bent passengers were handled without a single loss of life.

After the close of the fair, *Columbus* was purchased by the Hurson Line of Chicago. This company had been founded by Gregory Hurson, who was a former Goodrich employee and at one time secretary of the company. Hurson placed *Columbus* on the Chicago-Milwaukee route as an excursion steamer on a daily round-trip schedule. This action placed the Hurson Line in direct competition with Goodrich. To meet this challenge, Mr. Goodrich ordered the crack liner *Virginia* placed on an identical schedule during the summer season of 1894.

With identical schedules the north- and southbound trips became a race between these two giants of Lake Michigan. On calm days and fair weather the *Columbus* was usually the victor. In heavy weather, with big seas running, the winner was invariably *Virginia* as she was an exceptionally good seaboat.

When Hurson became involved in financial problems the control of *Columbus* was taken over by a group known as the Colum-

S.S. CHRISTOPHER COLUMBUS — A good view of the "pig boat" taken at the Manitowoc Goodrich dock.

Courtesy: Henry Barkhausen

bian Whaleback Steamship Company and they continued to operate *Columbus* on the excursion schedule.

In 1898, Mr. Goodrich made plans to acquire *Columbus*. His first step was to organize a company known as the Chicago & Milwaukee Transportation Company. The stockholders consisted of one or two others from the Goodrich company and the rest were cronies of Mr. Goodrich from Chicago.

Courtesy: Dowling Collection

CAPTAIN ALEXANDER McDOUGALL — He was the inventor of the whaleback vessel. He designed and built the *Christopher Columbus*, the only whaleback passenger steamer ever built.

His next move was to approach the Columbian Whaleback Steamship Company and, as an individual, purchase *Columbus* outright. Then he sold the big excursion boat, at a profit to himself, to the Chicago & Milwaukee Transportation Company.

A. W. Goodrich arranged for the Goodrich Transportation Company to charter *Columbus* from the Chicago & Milwaukee Transportation Company in 1899. Some years later, *Columbus* was actually sold to the Goodrich Transit Company for $290,000.

During the winter of 1899-1900 *Columbus* was sent to the shipyard at Manitowoc for a complete óverhaul and rebuilding. To increase her capacity as an excursion steamer, a third deck was added. Upon completion of the work, *Columbus* was given the traditional black hull, white topsides, and red stack which marked her as a steamer of the popular Goodrich line.

Her acquisition by Goodrich brought an end to the intensive competition between her and *Virginia* on the Chicago-Milwaukee excursion route. Upon her return to service after the extensive remodeling program, *Columbus* was given the day-excursion schedule and *Virginia* returned to her original schedule of day and night service between Chicago and the Cream City.

Columbus departed her dock in the Chicago River at the foot of Michigan Avenue at 9:00 A.M. every day except on Saturday. Her return trip from Milwaukee was scheduled to depart at 4:00 P.M. On Saturdays she departed at 1:00 P.M. from Chi-

STABILITY TEST — The *S.S. Columbus* is shown here in tow of the tug *Kenosha* during the famous stability test held in Chicago harbor on a busy Saturday afternoon, so that all might see that she was a safe and sturdy steamer.

Courtesy: Harry W. Thorp, Jr.

cago and returned from Milwaukee at 7:00 P.M. Her normal summer season was from mid-June until Labor Day and her daily schedule remained the same throughout her long life with Goodrich.

Refreshment stands, a large cafeteria, and a main dining room offered a wide range in food service and prices. Dancing, deck games, movies, and other forms of entertainment were provided for the passengers' comfort and pleasure. Her extreme popularity in the Chicago-Milwaukee service is attested to by the fact that the *Columbus* carried more passengers in her existence than any other Great Lakes ship in history.

As early as 1910 *Columbus* was equipped with wireless. Her "shack" was located on the upper deck on the starboard side.

After the tragic accident of the *Eastland* in the Chicago River on July 24, 1915, the Lake passenger business took a terrific beating. The traveling public lost all confidence in the stability and safety of the Lake steamers. As a result their normal passenger patronage came to a standstill. The ships remained tied to their docks, idle, because no Chicagoan in his right mind would board them to go anywhere. All kinds of wild statements, rumors, and accusations continued unabated. Because of her unusual design and different appearance, *Columbus* was the victim of some very vicious and wholly ungrounded rumors regarding her stability and passenger safety.

Things were so serious that a special meeting of the Goodrich Transit Company board of directors was called for the purpose of determining what should and could be done to restore the passenger traffic to a degree of normalcy. The board session had all the earmarks of a coroner's inquest into the sudden demise of a public idol. Every board member realized the seriousness of the situation but none, including the operating officers of the line, could offer a solution to the problem.

Finally one director, Mr. Charles Hermann, asked a pointed question that could only be answered by Messrs. Goodrich and Thorp: "If the whaleback were fully loaded with passengers and all of them went to one side of the ship at the same time, would it tip?" Both Goodrich and Thorp replied quickly and emphatically, "No!" "Well," replied Mr. Hermann, "then we must, without delay, but with plenty of publicity, make such a demonstration."

All present agreed that it would not be possible to assemble a sufficiently large crowd brave enough to make the test. It was agreed to secure as many as possible, including a band and some prominent city officials. On the basis of an average weight of 150 pounds per passenger, sandbags would be used to make up for the missing passengers.

The Chicago Hearst paper, the *Morning Examiner*, agreed

to run the advance story to inform the public of the unique test that would be held in Chicago's harbor area. The story broke on the front page and excited tremendous public interest in the event.

On a cloudy warm Saturday afternoon, August 24, 1915, the test was made just off the entrance to Chicago harbor. Among the passengers aboard were many gentlemen of the press and a few of the braver city officials. Five hundred tons of sandbags were placed aboard to compensate for the missing passengers who would not even avail themselves of an opportunity for a free boat ride.

When all was in readiness and the shore was lined with thousands of the morbid and curious, the sandbags were shifted to the extreme starboard side of the ship. Then all aboard took places along her starboard rails so that all on shore could see that all weight was on one side of the pig boat! With this tremendous load off-center and concentrated on her starboard side the big ship listed but a few scant degrees in that direction.

With much whistle blowing and accompanied by tugs, Coast Guard craft, and many sight-seeing vessels, *Columbus* triumphantly cruised about the harbor area for all to see that she was a safe and stable steamship!

The test was most conclusive and the press made the most out of the story, heaping high praise on the steamer and congratulating the Goodrich management for their daring and foresight. Only a few days after this spectacular show the gallant *Columbus* was again carrying capacity throngs of pleasure-bound passengers between Chicago and Milwaukee.

Up to this point in her existence, *Columbus* had a very remarkable accident-free record. In spite of the millions of persons handled, no passenger had ever lost his life.

On Saturday, June 30, 1917, this fine record came to a shattering end in one of the strangest accidents ever to befall a Great Lakes steamer. The big whaleback had arrived at Milwaukee on her regular northbound trip from Chicago at about 2:00 P.M. She was scheduled to depart on her southbound return to Chicago at 4:00 P.M.

Promptly on schedule the lines were cast off and the trip back was begun. The harbor tugs *Welcome* and *Knight Templar* took her lines to assist in backing *Columbus* down the Milwaukee River to its junction with the Menominee River, where she would be turned and headed, bow out, to the outer Milwaukee harbor and into Lake Michigan.

The tug *Welcome*, under command of Captain John McSweeney, took the stern line to guide *Columbus*, stern first, down

Courtesy: Marine Historical Collection, Milwaukee Public Library

S.S. CHRISTOPHER COLUMBUS — With the tug *Conrad Starke* at her stern, the *Christopher Columbus* is departing the Goodrich dock in Milwaukee. It was during this operation that the tragic incident with the water tank took place.

the river. The bow line of *Columbus* was being handled by the other tug, which was in charge of Captain F. C. Maxon.

Aboard the *Columbus* were 413 passengers, two hundred of which were students from the University of Chicago on an outing. The big whaleback was under command of Captain Charles Moody who had commanded her every season since 1904. His crew consisted of eleven officers and 139 men.

The maneuver about to be undertaken was a daily routine. The only thing unusual to cause Captain Moody any concern was the fact that the Milwaukee River was swollen from prolonged heavy rainfall, and as a result the current was somewhat swifter than usual. This fact was discussed on the bridge and Captain Moody dispatched an officer to the tugs to caution their captains to proceed as slowly as possible with the big ship.

As they neared the junction of the two rivers, about one-half mile from the Goodrich dock, the tug *Welcome* started to swing the stern of the *Columbus*. As was the usual procedure in turning the big ship at the fork of the two rivers, the bow tug *Knight Templar* shifted the tow line from the bow bitts by walking the line along the starboard side of *Columbus* and securing it to the stern bitts.

Whether it was the swifter current or just an error in judgment on the part of the captain of the tug *Welcome,* or a combination of both, is not clear, but as she began to swing around, Captain Moody became concerned that *Columbus* was bearing down too close to the dock of the Yahr-Lange Drug Company. He felt the tugs were not holding her in check as they should. To avoid striking the dock, he ordered her helm "hard-to-starboard" and moved the engine-room telegraph to "full astern." This action placed him in danger of striking the railroad bridge with his stern but it was imperative that the arc of swing of *Columbus* be checked.

Slowly she came around but, as she did, the long overhang of her snout came in over the pilings and began to sweep the dock itself! The danger signal was blasted on the deep-throated whistle of *Columbus.* From his vantage point on the bridge, Captain Moody shouted, in vain, for the passengers on the bow to run for their lives!

Without realizing the danger at the bow, *Welcome* continued to swing the stern. At this point the current in the river moved

Courtesy: Harry W. Thorp, Jr.

S.S. CHRISTOPHER COLUMBUS — This photo shows the extent of her damage to the bridge and foredeck during her bout with the water tank from the roof of the Yahr-Lange Drug Company at Milwaukee.

the long overhang of the bow along the dock with deadly determination. Suddenly the massive steel pig snout came in contact
with two of the four supporting legs of a large water tank used
for the sprinkler system in the drug company warehouse. With
a screech of tortured metal, the supporting steel girders, forming
the front legs of the tank framework, were sheared off cleanly
a few feet above the ground level. From its towering one-hundred-
foot height, the tank, filled with tons of water, came crashing
down on the upper parts of *Columbus!* The steel ship received
a major blow just a few feet forward of her wheelhouse, amidst
the screeching of ruptured steel, splintering wood and glass, followed by the cries of the injured and those trapped in the awful
wreckage!

The force was so tremendous that the falling tank rocked
the huge ship as though she were in mid-lake and at the mercy
of a big storm. A large hole was torn in the wheelhouse and the
entire area was a litter of twisted steel, broken timbers, smashed
equipment and broken bodies of the killed and injured. The swiftly
moving tank literally pulverized the forward portion of the upper
decks and finally came to rest on the forward turret top, just
above the main deck. When the water tank burst, it sent a wall
of water cascading down the upper decks from bow to stern. It
washed many clear of the vessel and deposited them in the dirty
waters of the Milwaukee River. Others became panic-stricken
and actually leaped overboard.

In just minutes, all type of craft in the river rushed to the
scene and began fishing the injured, the swimming survivors
and the drowned from the muddy, swollen waters. All available
ambulances were rushed to the docks along the river to receive
the dead and injured as they were brought ashore by the rescue
craft. Sixteen persons lost their lives and over twenty sustained
serious injury in this freakish accident. Many others received
minor injuries and bruises and several had swallowed too much
of the dirty river water and as a result became ill.

When the crash occurred, Captain Moody had jumped to the
port side of the bridge and sustained only a slight leg injury.
His wheelsman escaped with only bruises although a huge hole
was torn in the deck at the exact spot he had been standing. Later
he could not remember just how he had escaped.

Goodrich officials made arrangements with the railroad and
a special train carried about three hundred of *Columbus'* surviving passengers back to Chicago that evening. The special train
departed from Milwaukee at about 7:00 P.M.

Investigations by both federal and local authorities were
conducted immediately. The real cause of the accident was finally
blamed on the swollen condition of the Milwaukee River but the

Courtesy: Harry W. Thorp, Jr.

CAPTAIN CHARLES E. MOODY — He spent thirty-six years of his long career as a Great Lakes captain as master of the *Columbus*.

steamboat inspectors did rule that the horrible accident could have been prevented if the masters of *Columbus* and the tug *Knight Templar* had exerted more caution.

The *Columbus* was taken to Manitowoc for repairs. The work took most of her normal season and the amount of damage was placed at $25,000 by Mr. Goodrich. In 1918 the whaleback was back in her regular service with Moody again in command. Captain Moody was first placed in command of *Columbus* in the spring of 1904. For twenty-six years he remained in command of her and during that time it is estimated that *Columbus* handled over 2,600,000 passengers. During this long career the only accident suffered by this great team was the freakish one in the Milwaukee River. At no other time in her history did another passenger lose his life while aboard this great steamer. Captain Charles E. Moody retired from the Goodrich line on March 1, 1930, at the age of eighty years. His first employment on the Lakes was at the age of fourteen so at his retirement he had concluded sixty-six years of service on the Great Lakes.

Throughout his career, Captain Moody was as colorful a character as ever tramped the bridge of a Lake steamer. With thirty-six years of his long career spent on *Columbus*, he not only grew very fond of the big "pig boat" but he became amazingly adept at handling her.

Only on rare occasions would Captain Moody entrust her to the care of a wheelsman when entering or leaving port. His confidence and skill with the big ship resulted in his running much faster in tight places with her than was customary with other steamers. If someone got in his way or was the cause for him to have to ring down her speed, the captain would become quite vocal and as efficient with words as he was with the wheel of the whaleback. Some of his more choice exclamations and opinions of those who got in his way do not lend themselves to be included in these pages!

The poem "The Passenger Hog" is reproduced here for our reader's amusement. The author is unknown but the story told was very familiar along the Milwaukee River, where the wake of the fast-moving *Columbus* often raised havoc with ships that were moored to the various docks. This was especially true if a shipmaster, unfamiliar with Captain Moody's habits, had been a little careless in his manner of tying up!

THE PASSENGER HOG*

She comes up the river, an' all in her wake
There's trouble she don't care to heed,
The water's kicked up an' the hawsers all break;
Why can't she come down in her speed?
She noses along like a grouchy old sow,
Then she lets out her engines a cog,
An' all along the river she raises a row,
The clumsy old passenger hog.

The Northwest's a lady, the Northland's the same,
An' the others is mostly all right.
But the passenger hog is a portly old dame,
That ain't at all nice or polite.
She hasn't no likin' for freighters or those
That happen her pathway to clog;
An' the freighters they hates her from rudder to nose,
The ugly old passenger hog.

The hogs that are loaded with iron or wheat
They seem to be handy fer use,
But the passenger hog is a mean one to meet,
An' when you're in dock she's the deuce.
She'd ought to be given a port all her own,
Where no one would care how she'd jog,
Where she'd leave us poor freighters an' others alone,
The ugly old passenger hog.

Right through World War I, and on into the roaring twenties, *Columbus* continued her daily round-trip service between Chicago and Milwaukee. Each year she operated she set new records for the total number of passengers handled by any American flag vessel. Other steamers were acquired and still others were sold or retired from service with the Goodrich fleet, but Old Reliable continued to operate, thereby justifying the faith of Captain McDougall, her designer and builder, by her continuous and very efficient performance year after year. No steamer in Goodrich history earned the total profit produced by *Christopher Columbus*. As a result, she remained in Goodrich service until the bitter end.

Columbus was last operated in 1932. In 1933 she was purchased by interests in Manitowoc. After that she remained idle until 1937. The long idleness rendered her useless for further service and in the same year the famous old excursion whaleback fell victim to the cutting torch. The very fine steel salvaged from her hull was sold to Japan.

For a "one-of-a-kind" steamboat, *Columbus* certainly produced an enviable record. While all of the whalebacks performed very well, none did more to dispel the nickname "McDougall's dream," given the very first pig boat, named only "Hull Number 101," and produced back in the year 1888. The memory of *Christopher Columbus* is fondly treasured by those of us who were privileged to be a passenger in search of fun and pleasure as she plied beautiful Lake Michigan.

*A "hog" is Lake parlance for a whaleback vessel.

For eight years after placing *Columbus* under the Goodrich flag, no new steamers were added to the fleet. As the year 1900 was ushered in, and the era of the gay nineties ended, the fleet roster of the Goodrich Transportation Company read as follows: *Atlanta, Chicago, Christopher Columbus, City of Racine, Georgia, Indiana, Iowa, Sheboygan, Virginia,* and tug *Arctic.*

With the exception of the side-wheelers *Chicago* and *Sheboygan,* all nine of the steamers were new or nearly so. Collectively the Goodrich fleet was larger and in a more nearly new condition than at any time in the history of the line. Financially, the company was producing exceptionally good earnings and the total indebtedness was at a low and reasonable level. All of these facts were a fine tribute to the man that had stepped into the shoes of his remarkable father only ten years previous.

In the year 1900, the routes served by the line and the assignment of the steamers were about as follows:

Christopher Columbus was alone on the daylight excursion run to Milwaukee. Fare was $1.00 for a round trip.

Virginia and *City of Racine* ran opposite each other in the night service between Chicago and Milwaukee with a stop in each direction at Racine.

Iowa and *Indiana* handled the cross-lake route from Chicago to Grand Haven and Muskegon.

Atlanta, Chicago and *Sheboygan* handled the west-shore route, serving Manitowoc, Sheboygan, Green Bay and Door County ports. This four-day trip cost $13.00, including meals and berth.

Georgia departed from Chicago at 8:30 P.M. on Saturday on a cruise to Mackinac Island. En route to the island she stopped at Milwaukee, principal west-shore ports, and Washington Island. She returned to Chicago at 7:00 A.M. the following Saturday. The fare for this seven-day trip was $25.00 with meals and berth included. Parlor room berths were $5.00 extra.

The tug *Arctic* continued to base in Manitowoc in summer and in Milwaukee harbor in winter. Her ability as an icebreaker had been proven many times since her building and she greatly aided the winter service along the west-shore routes.

The city of Manitowoc continued to be the operating base for the Goodrich line. A large storage yard, shops, and coal bunkers were maintained there. This was also the winter lay-up port. The port-of-hail continued to be shown on the stern of all Goodrich boats as Kenosha.

Passenger and freight traffic on the Great Lakes in general, and on Lake Michigan in particular, was setting new records each season. With the exception of the Chicago-Mackinac Island route, Goodrich had pretty well outdistanced its competitors on the routes

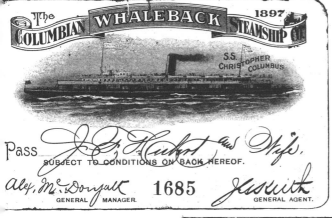

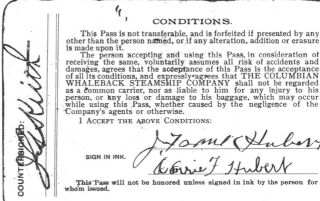

OLD PASSENGER PASS — The front of this passenger pass, in actual size, shows that the original was issued to Mr. and Mrs. J. F. Hubert, in 1897 ("J. F. Hubert and Wife"!), for travel on the *Christopher Columbus*. It bears the signature of Alexander McDougall, then General Manager of the old Columbian Whaleback Steamship Company. The back shows the signatures of the couple.

they had concentrated on these many years. Goodrich, by now, was not only the largest steamboat operator on Lake Michigan, but did a larger volume annually than any other passenger line on any of the Lakes.

Up to this milestone in Goodrich history, only three steamer losses involving the loss of life of passengers had been sustained. These were the *Sunbeam, Seabird* and *Alpena*. Other steamers flying the Goodrich flag had been lost but only these three had taken the lives of passengers who entrusted their safety to the Red-Stack line. This is a truly remarkable record, considering the fact that Goodrich had actually owned a total of thirty-eight steamships since George Drew and Captain Goodrich first chartered the little *Huron* from Captain Ward, forty-five years before!

S.S. ALABAMA — This is a view of her engine room.

Courtesy: Muskegon Chronicle

Chapter Nine

A NEW PORT-OF-HAIL

Early in 1906 it was the decision of Mr. Goodrich and his staff, that the best interests of the corporation would be served by changing the state, under whose laws the company existed, from Wisconsin to Maine.

Acting on this decision, the old Wisconsin corporation was dissolved and a new company was chartered under the laws of the state of Maine. The name of the new corporation was Goodrich Transit Company. The new charter was granted on April 7, 1906, at Augusta, Maine. The following gentlemen were appointed as officers of the newly founded company: A. W. Goodrich, President; E. L. Upton, Vice-President; H. W. Thorp, Secretary; W. S. Willard, Assistant Secretary; W. J. Louderback, Treasurer.

By this time the great Captain Thomas G. Butlin had stepped down and the post of superintendent was filled by Captain David Mitchell Cochrane, a Scotchman, who had been with the original A. E. Goodrich's Steamboat Line.

The corporate offices were continued in Chicago at their old location at the foot of Michigan Avenue and the Chicago River. The shops and the base of the shore operations remained, unchanged, at Manitowoc, Wisconsin. There was no change in the standard color scheme for the steamers. The former name on the bow read "Goodrich Trans. Co." This was changed to read "Goodrich Transit Co." The port-of-hail on the stern was changed from Kenosha to Duluth as was the port of registry with the Federal Government.

With exception of the *Atlanta,* which burned in Lake Michigan on March 18, 1906, less than a month before the birth of the Goodrich Transit Company, the ship roster for the new company was identical with that in effect in 1900. No new steamships were added to the Goodrich line from 1898 to 1906.

The loss of the relatively new *Atlanta* was a serious blow financially as well as operationally. An immediate replacement for the burned steamer became a matter of great urgency for Mr. Goodrich. The search for a replacement led to negotiations with the Hackley Transportation Company of Muskegon, Michigan, for the purchase of the twin-screw *Charles H. Hackley.* Upon the acquisition of the *Hackley* her name was changed to *S.S. Carolina* and her story is an interesting one.

Travel between Boston and New York had always been popular but this traffic really began to boom when the New Haven Railroad began operation of the so-called "boat trains" from Boston to the Long Island Sound ports of Fall River, Newport, and Stonington, about 1870. The boat train would depart from Boston

Courtesy: Dora B. Goodrich

CHICAGO RIVER SCENE — This scene was taken in 1905. The *S.S. Charles H. Hackley* is in the foreground. Note the Hackley Line square trademark on her bow.

Courtesy: Dowling Collection

S.S. CHARLES H. HACKLEY — This is what she looked like while in the service of the Barry Line on her Chicago-Muskegon run. Afterwards she was purchased by Goodrich and rebuilt as the *Carolina*.

in late afternoon and arrive at Fall River the same evening. On arrival the passengers for New York City would board the steamship for an overnight trip down Long Island Sound to New York. From this combination rail-and-water route, several steamship companies sprang up and the competition became quite keen. Those that survived, and are best remembered, are the Fall River Line and the Eastern Steamship Company.

Fire, being the dreaded threat that it was to ships of this era, caused the average traveler to look upon the steel-hulled ships as much safer and more desirable than the wooden-hulled vessels. Generally speaking, the traveling public also expressed a preference for propeller-driven craft, believing them to be faster and more dependable than the side-wheel-driven ships, although this was certainly not necessarily true. As a result of this feeling, more and more steel-hulled, propeller-driven steamers began to make their appearance on the Sound.

On this mooted question of propellers versus side-wheelers, it is interesting to note that the most famous of the steamship companies operating on Long Island Sound, the Fall River Line, never did build or own a propeller-driven steamer in its entire history. It was the ability of the side-wheel steamers to reverse engines and stop much more quickly, especially when running in the dense fogs encountered on the Sound, that endeared the paddle-wheel ships to the Fall River Line management.

In keeping with the trend towards propeller-driven ships, there was launched at the Neafic & Leavy Shipyard in South Philadelphia, in early 1892, a twin-screw, steel-hulled combination passenger and freight vessel named *S. S. Hartford*. After fitting out, *Hartford* entered the service on the Sound for the Hartford & New York Transportation Company that same year. Her record in the Sound service is very good and there is every indication that she was a satisfactory steamer in every way.

The next we hear of the *Hartford*, she was in the custody of the United States Government on a charge of running contraband guns and war material to the Cuban rebels. This incident took place just before this country entered the Spanish American War.

About this time, according to legend, *Hartford* was acquired by Miss Helen Gould, philanthropic daughter of the wealthy and famous Jay Gould. According to rumors of the time, Miss Gould acquired the ship to be converted to a private yacht, but when war broke out she had it converted to a hospital ship and then presented it to the United States Government.

Regardless of these rumors and the legend, the fact does remain that there is no record in the documentation of the vessel to indicate that she ever was the property of Miss Gould. The record does show, however, that on December 8, 1898, she was registered to the Quartermaster Department, U. S. Army. On March 31, 1899, her name was changed to *U. S. Q. D. Terry*. There is nothing in the record to indicate that the *Terry* did anything to distinguish herself as an Army ship.

In 1901 *Terry* had been decommissioned and laid up in a southern port on the Atlantic seaboard. Being, at this time, surplus to the Government's need, she was offered for sale. It was at this time that Captain Miles Barry, of Chicago, found her and decided that she would make a fine Lake steamer.

Captain Barry owned and operated the Chicago & Muskegon Transportation Company. This line operated in direct competition with Goodrich by offering a service between Chicago and Muskegon. The line was organized in 1900 and the first steamer operated by Barry was the small wooden steamer *Mabel Bradshaw*. Later this steamer was replaced by the former package freighter *Alice Stafford*. The *Stafford* had been rebuilt for the Muskegon route and had some passenger accommodations. At the time of the purchase of *Terry* this was the Barry Line's only ship.

Financial backing for the purchase of *Terry* from the Government was secured by Captain Barry from two prominent lumbermen from Muskegon. The name *Hartford* reappeared on her documentation record as she was prepared for her trip to Muskegon.

Upon being recommissioned she started north for her new home port. The long trek took her up the Atlantic seaboard to the St. Lawrence, thence through the Welland Canal to the Great Lakes and then around to Muskegon. En route, *Hartford* encountered many troubles including a major boiler failure at Montreal.

While traversing the Welland Canal, she struck and inflicted damage on the Grand Trunk Railroad bridge. Canadian authorities attempted to intercept her and assess a fine for the bridge damage, but she managed to elude them until safely in American waters.

After what proved to be a long hard trip, *Hartford* arrived in Muskegon on September 14, 1901. Her new owners lost no time in putting their new steamer to work. On September 15, 1901, there was a brief ceremony and she was renamed *Charles H. Hackley,* in honor of her most substantial backer. That same evening the *Hackley* departed from Muskegon on her first trip under the Barry Line flag.

During the next three years the two Barry Line steamers *Hackley* and *Stafford* became very active and enthusiastic competitors of Goodrich. The keen and spirited struggle for the cross-

Courtesy: Father Edward J. Dowling, S.J.

S.S. HARTFORD — She is shown here when she was in the Long Island Sound service. She was destined to become the *S.S. Carolina* of the Goodrich line later on.

lake traffic is very graphically illustrated in the photo showing the *Hackley* racing the Goodrich steamer *Iowa* from Grand Haven to Muskegon in order to lay first claim on the Chicago-bound passenger and freight business.

At the close of the third season of this competitive situation, it was apparent that the Barry Line could not stand the furious pace. On March 20, 1905, decrees were granted to the Barry Line for their two steamers to be sold. At a public auction, held April 6, 1905, the *Alice Stafford* was sold to J. O. Nessen of Manistee, Michigan. The *Charles H. Hackley* was sold to Thomas Hume of the Muskegon lumber firm of Hackley & Hume. It was quite obvious that this bid on the *Hackley* had been placed to protect their previous interest in the Barry Line properties. Effective April 21, 1905, the *Hackley* was registered in the name of the Hackley Transportation Company of Muskegon.

The Hackley Transportation Company had no choice but to resume the competition with the strong Goodrich line. This new rivalry was not very spirited and was of brief duration, lasting only through the season of 1905.

On March 18, 1906, the *Atlanta* burned and was a total loss. Mr. Goodrich lost no time in approaching the owners of the *Hackley*. On March 28, just ten days after the loss of *Atlanta*, the *Charles H. Hackley* became the property of the Goodrich Transportation Company at the price of $80,000. By this action Mr. Goodrich not only acquired a badly needed replacement for the burned *Atlanta* but he eliminated a competitor on the cross-lake route as well. With the exception of one feeble effort, which only lasted one season, no other steamship operator attempted to compete with Goodrich for the Chicago, Grand Haven, and Muskegon traffic.

Goodrich immediately sent the *Hackley* to Manitowoc for rebuilding and a face lifting. This work included the installation of steel above her main deck, changes in her promenade deck and the installation of fine accommodations for overnight passengers. The ship was renamed *Carolina* and entered regular Goodrich service on June 16, 1906. In her glistening new Goodrich colors, *Carolina* was indeed a proud addition to the Red-Stack fleet. She had the following principal dimensions: hull, iron; length, 220 feet; beam, 40 feet; draft, 13 feet; gross tons, 1304; net tons, 887; propulsion, twin screw; engines, two compound, 20 x 40 x 26″ stroke; service speed, 14 mph; maximum speed, 16 mph.

From time to time during her life with Goodrich, *Carolina* was subjected to various changes in her cabin and topside layout. These changes gave her silhouette a typical "Goodrich look:" Many referred to her as a "little sister" to the famous *Alabama*.

Carolina's first assignment was the fashionable Mackinac Island route from Chicago with stops at Milwaukee and other principal ports along the west shore. On week-ends during the summer season she made the White Lake route, returning on Monday morning.

The first Goodrich master assigned to *Carolina* was Captain Cornelius ("Con") McCauley who commanded her until April of 1914. After that and well into the late twenties it was Captain Daniel J. McGarity, whose life story is told in detail in the next chapter.

Late in the afternoon of Saturday, June 16, 1908, the sailing yacht *Vandura* departed from Milwaukee harbor bound down for Racine. Shortly after dark the yacht was caught in a furious squall and capsized. The three men aboard, Harry Berman, James Norton, and Fred Fredstorf, were thrown overboard into the towering seas.

For hours the three men clung desperately to the overturned hull, from which they were frequently torn by the big waves. By daylight their strength was ebbing fast and they were about to give up hope.

Carolina, under the command of Captain Con McCauley, was bound up for Milwaukee from Chicago. First mate James Smith, known as Kewaunee Jim, was on the bridge when he and the wheelsman noticed a strange object in the water. Upon investigation it proved to be the overturned *Vandura*.

S.S. CAROLINA — She was often referred to as a little *Alabama* and was a truly beautiful ship after her rebuilding by Goodrich.

Courtesy: Edward N. Middleton

Courtesy: D. J. McGarity Collection

S.S. CAROLINA — Here she is shown in dry dock at Manitowoc for propeller repair.

The ship hove to, Captain McCauley was notified, and Jim Smith commanded the lifeboat that put out from *Carolina* and made the rescue just in the nick of time.

For most of her career as a Goodrich steamer, *Carolina* had a very significant, accident-free record. The only really serious accident that happened to Captain McGarity and his beloved *Carolina* occurred on December 3, 1916. A detailed account of this foundering is included in the story of Captain McGarity's career.

After this regrettable incident, all went well with *Carolina* until the night of December 12, 1921. All day long a strong northeasterly wind had been blowing and as a result there was a strong sea running when *Carolina* came around the Chicago harbor light and started on her way north. The seas, quartering as they were, caused the stern frequently to come clear out of the water. Every time this happened the propellers raced madly until the engineer could throttle them down. All night the ship battled the increasing winds and heavy seas. About 2:00 A.M. the port propeller threw two of its blades. At about 8:00 A.M. Captain McGarity received word that the storm had abated somewhat at Chicago, so he decided to return there. In the process of trying to come about to change course, the remaining two blades on the port wheel gave way!

A slight break in the heavy snowstorm afforded the captain a quick glimpse of Wind Point, just off the entrance to the harbor at Racine, Wisconsin. In spite of the difficulties involved in keeping a twin-screw ship on course with one wheel dead, the captain managed to bring the *Carolina* into Racine and dock her without mishap. When the wild storm finally abated, *Carolina* made her way to Milwaukee, and still with only one screw made her passage up the river and through the many bridges to the Goodrich dock where she discharged her passengers and cargo. She then went to Manitowoc under her own power to have her wounds healed at the Manitowoc Shipbuilding Yards.

During 1925, while bound down from Sturgeon Bay to Milwaukee in a heavy northeast sea, *Carolina's* steering engine became disabled when abeam of Kewaunee, Wisconsin. Fortunately the rudder was about on center when the failure occurred so Captain McGarity was able to steer the ship by her engines. During the remainder of the trip to Milwaukee, he was not only able to keep *Carolina* "on course" but he entered the Milwaukee harbor, traversed the river, negotiated the bridge draws, and docked the vessel entirely by use of her engines alone! Repairs to the steering engine were made at her regular berth.

In June of 1924 *Carolina* was chartered by the Milwaukee Association of Commerce for an extended tour of the lower half of Lake Michigan. During this trip she entered many ports on the east shore of Lake Michigan that she had never previously entered. The same group chartered *Carolina* again in 1925 for a ten-day cruise on Lake Michigan. This time the trip included a cruise into Lake Superior. Two ports of call were Washburn and Bayfield,

Courtesy: D. J. McGarity Collection

S.S. CAROLINA — This photo shows the amazing manner in which the blades sheared off, with less than a quarter of an inch difference between the remainders of the blades.

Wisconsin. *Carolina* was the largest steamer ever to enter these two small Lake ports.

For many years every summer thousands of Boy Scouts from the Chicago area were treated to a big thrill when they made the trip from Chicago to Whitehall, Michigan, on *Carolina* en route to their summer encampment known as Camp Owassippi. This famous Boy Scout Camp is still in existence.

When Goodrich suspended operations, the *Carolina*, like all other Goodrich steamers, was idle until they were all finally sold at auction. *Carolina* was sold to the Manitowoc Shipbuilding Company for a reported $3,000! The original intention was to make a barge out of the fine old ship but this never came to pass and in 1937 she was sold to Captain John Roen after having been cut down to the main deck. Her hull was used as a stone barge until 1950, when she was cut up for scrap at Sturgeon Bay. Speaking as one who in his youth was one of the Boy Scouts who so thoroughly enjoyed the cross-lake trip to Whitehall on the *Carolina*, I fervently hope that some day the traveling public will again turn to our inland seas for recreation and that fine passenger steamers will again dot the horizons of our beautiful Great Lakes.

After the purchase of *Carolina* in 1906, there were no further acquisitions or changes in the Goodrich fleet until the year 1910. It was in this year that the most photographed Goodrich steamer of all times was launched.

The beautiful steel steamer *Virginia* had been a fantastic success for the Goodrich company. Inspired by the experience with *Virginia*, the Goodrich management wisely decided to construct another steel, combination freight and passenger ship to replace the aging *Sheboygan* and *Chicago*.

Design work on the proposed new steamer was done under the personal direction of Mr. Elias Gunnell, president of the Manitowoc Shipbuilding Company. Plans were drawn and redrawn. A great deal of thought and attention was given to every detail of the new ship.

To combat the Lake Michigan ice meant that she had to have unusual ice-breaking ability. To be able to operate profitably in the fall, winter, and spring, when the passenger load was at low ebb, she had to have substantial cargo capacity. To meet competition and to satisfy shipping schedules, she had to be capable of a cruising speed of not less than seventeen miles per hour. To accommodate overnight passengers on the Grand Haven-Muskegon route, her sleeping quarters and public rooms had to be the very finest. To feed the travelers on this route meant providing a superb cuisine with an elegant dining room and top-grade kitchens.

All of these pertinent factors were given careful and indiv-

Courtesy: Dora B. Goodrich

ELIZABETH GOODRICH — A. W. Goodrich's daughter christened the
S.S. Alabama on a cold day in December, 1909.

idual study. Mr. A. W. Goodrich spent almost all of his time at Manitowoc, as the new ship was to be his pride and joy. Finally, in the spring of 1909, all details had been agreed upon and a contract to build the new ship was awarded to the Manitowoc Shipbuilding Company. Her cost was to be $386,272 and her name *Alabama*.

The dimensions of the *Alabama* were as follows: hull, steel; length, 272 feet overall; beam, 45 feet 5 inches; depth, 26 feet; draft, 14 feet; gross tonnage, 2,626 tons; net tonnage, 1,684 tons; engine, triple expansion 23-38-62 x 36; horsepower, 2,500; propulsion, single screw; fuel, coal; service speed, 15 mph; top speed, 17 mph; passenger capacity, 300 overnight guests; cargo capacity, 2,500 tons.

Alabama was fitted with two steel pole masts, equipped with gaff booms. The forward mast also served as a stack for the galley. Her large, single funnel was located amidships and all three were medium raked, giving her a very impressive silhouette. Like all Goodrich steamers, she was equipped with the traditional, melodious, chimed whistle. The color scheme was the Goodrich standard — black hull, white cabins and topsides, with the well-known bright red stack.

Designed for year-around operation on the cross-lake route, much care was given to her bow construction as ice-breaking would be an important part of her winter duties. Over her five-eighths-inch steel hull plates was placed a one-inch steel doubling plate. This

S.S. ALABAMA — Her side launch was a success in spite of the ice in the Manitowoc River.

Courtesy: Harry W. Thorp, Jr.

doubling plate extended for about six feet on either side of her water line to give additional strength when breaking heavy ice. In addition, her sixteen-inch frames were placed on ten-inch centers which made for a very stiff and sturdy ship. Her exciting record over the years is mute testimony to her ability as an icebreaker. During her career, she rescued many ships caught in the frustrating Lake Michigan ice.

When completed, *Alabama* had a somewhat stubby appearance, due to her great height. This feature tended to give the impression that she was a clumsy ship. Actually, just the opposite was true. She was an extremely good steamer in rough weather and thoroughly dependable in every way. In a recent interview Captain D. J. McGarity had this to say about her:

"The *Alabama,* without question, was probably the finest passenger-cargo ship to be built on the Great Lakes and an entire story could be built around her marvelous record. During the eight winters that I commanded her I had an opportunity to learn what a fine, able ship she was, not only as a seaboat, but also as an icebreaker."

Construction work progressed on schedule and *Alabama* was launched on Saturday, December 18, 1909. The new ship was christened by Miss Elizabeth Goodrich, oldest daughter of A. W. Goodrich, who was then eleven years of age. The *Inter-Ocean* of Chicago carried the following news item on December 19, 1909. This article ran beneath a large photo of Elizabeth Goodrich:

S.S. ALABAMA — Workmen are completing her superstructure after her winter launching. Note the ice in the Manitowoc River.

Courtesy: C. P. Labadie

Courtesy: Harry W. Thorp, Jr.

S.S. ALABAMA — Here she is seen departing from Grand Haven in a big blow.

Miss Elizabeth Goodrich, daughter of Albert W. Goodrich, President of the Goodrich Transit Line, yesterday christened the new steamship ALABAMA by breaking a ribbon-bedecked bottle of champagne over the bow of the vessel as it started down the ways of the Manitowoc (Wis.) Dry Dock Company. Officials of the Goodrich Transit Company and their families attended the launching of the new boat, which is said to be the strongest steamship ever built for passenger service on the Great Lakes.

The ALABAMA is entirely of steel construction of unusual heaviness throughout, being designed for passenger service all the year around between Chicago, Grand Haven and Muskegon. The average thickness of its hull plating is one inch, being heaviest at the bow and along the keel. The boat will be able to break its own channel through any ice it may encounter. It has a double bottom with six water tight compartments.

The new steamer is 271 feet long, having a 44 foot beam amidships and a draft of 12½ feet. A triple expansion engine of 2,500 horsepower will give the boat a speed of eighteen miles per hour.

The ALABAMA will be licensed to carry 2,000 passengers, and will have sleeping accommodations for 300. It has three tiers of cabins and many of the staterooms have private bathrooms. The salons are finished in mahogany, inlaid with various woods. The staterooms are finished in white enamel. The main dining room has a capacity of 125, and there are two small dining rooms for private reservations.

The ALABAMA will be in commission next June, starting that day from Chicago for Grand Haven and Muskegon. Her cost was $400,000.

After the launching, fitting-out work on the new ship progressed according to schedule and on June 12, 1910, she was formally delivered to Goodrich. Her maiden voyage was from Manitowoc to Chicago with stops at Milwaukee and Racine in order that the public could have a look at the beautiful new ship. At each stop and at Chicago thousands of people made their way through the new steamer and the press acclaimed her to be the finest passenger vessel ever built for the Lake service. Immediately on delivery, *Alabama* was designated as the flagship of the Goodrich line, a distinction that she retained throughout her illustrious career as a member of the Red-Stack fleet.

Shortly after *Alabama* was built Mr. Goodrich contacted a famous ship-model builder in Scotland to build a model of the

Courtesy: Manitowoc County Museum

S.S. ALABAMA — View of the purser's office and the main stairway.

new Goodrich flagship. When completed this beautiful and very accurate model was five feet in length and was enclosed in a glass case. For all of the life of the Goodrich Transit Company this attractive model adorned its general office at Chicago.

Alabama made her first trip in regular service from Chicago to Grand Haven and Muskegon on June 29, 1910. On this assignment she replaced *Indiana* who then served opposite *Arizona* as a night boat between Milwaukee, Racine and Chicago. During the summer season, when week-end travel was very heavy on the cross-lake route, *Indiana* was used as an extra boat.

From 1910 to 1917 *Alabama* and *Virginia* ran opposite each other in the Muskegon-Grand Haven service. This meant that for seven very prosperous years Goodrich kept two of the finest steamers on the Lakes on this popular route. *Virginia* would lay up at Manitowoc each winter but the sturdy *Alabama* ran on a year-around basis and during the early part of her career she was commanded by Captain E. E. Taylor, who later became president of the line.

S.S. ALABAMA — The main dining room as it looked during her career as a cruise ship for the Georgian Bay Line.

Courtesy: Georgian Bay Line

In the period from 1912 to the early twenties, a popular way to spend a Saturday or Sunday was to board the Chicago boat at Muskegon for Grand Haven. By purchasing a special round-trip ticket the return portion was honored on the electric Interurban Line that operated between Grand Haven and Muskegon. So many availed themselves of this delightful transportation "bargain" during warm summer week-ends that the Interurban Line ran a special "boat train." This trip was referred to as "looping the loop" by local residents. Departure of the "boat train" for Muskegon was scheduled just after the Chicago boat departed from Grand Haven. In this manner the hustle and excitement of the steamer's departure for Chicago could be enjoyed to the fullest before starting back to Muskegon.

At 9:00 P.M. on January 12, 1918, *Alabama* departed from Chicago for Grand Haven and Muskegon. Captain Stufflebeam was in command. A roaring blizzard was battering the Michigan shore line when *Alabama* arrived off Grand Haven the next day. The strong winds from the west-northwest had driven in a huge ice floe. In attempting to force her way through to Grand Haven harbor through the mass of heavy ice, the great steel steamer found herself firmly locked in its relentless grip. *Alabama* found that she was not alone in this predicament. The Grand Trunk car ferries *Milwaukee* and *Grand Haven* were victims of the same ice field. Unable to free themselves, all three steamers remained as prisoners of the ice for the next two weeks.

A change in wind direction caused the ice field to break up and *Alabama* was finally able to work herself free. The ice conditions at the entrance to Grand Haven were still impossible, so Captain Stufflebeam elected to bypass Grand Haven and so headed north in Lake Michigan for Muskegon.

Upon entering Muskegon Lake *Alabama* encountered solid ice over eighteen inches thick. In attempting to smash her way through en route to the Goodrich dock, she broke a blade off her propeller. Then, trying to back down from the solid ice into which she had driven a wedge, she severely damaged her rudder and steering engine. This terminated her struggle to reach the Goodrich dock, still some five miles distant.

Upon learning of her predicament the Muskegon office of Goodrich contacted Grand Haven and a tug was dispatched from there to aid the Goodrich flagship.

The tug failed to get through to the *Alabama*. An examination of the damaged steering engine revealed that several new parts would be required to put the engine back in operating condition. World War I was then in full swing and a delay in securing the badly needed repair parts was inevitable. After weighing all fac-

Courtesy: Daryl Cornick

S.S. ALABAMA — Bath facilities for a deluxe suite aboard the Alabama about 1912. Note ornate old-fashioned tub and plain bulb lighting.

tors, the Goodrich management then decided to lay the big ship up until conditions improved.

Part of the cargo aboard *Alabama* consisted of about a hundred tons of staples and groceries consigned to Grand Haven, Grand Rapids and Muskegon. Over six thousand pounds of this was bagged sugar destined for Muskegon and Grand Haven grocery stores. Because of the war situation, sugar was in short supply and the nearly three-week delay would have been severely felt by the housewives in the area.

As quickly as it could be arranged, several two-horse sleighs were contracted for and the task of removing the precious cargo was begun. The Interurban Line made up a special train and the

Courtesy: Harry W. Thorp, Jr.

S.S. ALABAMA — Here she is struggling through the ice as she fights her way to the Muskegon dock, January 22, 1918.

freight was rushed to its destination in Grand Haven and Grand Rapids. The arrival of the much-needed sugar was happily hailed by the local newspapers!

On February 9, 1918, Lake Michigan was completely frozen over. For the fifth time in the fifty years since the incorporation of the Goodrich Transportation Company, there were no Goodrich steamers on Lake Michigan.

Due to the severity of the winter there was a shortage of coal in the city of Muskegon. Retaining only enough coal in her bunkers to keep the boilers warm, *Alabama* made the rest available for use by the townspeople. Then most of her crew were paid off and the big steamer remained inoperative in Muskegon Lake until March 17 of 1918.

On that day the *Georgia* worked her way alongside of *Alabama* and delivered a cargo of coal to replenish her nearly empty bunkers. When a full head of steam was up and the big icebreaker was ready to move, her crew went out on the ice with axes to assist in freeing her. This was not accomplished until late Monday afternoon, March 18.

After gaining the open Lake, *Alabama*, still with her damaged propeller, managed to limp into Manitowoc under her own power. There she was placed in dry dock for much-needed repairs.

Throughout her entire life *Alabama* had a remarkably clean safety record. Only one serious accident marred her twenty-three years of year-around service in the cross-lake run for Goodrich. On the morning of February 22, 1920, *Alabama* was approaching the Chicago shore on her regular night trip from Muskegon. She had been in ice for most of the night but as she approached the west shore the ice was somewhat broken. From this water steam was rising which greatly obscured visibility.

The first object sighted from the bridge of the *Alabama* was the water-intake crib just off Lawrence Avenue. Inasmuch as this crib was only about a thousand feet off shore, Captain E. E. Redner realized that he was in too close, and he immediately ordered the ship hauled on to a southeast course. The big steamer made the turn and squared away on the new course. After traveling only about two miles she fetched up sharply with a grinding of her steel bottom plates. Had she been only fifty yards either way she would have missed the underwater, concrete obstruction that caused the accident. This concrete was believed to be the foundation

S.S. ALABAMA — The terrible winter of 1918 is graphically illustrated in this view of Muskegon Lake as the ship tries to make her way through the heavy ice.

Courtesy: Harry W. Thorp, Jr.

of an old water-intake crib but it was sufficient to hold *Alabama* firmly in its grasp. The site of this accident was off Belmont Avenue.

Examination revealed that *Alabama* rested on this obstruction, just abaft of amidships and her stern was in the air, quite a bit above her lines. Some of her bottom plates were sprung and water entered one of her holds. The flooding was controlled by her huge pumps so that the water did not gain the fireholds or the engine room.

Goodrich engaged the small package freighter *S. S. Sidney O. Neff* to go alongside the *Alabama* and remove her cargo. Then harbor tugs from Chicago were able to pull her free. She was taken to dry dock where it was found that she sustained considerable hull damage. Repair work consumed the balance of the winter and *Alabama* returned to her regular route in May of 1921. During her lay-up for repairs, the *S. S. Missouri* was chartered from the Michigan Transit Company to replace *Alabama* on the Grand Haven-Muskegon route.

The winter of 1923-1924 was another severe one and again *Alabama* had her share of problems with ice and winter storms. On Saturday, January 19, a gale-force southwest wind drove ice floes into the channel at the entrance to Muskegon Lake. That

S.S. ALABAMA — This view shows the *Alabama* and two Grand Trunk car ferries locked in the ice just off Grand Haven.

Courtesy: Harry W. Thorp, Jr.

Courtesy: Harry W. Thorp, Jr.

S.S. ALABAMA — Here she is aground on an underwater obstruction just off Belmont Avenue, Chicago.

evening *Alabama* departed from Muskegon for Chicago. She could not force her way through the packed ice and was delayed nearly twenty-four hours.

January 22 found *Alabama* again locked in the ice. This time she was off the entrance to Grand Haven and her schedule was disrupted by a four-day delay before she finally reached her dock at Grand Haven. On January 28 she was again attempting to enter the channel to Muskegon Lake. A small steamer, the *Sheboygan*, was in distress about two miles off the pier heads. Hearing her distress signal, Captain McGarity turned *Alabama* and went to the smaller vessel's aid. Making a tow line secure he brought the disabled *Sheboygan* into the Coast Guard Lifeboat Station in Muskegon channel. This was just one instance where the *Alabama* gave aid to another steamer less fortunate in the battle with Old Man Winter. Her list of assistance rendered to other ships was long and impressive and *Alabama* had many friends and admirers among Lake sailors.

To give our readers some idea of the conditions often en-

Courtesy: Marine Historical Collection, Milwaukee Public Library

S.S. MISSOURI — This ship was chartered by Goodrich to replace *Alabama* while she underwent repairs to hull damage suffered when she struck an underwater obstruction off Belmont Avenue, Chicago.

countered in the winter service, the following incident was told to the author by Captain McGarity.

"In the big storm of February, 1925, I received a wireless distress signal from the Ann Arbor Car Ferry Number 4. Immediately on receipt of the distress call I headed the *Alabama* on a north-northwesterly course. During the night the temperature dropped to twenty below zero which caused very heavy steam or frozen fog. I ran *Alabama* on this course from midnight until noon the next day in a terrifically heavy northwest sea. At noon I managed to catch a glimpse of the land at Port Washington, Wisconsin. With this bearing I set a course for Milwaukee and on arrival there I learned that the Ann Arbor No. 4 had just managed to get back to Frankfort, Michigan, where she sank just inside the end of the south pier."

When the *Virginia* left Goodrich for service in World War I, her place as a running mate to *Alabama* was taken first by *Carolina* and then *Indiana*. After the merger with Graham & Morton in 1925 the former G & M flagship *City of Grand Rapids* was placed on the cross-lake route opposite *Alabama*. Once more the popular Muskegon-Grand Haven route was served by two of the finest steamers on the Lakes. The *Grand Rapids*, like *Virginia*,

Courtesy: Georgian Bay Line

S.S. ALABAMA — This is the way she appeared in the colors of the Georgian Bay Line.

operated in the summer season and *Alabama* continued on the gruelling year-around schedule. This arrangement lasted for another seven-year span until the end of the season of 1932.

Alabama was perhaps the first Goodrich steamer allowed to remain in her original form after building. Her predecessor, the *Virginia,* was altered several times during her life as a Goodrich ship. As business increased, *Virginia* was returned to the shipyard for the addition of cabins and other changes that affected her silhouette, but not so *Alabama.* The only change in her outward appearance during her entire career with Goodrich was the addition of two very large lifeboats. These were placed port and starboard on the boat deck, just forward of the bridge wing, and were installed in 1912, following the tragic loss of the *Titanic* in the Atlantic. Much publicity was given the lack of sufficient lifeboats on the *Titanic* and the addition of these two fine lifeboats on *Alabama* was Goodrich's indication to the traveling public that there was no such shortage aboard its flagship. Incidentally, these large lifeboats were something of a hazard and inconvenience as they interfered with a clear view of the dock from the bridge. They were removed when *Alabama* came under the management of the Georgian Bay Line some years later.

Following the cessation of operations by Goodrich Transit Company in 1932, *Alabama* was chartered from the bondholders by the Gartland & Sullivan Steamship Company. During the summer of 1933 she was operated on the Chicago-Grand Haven-Muskegon route.

In 1934 the Sullivan Line changed her color scheme to all white, and that season she operated to Isle Royale for "Journeys Inc."

Earl G. Kirby of Detroit purchased her in 1937. Mr. Kirby spent in excess of $125,000 reconditioning her to operate between Cleveland and Isle Royale.

In 1939 *Alabama* was chartered by the Chicago, Duluth & Georgian Bay Line. At this time she was again remodeled extensively for cruise service. She was painted in the standard Georgian Bay Line colors and operated from Buffalo to Duluth on the well-known "adventure cruise." She remained in this service until the close of the season in 1940.

In 1941, business had ·fallen off and *Alabama* was replaced by the *S. S. South America,* which still maintains this service as this book is written. During the seasons of 1941 and 1942 she

Courtesy: Georgian Bay Line

S.S. ALABAMA — After having been long out of service, she is shown here at the Georgian Bay Line dock in Holland, Michigan, prior to her being dismantled and converted into a work barge.

Author's Collection

ALABAMA OF BAY CITY — The former *S.S. Alabama* as she looks today in her capacity as a work barge.

was used for five-day week-end cruises out of Chicago to Sturgeon Bay and Mackinac Island. Due to the pressure of wartime conditions, she was laid up at the close of the 1942 season. Title to *Alabama* was assumed by the Georgian Bay Line in 1943.

The newly organized Cleveland & Buffalo Transit Company (an Illinois corporation) purchased *Alabama* in 1945. Again she was remodeled, this time by the Toledo Shipbuilding Company at Toledo, Ohio.

June of 1945 saw the former Lake Michigan queen on a daily run from Cleveland to Put-in-Bay by the Islands-Bay Steamship Line. Late in the season of 1945 she made several runs between Cleveland and Leamington, Ontario, so that Americans, still under wartime rationing, could buy unrationed Canadian merchandise. Many Canadian citizens resented these American raids and as a result some stores would close shop while *Alabama* was in port.

During the season of 1946 she was operated as an excursion steamer between Cleveland and Cedar Point. Business on this route was not profitable and at the close of the season the Cleveland & Buffalo Transit Company turned *Alabama* back to the Georgian Bay Line.

She was then retired to a berth in their winter quarters on Lake Macatawa near Holland, Michigan. Gradually she deteriorated and during 1960 she was dismantled and cut down to her main deck. Some of her beautiful woodwork adorns the interior of a summer home on Mackinac Island.

The Stender Construction Company purchased the stripped-down hull of this great ship on March 4, 1963, for use as a construction barge in the Saginaw Bay area. As this is written she is known as the *Alabama* of Bay City.

Probably no Lake steamer had more friends or was better known than *Alabama*. Because of her striking appearance and her many bouts with Lake Michigan ice she appeared in many press photographs and soon earned the title "most photographed ship on the Lakes." With never a change she still proudly carries the original name given her by Elizabeth Goodrich in Manitowoc on that cold day in December, 1909.

CAPTAIN DANIEL J. McGARITY — Here he is shown on the bridge of his beloved *Carolina*.

Courtesy: Captain McGarity

Chapter Ten

D. J. McGARITY—
A GREAT GOODRICH CAPTAIN

THE MARRIAGE OF JAMES PATRICK McGARITY OF BIG Rapids, Michigan, to the lovely Ellen Hanley of Topeka, Kansas, produced six children, four girls and two boys. The eldest, a son, born October 19, 1889, in Big Rapids, was Daniel J. McGarity. When Daniel was seven years old the family moved to Grand Rapids, Michigan, where his father felt his skill as a carpenter would be more in demand.

The McGaritys were a happy family until 1898. In November of that year the mother passed away. Not long after this saddening blow Daniel, now nicknamed Jerry, had to seek employment to help keep the family together.

In early 1904, Jerry secured employment with a local brewery. His father, being quite religious, resented his son's action and a serious quarrel resulted. On March 25 of that year Jerry took stock of his possessions and found exactly $2.80. To attract the perch fishermen, the Grand Rapids and Indiana Railroad was offering a special excursion rate to Muskegon, Michigan. The rate was 50¢ for the round trip. Our young adventurer purchased a ticket and then and there left home to make his own way.

Upon arrival in Muskegon his inventory consisted of $2.30 and the return-trip ticket to Grand Rapids. His first glimpse of water was Muskegon Lake which he believed to be Lake Michigan. After engaging a man on the Goodrich dock in conversation, he learned his error. His informant directed him to a trolley car which carried him to the shore of Lake Michigan.

Jerry McGarity's first glimpse of Lake Michigan was overwhelming. As he stood on the pier head, gazing in awe at the vast, deep-blue expanse of water, the *S.S. Atlanta* of the Goodrich line came up over the horizon. The *Atlanta* was fresh out of the shipyard at Manitowoc where she had undergone a complete overhaul in anticipation of a heavy summer schedule. Her newly painted black hull and white cabins literally gleamed, and young McGarity immediately fell in love with her. This was the first ship he had ever seen and the sight aroused a passion in the young man that determined his future career.

Again boarding the streetcar, he spent five cents of his small cash reserve to return to the Goodrich dock where he was determined to gain employment aboard the *Atlanta*.

Upon approaching an officer of the ship his request for a job evoked one quick question, "Can you scrub?"

Assuring the officer that he could and would "scrub," he was delivered to the bos'n and immediately put to work. His starting salary that fateful March 25, 1904, was exactly $15.00 per month.

Two weeks after gaining a berth on the *Atlanta* the bos'n got roaring drunk and was discharged. Young McGarity was his replacement.

Ship work fascinated Jerry McGarity and he was a hard worker and eager to learn. In November he was promoted to watchman and his salary raised to $40.00 per month.

From the very beginning of his working life, Jerry sent most of his earnings home to assist in the raising of his brothers and sisters. There was no deviation from this policy until his kin were able to carry on without his help.

In early 1905, McGarity was promoted to able-bodied seaman and transferred to the *Indiana*. He remained aboard this ship until she went to the shipyard at Manitowoc in February, 1906.

Early in March McGarity was assigned as quartermaster on his first ship, the *Atlanta*. He was on watch in this capacity when the *Atlanta* caught fire. It was thus that McGarity witnessed the complete destruction of the first vessel he had ever seen; the ship on which he had begun his long career with the Red-Stack line.

Following this harrowing experience he returned as quartermaster on the *Indiana*. In this capacity young Jerry had opportunity to gain knowledge of navigation and ship handling which he so eagerly sought. His enthusiasm and thirst for knowledge were rewarding for in June, 1907, he successfully passed an examination and was awarded second mate's papers.

That same year he was assigned to the great whaleback *Christopher Columbus* as second mate. In this new capacity his salary was raised to $70.00 per month. For three years he served in this capacity aboard the *Columbus* during the summer season. The winters were spent aboard the *Arizona* under Captain John Wilson. Captain Wilson diligently instructed his young second mate in the art of ship handling, navigation and, most important, ice-breaking.

In June, 1910, McGarity took the examination for first mate, and passed with flying colors. As first mate he was again assigned to the *Columbus* at a salary of $100.00 per month.

In January, 1911, McGarity was assigned as first mate aboard the *Indiana*. Captain John Wilson was also transferred to the *Indiana* as master. McGarity was delighted to serve again under his old skipper and good friend. They proved an excellent team and remained on the *Indiana* till the middle of 1913. Captain Wilson turned the ship over to his first mate as often as he could when docking, undocking, and turning so McGarity could become thoroughly experienced in these maneuvers.

October, 1912, was a real highlight in the career of the young officer. He took the Federal Government's examination, passing with honors, and was awarded his master's license. At the age of twenty-three, he was one of the youngest men to receive captain's papers in the history of the Great Lakes. Only eight years had passed since the runaway youth had stood in awe of the *Atlanta*, when it entered the pier heads at Muskegon! Now he was a full-fledged captain, fully qualified to command any ship on the inland seas. For a green youth, who had never glimpsed a ship before signing on as a deck hand, to rise to rank of captain in so short a period of time was a significant accomplishment. The fact that it has rarely been done, before or since, is a fine tribute to a truly great shipmaster.

Captain McGarity's first command was the side-wheeler *Chicago*. He placed his flag in her June, 1913, and remained her master until she was placed in winter lay-up in September.

Early in the season, in a dense fog with a very heavy sea running, the *Chicago* came upon the sand barge *Reliable*, which was in dire trouble. The *Reliable* had taken a terrific pounding and was in a sinking condition. Her crew was unable to launch her boats and she finally rolled over and sank.

Captain McGarity maneuvered the *Chicago* close to the wreckage that her crew was clinging to. A boat was quickly launched which picked up the survivors. This gallant rescue took place just off Milwaukee harbor.

After the winter lay-up of the *Chicago*, Mr. Goodrich assigned Captain McGarity to the *Iowa* with a salary increase to $150.00 per month. The *Iowa* was known to all Goodrich line captains as the "hard-luck ship" and no one received assignment to her with glee.

All went well aboard the *Iowa* until November 10, 1913. On this day a bad storm raged, respectfully referred to by Great Lakes sailors as the "Big Storm." No storm in the annals of Lake history surpassed this one of three days' duration from Sunday night till Wednesday night.

During these tragic, wild, snow-filled days, some sixteen or seventeen ships were wiped off the face of the Lakes. Some just "sailed away" with no trace of where they had met their doom. Many others were driven ashore and wrecked; still others were grounded and later salvaged. The total loss of life exceeded two hundred and fifty, an all-time sad record of big Great Lakes storms.

The *Iowa* had left Milwaukee, bound down for Chicago. When off Kenosha, the storm, accompanied by snow, struck with the speed of an express train from the dreaded northeast. Winds reached a velocity of eighty-five miles per hour. In moments the shore lights were blotted out and visibility reduced to absolute zero. Great seas, thirty to forty feet high, began to pound the ship. Soon it was impossible to hold the *Iowa* on course. Captain McGarity, fearful of being driven ashore or, worse yet, completely rolled over, ordered the course changed to east and then east-northeast to run into the wind and ease the strain on the old

S.S. CAROLINA — This ship was commanded by Captain McGarity for many seasons. Together, they were extremely popular with summer travelers. Here the ship is shown downbound in the St. Mary's River.

Courtesy: A. E. Young

wooden hull. With anything like normal shaft speed it was impossible to hold her head up in the gigantic waves. Finally the captain rang for "slow ahead" and the *Iowa* settled down to a rough but safer ride in the troughs of the big waves.

After sailing blind for two days Captain McGarity caught a glimpse of the Chicago harbor light and managed to bring the *Iowa* to dock with only minor damage. This was truly a great piece of seamanship in the worst storm ever to strike the Great Lakes. Fortunately, the rest of the winter aboard the *Iowa* was routine.

In April, 1914, Captain McGarity took command of the *Carolina*. She was a fine steel, twin-screw ship. Not being equipped for winter service, she was usually laid up in early fall. McGarity commanded the *Carolina* continuously every season up to and including 1927.

When the *Carolina* stopped for the winter, Captain McGarity would relieve other masters for vacations. When these were completed he would transfer to the winter run from Chicago to Grand Haven and Muskegon commanding the flagship of the fleet, the renowned *Alabama*.

Winter sailing across Lake Michigan is the most hazardous service on the Lakes. Heavy ice, snowstorms, and big seas combine to reserve these trips only for the brave and thoroughly experienced. Captain McGarity commanded the very capable and reliable *Alabama* from December 1 to April 1 for eight winters. The tale of his experiences in this winter service would make an additional book.

Heroic rescues of other vessels trapped in the ice, entering and leaving the pier heads under impossible conditions, being herself trapped in the ice for days, all contributed to a fabulous history in a trying service. Another tribute to the fine seamanship of the captain is that both he and the *Alabama* came through those eight long, severe winters without a single serious mishap.

The only serious accident that occurred to a ship under Captain McGarity was with the *Carolina*.

Carolina was usually laid up in the winter; nevertheless, she had her share of exciting incidents because it was usually December when she made her last trip northbound from Chicago. A typical experience occurred on December 3, 1916, when she was upbound on her last round trip of the season. As she approached the north end of Lake Michigan, she encountered heavy snow. Very soon the ship was entirely dependent on her compass for course and position. The snow was so dense that the captain wisely decided to bypass two regular stops, Kewaunee and Algoma, in the hope that these could be worked in on the downbound trip.

This being before the days of gyro compass, radio navigation aides, radar and depth finders, the floating card compass was the only means of determining course and position. With a large cargo of automobiles between decks, Captain McGarity purposely held a course further off shore than usual because he feared for the accuracy of his compass with so much additional metal aboard. In modern navigation terminology, he was concerned with the possibility of deviation problems in the compass, particularly since, due to the heavy snow, he was unable to check the compasses on pier ranges when leaving Manitowoc.

Just after dark the *Carolina*, without any warning, plowed onto a reef just off Stony Creek. With a terrific grinding and crunching of steel, the proud ship slid along the reef on her bottom plates for over forty feet before fetching up to an abrupt and jarring stop. Water immediately began to rise in the firehold and engine room. The captain gave the order to "stand by" to launch the lifeboats as a precautionary measure. A survey of possible damage was ordered to ascertain whether or not it would be necessary to abandon ship. It was revealed that the bow was four feet out of the water. To offset this, the after compartments were pumped out, bringing the ship to a more even keel. Exact extent of the damage to her bottom plates could not be determined under these conditions, but the captain was satisfied that the *Carolina* was in no immediate danger of foundering.

In the meantime, the wireless operator had contacted Milwaukee and made their plight known. A message giving the ship's position and general conditions was then telegraphed to the Lifesaving Stations at Sturgeon Bay Canal and Kewaunee, Wisconsin. Shortly after, all contact was lost. The rising water in the firehold made it necessary to draw the fires to avoid the possibility of an explosion. The ship was now without contact, steam, lights, heat or power. The eighty souls aboard, making up the crew and passengers, began to be very uncomfortable in the cold air of upper Lake Michigan in December. Later that night, the wireless operator demonstrated his ingenuity by using the batteries from some of the automobiles to make his transmitter function again and contact with shore points was re-established.

Immediately upon receipt of the message from Milwaukee the Lifesaving crews set out for the scene to render assistance, but the dense fog was impenetrable. In spite of bells that were rung and signal guns that were fired, it was nearly 3:00 A.M. before the first rescue boat located the stranded vessel. The Canal Station crew was the first to locate the ship. They immediately began to disembark the passengers from the darkened and heatless vessel. The Kewaunee Station crew arrived at daylight and assisted with the removal of passengers and crew. When evacuation was completed, the two crews stood by, awaiting additional forces that were needed to float the *Carolina* off the reef.

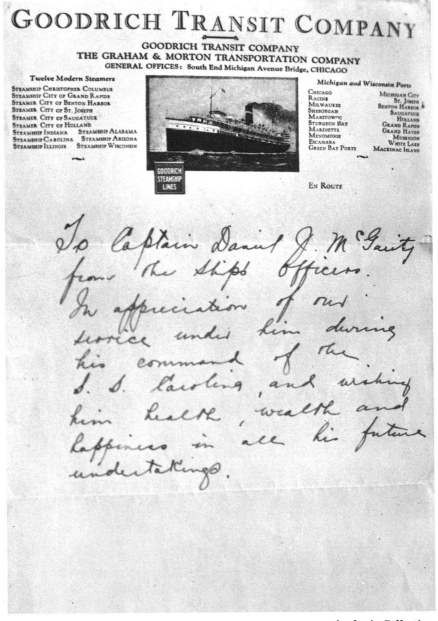

Author's Collection

TESTIMONIAL LETTER — When Captain McGarity gave up the command of the *Carolina,* the ship's officers handed him this letter of appreciation.

Daylight on Monday brought no improvement or lessening of the cold, dense fog. The harbor tug *Arctic* came up from Manitowoc, but was unable to find the *Carolina*. After a long search, she groped her way into Sturgeon Bay to refuel and await better weather on Tuesday.

Later on Monday, the *Saugatuck*, owned by the Escanaba & Garden Bay Transportation Company, sighted the grounded ship and began to remove the 'tween deck cargo of automobiles and such general freight that was not already ruined by the water. On Tuesday the *Saugatuck* completed the task and it was hoped this would lighten the ship sufficiently to drag her off. The reef was not that easily thwarted and had other notions about releasing the ship it so firmly held. In the next couple of days, the combined service of the tugs *Arctic, O. McMullen,* and *Meyers,* the steamers *J. S. Crouse* and *Saugatuck,* and the lighter *Advance* were to no avail. It began to look hopeless until the big sea-going salvage tug *Favorite* arrived.

By covering the holes in her bottom with canvas wrecking cloths, the big pumps on the *Favorite* were able to gain enough on the water to cover the canvas with cement to keep the sea out. Once dragged clear of the reef, additional shoring was placed over the patches and the tug *Favorite* set course for Manitowoc and the damaged ship was delivered to the shipyard for badly needed repairs to her bottom plates without further incident. By the next spring, she was completely repaired and renovated, and returned to her old regular run from Chicago to Mackinac Island.

Mr. Goodrich had a strict rule that when one of his captains stranded a ship or was involved in a serious accident, he was discharged. Mr. Goodrich insisted that the captain was to blame but if he was retained and it happened again the company was to blame. As a result of this rule many fine, experienced men were discharged. When the *Carolina* was released and taken to dry dock, McGarity's first act on getting ashore was to mail his resignation to the general superintendent of the company. Some weeks later he was agreeably surprised to have the letter returned unopened with instructions not to destroy it until after a hearing by the Government steamship inspectors. If the inspectors did not clear him he was to return the letter to the superintendent.

After a lengthy hearing he was completely cleared of responsibility for stranding the *Carolina* and was again given her command when she was released from dry dock. He commanded her and other ships of the line for many years without an accident. He never learned why he had not been discharged. Retaining him broke a rule of many years and later worked to the benefit of two veteran captains who were unfortunate enough to get into trouble. One captain got too close in off South Point, Milwaukee, causing

Courtesy: Harry W. Thorp, Jr.

S.S. ALABAMA — Captain McGarity and his first mate Edward Wilson are shown here on the bridge of the *Alabama* as she fights her way through the ice at the entrance to the Grand Haven harbor.

some slight damage with no loss of life. The other captain ran his ship into the breakwater at Chicago in a blinding snowstorm, badly damaging the ship but with no loss of life. Both were cleared by the inspectors and were retained by the Goodrich company and gave many more years of successful service.

After the Stony Creek accident no other outstanding events occurred in the life of Captain McGarity until 1920. That year he met and began courting the secretary of the president of a large advertising firm located in the Wrigley Building in Chicago. This vivacious redhead was Ethel Wallace of Warrenville, Illinois. She was the daughter of William and Clara Wallace and a graduate of Wheaton College. Ethel, accompanied by two girl friends, properly chaperoned, made a trip on the *Carolina* to Mackinac Island. This settled things for the young master of the ship. He vowed he would change the name of this delightful girl to McGarity. The year 1921 was the most important one in his life for then Ethel Wallace consented to be his bride.

When the *Carolina* was laid up in September of 1926, Captain McGarity was brought ashore as assistant superintendent. In his new position he did not relieve the west-shore captains for their vacations. Instead, he remained at Manitowoc where he supervised the lay-up and repair of those ships taken out of service for the winter months. Due to the change of responsibility he now earned $250.00 per month.

On December 1, 1926, the work at Manitowoc was completed and Captain McGarity returned to the command of the *Alabama* on her winter runs from Chicago to Muskegon and Grand Haven. On April 1, 1927, he was named acting superintendent and he assumed the responsibility of fitting out the fleet for the 1927 season.

After all the work of painting, repairs and dry-docking was completed and the ships had all left Manitowoc, Captain McGarity returned to his beloved *Carolina*.

The fall and winter of 1927-28 were a repetition of the previous year, with the exception that the title of general superintendent was bestowed on McGarity in the spring of 1928. As a result he did not command the *Carolina* or the *Alabama* that year and spent most of his time in the Chicago office of the line.

In his new capacity, Captain McGarity had the responsibility of assigning the captains, mates and engineers to the various ships. While ashore in this work, McGarity was paid an additional $100.00 per month for living expenses. His base pay of $250.00 per month for twelve months remained the same although some years he was required to work only eleven months.

During the winter that Captain McGarity stayed ashore as superintendent an amusing incident that could have been tragic happened.

WATER-FRONT PASS.

Port of... Milwaukee

Pass... Daniel J. McGarity

Residence... Chicago, Ill.

Nationality... American

Occupation... Master SS Carolina

Employed by... Goodrich Transit Co.

Date... 6-17-18   Pass good at... Universal

No. 910650   Samuel M. Randolph

07—1108   United States Marshal.

Author's Collection

WATER FRONT PASS — This pass, giving access to the water front, was issued to Captain McGarity during World War I.

A sand bar had been building up in the entrance between the pier heads at Grand Haven. Several reports had come to Captain McGarity of ships scraping bottom at this point in heavy weather. This was particularly true when the wind was in the southwest quarter. To avoid possible hull damage, Captain McGarity issued a letter to all masters advising that Grand Haven should be by-passed when these conditions existed.

Late one afternoon in February, Captain Gerald Stufflebeam, then captain of the *Alabama,* was called away on an emergency. To keep the schedule Captain McGarity took the *Alabama* on her night trip to Muskegon with a scheduled stop at Grand Haven. During the night the wind built up from the southwest. In the early morning hours, as the Grand Haven light loomed on the horizon, a very heavy sea was running and it appeared that it would be necessary to bypass this popular stop.

After studying the seas for a while the captain had a conference with Mr. Thomas Fitzpatrick, his chief engineer. The captain explained he felt that by staying close to the south pier head and putting on a slight burst of speed, the entrance could be safely negotiated. The *Alabama* was known to be under-powered. It was agreed that when the engine room telegraph signaled "full ahead," her throttles would be opened wide to make certain the ship would hold up her head during the minutes it took to get safely inside the pier heads.

When McGarity felt the right moment had arrived, the signal was given and the *Alabama* picked up speed and started in. No sooner had her bow passed the west end of the south pier head when she started directly for the pier itself. Actually the big, steel ship traveled almost the entire length of the channel nearly sideways to the wind and the sea!

After a yeoman effort at the wheel and the engine room telegraph the pride of the Goodrich line was brought under control and safely docked. It seems that live steam passed over into her low-pressure cylinders and her usual 96 rpm were greatly exceeded.

When the excitement of the wild ride and docking had subsided, Captain McGarity retired to the captain's quarters for a well-earned rest. There, pasted on the dresser mirror by Captain Stufflebeam, was the letter admonishing all concerned not to attempt to enter Grand Haven harbor under the conditions just experienced. Captain McGarity sheepishly turned out the lights and went to bed.

1928 was the beginning of the twilight for the Red-Stack fleet. The automobile was making deep inroads in the summer tourist traffic from Chicago to west Michigan and Wisconsin. Highways were being rapidly improved and the automobile was looked upon as a reliable and fashionable means of travel. The railroads were also making a concentrated effort to attract business. Patronage, especially on the overnight boats, fell off drastically.

The merger of the Graham & Morton Line with Goodrich in 1924-25 brought several G & M officials into the Goodrich family. As profits fell and things began to look glum, internal strife developed between the old G & M officers and some of the Goodrich officials. The company finished in the red in 1928 and hard times ahead for the old Lake Michigan line seemed a certainty.

With the outlook not too bright and the internal strife within bound to take its toll, Captain McGarity reluctantly reached a decision — he would resign. On September 1, 1928, his resignation was submitted and so ended a distinguished career on the part of the Goodrich's best-known master.

After his departure, Captain McGarity continued a distinguished career in shipping circles and only as late as January 1, 1965, did he retire as vice president of the well-known Great Lakes Towing Company.

As these lines are written Captain McGarity and his wife are living in blissful retirement at St. Charles, Illinois. This story of his great career with Goodrich was told to the author personally over a series of most enjoyable sessions.

THE GOODRICH DOCKS, CHICAGO, 1915 — A view from the south end of the Rush Street bridge, looking east up River Street.

Courtesy: Chicago Historical Society

Chapter Eleven

THE LAST NEW STEAMER

Robert M. LaFOLLETTE, KNOWN FOR MANY YEARS IN political circles as "Battling Bob," was United States senator from the state of Wisconsin from 1905 to 1925. As far back as 1885, when he was elected a United States congressman, he was known as a liberal and was outstandingly progressive. Upon his election to the Senate he advocated strict railroad regulations, lower tariffs, and better working conditions for American seamen.

Senator LaFollette wrote, sponsored, and succeeded in having passed, a law known as the LaFollette Seaman's Act. This law in its original concept was very far-reaching and its enactment struck a serious blow to the steamship business on the Lakes. The Seaman's Act was passed in 1912.

The operation of the excursion steamer *Columbus* is a good illustration of the added operating expense brought about by the restrictions imposed by the LaFollette Act. While the *Columbus* was always operated as strictly a day-excursion ship and carried no overnight passengers, a large duplication of officers and crew was necessary to comply with the new law. Her normal rated capacity of approximately four thousand day passengers was reduced to about 2,200.

The normal summer season for *Columbus* was from June 15 until Labor Day. It was customary to hire a crew at the beginning of each season and lay them off right after Labor Day. The best of the crew were often retained for service on those ships used on the year-around routes. Under the stipulations of the LaFollette Seaman's Act, a man had to have four years' experience to qualify as an able-bodied seaman. This rule forced the line to carry a larger payroll through the winter months, thereby greatly increasing operating costs.

The real decline in profitable Lake steamship operations throughout the Great Lakes began with the enactment of the La-Follette Act. Later some of the requirements were tempered but not until after much damage to Lake shipping had been done.

Mr. A. W. Goodrich joined with other Lake steamship operators in a strong fight against the passage of the LaFollette bill, but to no avail. They did their best to convince the senator that operating conditions on the Lakes were seasonal and therefore vastly different from those encountered in salt-water ships. By 1912 the Goodrich profit picture was still good but the need for additional operating capital was making itself felt.

Up to this time in Goodrich history it had never been necessary or was it deemed advisable to issue preferred stock. The situation he now found himself in convinced Mr. Goodrich that an issue of preferred shares would be the best way to meet the need for additional funds. Still not wishing to offer preferred shares to the public in general, he decided on a private sale of the stock.

About twenty close friends were invited to a private dinner and Mr. Goodrich carefully explained the problem that confronted his company. Before the dinner was over the entire issue of $500,000 had been subscribed to.

LAUNCHING DAY—The *Nevada* in the stocks at Manitowoc Shipbuilding and all ready to enter the water.

Courtesy: Dora B. Goodrich

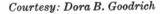

Courtesy: Harry W. Thorp, Jr.

CHRISTENING OF THE NEVADA — On board the *Alabama* are, from left to right, A. W. Goodrich, Albert E. Goodrich II, and Harry W. Thorp, Sr. The badges they are wearing state, "NEVADA — Made in Manitowoc."

Following this generous response to his appeal, a new seven-man board of directors was selected. Except for Mr. Harry Thorp and himself, the balance of the new directors were selected from the group that purchased the new stock issue. The new board consisted of the following: Albert W. Goodrich, Chairman; Harry W. Thorp, Vice President; C. H. Hermann; W. L. Phelps; A. A. Sprague; B. M. Winston; F. L. Whitcomb.

When the *Iowa* was crushed and sank in the ice just off Chicago harbor in February of 1915, a replacement for her was badly needed. For immediate relief the steamer *Holland* was chartered from the Graham & Morton Line until a new ship could be built.

The first consideration by Mr. Goodrich for a replacement for the *Iowa* was a steel combination passenger-and-freight ship similar to *Virginia* and *Alabama*. Both of these steamers had been highly successful but the terms of the LaFollette Act were such that he was convinced a straight-package freighter could be operated much more profitably because fewer crew members would be required. This was especially true during the winter months when the passenger travel would be at a low level.

Again Mr. Elias Gunnell, president of Manitowoc Shipbuilding, se̲t ̲bout to design a ship that would best meet the needs outlined by Mr. Goodrich. After complete agreement on all details, a contract to build the new steel ship was awarded to Manitowoc Shipbuilding on May 10, 1915.

Like the *Alabama*, she was intended for winter service, and much thought was given to her ice-breaking ability. Her hull construction reflected this thinking with extra heavy plates in the bow. The principal dimensions of the new steamer were as follows: hull, steel; length, 220 feet; beam, 42 feet; depth, 24 feet; draft, 14 feet; gross tons, 2,122; net tons, 1,078; propulsion, single screw; engine, triple expansion 21½-34½-56 x 36; horsepower, 1600; revolutions per minute, 105; service speed, 16 mph; top speed, 18 mph; fuel, coal.

This steamer, the forty-fifth to be owned by Goodrich, was built at a cost of $411,000 and was christened *Nevada*. She was launched at 9:00 A.M. on Wednesday, September 15, 1915, at Manitowoc. This was a gala event and was well attended by many dignitaries from Chicago and Milwaukee. All wore badges of silk that read: "*Nevada* — Built in Manitowoc." Representatives from other steamship lines on the Great Lakes were on hand to inspect the newest idea and latest design in package freighters.

Mr. Goodrich had *Alabama* taken off her regular run to Muskegon and instead she took aboard company officials, their families, representatives of the press, and steamship dignitaries from Chicago. *Alabama* departed for Manitowoc on the afternoon of Tuesday, September 14, with a stop at Milwaukee en route.

At this time Mr. Goodrich's only son, Albert E. Goodrich II, was just nine years old. There was a firm superstition and conviction among shipping men that a new vessel had to be christened by a woman or a girl. The last new Goodrich steamer, *Alabama*, had been christened by Mr. Goodrich's second daughter, Elizabeth, in keeping with the best tradition.

Precedent and superstition were dealt a severe blow when Mr. Goodrich elected to have his son Albert II do the christening of *Nevada*. This caused quite a stir among the visiting dignitaries of the shipping world.

The announcement of the event as described in the Chicago newspapers read as follows:

BOY WILL CHRISTEN A BOAT

Albert Goodrich II will christen the steamship NEVADA of the Goodrich Transportation Company when she is launched September 15th at Manitowoc, Wisconsin. There will be a gallery of Chicagoans to witness the ceremony. The boy will upset precedent, as usually a girl officiates at the christening of ships.

"My boy asked me one day while looking at the NEVADA, if he could christen her," said President A. W. Goodrich of the Company. "It was the first flash of interest he had shown in the calling the Goodrich family has followed for three generations. The NEVADA is a boat built for the business world and I could not frame in my mind a reason why the boy's healthy ambition should not be gratified, so christen her he will. My only regret is that NEVADA is not the $500,000 passenger boat we had planned, the building and operating of which was prevented by the seaman's bill."

The NEVADA will be completed this fall for winter service. She will be 232 feet long with a breadth of 42 feet for stability. Her bow is a veritable battering ram, for her appointed task is to batter her way into Chicago, Milwaukee, Muskegon, Grand Haven and other harbors when the winter ice is piled high along the shore. She will be driven by engines giving her a speed of seventeen miles an hour. Chicago shippers will be able to lay down across Lake Michigan the next day, goods ordered as late as 4 P.M. the day before.

Courtesy: Harry W. Thorp, Jr.

S.S. NEVADA — When launching the ship, a near accident happened. Her stern entered the water first. A little more, and the *Nevada* could have rolled over.

The launching of *Nevada* very nearly ended badly. To accomplish the side launch smoothly there were two triggers rigged, one at the bow and the other at the stern. These were tripped by cutting a taut line with a blow of an axe by the yard workmen at a given signal from the yard foreman.

When all was in readiness, the signal was given. The man at the stern swung his axe with unerring accuracy and immediately that end of the vessel began to move down the ways toward the river. The man on the bow also swung his axe at the given signal. Due to overanxiety or some other unexplainable reason, he missed the taut line with his first blow! By the time he recovered and managed to strike a second and more accurate blow, the stern was already moving. For a few breathless seconds it appeared that the new *Nevada* would end up on her beam ends! As things turned out, the second blow came in time to prevent this but the new freighter did enter the Manitowoc River stern first. Had she actually turned over, the superstitious would have immediately blamed the fact that *Nevada* had been christened by a boy and not, as tradition dictated, by a girl or a woman.

Nevada had many innovations designed to aid in the rapid handling of her package freight cargo. She was equipped with three freight gangways on each side and in addition she had a special gangway for the use of her crew. The forward gangway measured nine feet by nine feet to facilitate the loading of automobiles.

Her ground tackle was the finest of any vessel on the Lakes. She had two stockless anchors weighing 4,000 lbs. each and 1,260 feet of 1-7/8-inch stud-link chain. The windlass was on the spar deck and operated a capstan on the deck above. She also had two two-drum mooring winches, one fore and the other aft.

The coal bunkers had a capacity of 190 tons but the cargo hold just forward of the coal bunkers was arranged so that it could also be used as an additional coal bunker. This gave *Nevada* a total bunker capacity of 550 tons. At full speed she consumed 2,400 lbs. per hour.

Being a freighter, she had no regular passenger accommodations. On the boat deck she had a sumptuously outfitted owner's quarters. These were complete with bath and private dining room. Aft on the spar deck were six "director's rooms" that were finished in elaborate style.

One leading idea in her design was to render her as fire-proof as possible. The cargo holds were arranged so that they could be completely shut off from the quarters above. When the doors in the upper house were locked no one but the officers in charge could gain access to the freight holds. All cargo holds were protected by an automatic sprinkler system.

S.S. NEVADA — She was a very fine-looking package freighter.

Nevada was equipped with a single stack and two steel pole masts each having the traditional gaff boom found on all Goodrich steamers. On the aft side of the main mast there was a five-ton, forty-foot cargo boom with hoist.

She was the first vessel on the Lakes to be built with the "cruiser" type stern. This was in order to save as much length as possible to enable her better to turn in rivers with very little clearance between the banks.

All work and her time trials were completed by December 6 and on that Monday morning, at 10:40 A.M., the new ship departed Manitowoc, bound down for Chicago.

In short order *Nevada* proved herself to be a very fine ship. She was an exceptionally good rough-weather boat and experienced no difficulty in the heavy ice of the winter of 1915-1916. This, in spite of the fact that temperatures that winter were far below average and the Lake Michigan ice was unusually heavy.

Winter persisted until late spring of 1916. The ice lasted well beyond the time it usually broke up. In late April, the big bulk freighters started their trek to the head of Lake Superior to begin the never-ending task of supplying the precious red iron ore to the hungry furnaces in the steel-making centers of the Midwest.

The winter ice in the north country, like the rest of the Great Lakes area, was unusually heavy. A sudden drop in temperature and the big ships found themselves securely locked in the ice

Courtesy: Henry Barkhausen

S.S. NEVADA — An unusual bow view.

all the way from Whitefish Bay to the mouth of the St. Mary's River at Detour. The situation was desperate.

In a frantic effort to get the ore traffic off to a good start, the Lake Carriers Association requested permission from Mr. Goodrich to charter the *Nevada* to help free the stricken freighters.

Nevada, by this time, had earned a fine reputation as an ice-breaker. Mr. Goodrich agreed to the charter and on April 20 the sturdy package freighter departed Manitowoc on her unusual charter assignment.

Up around the north end of the Beaver Island group she made her way. While the going was a little slow, the ice encountered was nothing compared to the high windrows and heavy sheet ice she encountered in passing through the Straits of Mackinac. Ahead, back, ahead, smash, smash, she slowly made her way to the entrance to the St. Mary's River. As she continued her grinding progress up the river she released the trapped steamers one by one. As soon as they were free, they fell in line behind *Nevada* and the group slowly and in majestic splendor made its way toward the Soo Locks.

The odd parade passed through the locks and on out across Whitefish Bay. In a surprisingly short period of time the bulk carriers were clear of the ice jams and running free in the cold, deep waters of Lake Superior en route to their waiting cargos of heavy iron ore at the head of the Lake.

The *Nevada,* with a "well done" blast from the deep-throated whistles of her consorts, made her way back to Lake Michigan to resume her regular duties for her proud owners. Word of her accomplishment flashed through shipping circles all around the world.

Not long after this thrilling episode, the Goodrich management was approached by a Captain Mishtowt, an official representative of the Imperial Russian Navy Department. Ice was a continual and serious problem in the harbor of Vladivostok and the Russians desired to purchase *Nevada* to serve as an icebreaker in that far Russian port in the north.

Negotiations were carried on and it was finally agreed that Goodrich would sell *Nevada* to the Imperial Russian Navy for $725,000 delivered at Montreal, Canada. A deposit was placed in escrow in the National City Bank of New York in the amount of $125,000. The balance of $600,000 was payable on delivery of the vessel at Montreal.

Under command of Captain D. J. McGarity, *S.S. Nevada* departed from Manitowoc on the morning of May 10, 1917, bound up for Montreal. En route, two furnaces in the starboard boiler collapsed. Upon arrival in Montreal, in this condition, the representatives of the Russian Government refused to accept delivery of the ship.

Captain McGarity immediately communicated the facts to Mr. Goodrich in Chicago. Steps were then taken to secure a court order restraining the National City Bank of New York from returning the deposit of $125,000 to the Russians. While the transaction was thus deadlocked, the Imperial Russian Government was deposed.

As soon as things in Russian Government affairs were a bit
more settled, the sale of *Nevada* to the Provisional Government was
undertaken. In the meantime necessary repairs to place the ship
in top condition–were completed at Montreal.

On July 23, 1917, the sale was completed to the new Government for the sum of $600,000. Actually, the board of directors dis-
liked the idea of disposing of the *Nevada* as she had proven herself
to be a fine ship and an excellent money-maker. But the temptation
of the substantial profit was too attractive to pass up. Of the funds
received from the sale of the ship, $500,000 was used to retire the
bonds in that amount, issued during the reorganization of 1906.
These bonds were due for redemption April 1, 1918, and were
actually called on August 25, 1917. This action left the Goodrich
Transit Company practically free of all indebtedness with the exception of the preferred stock issued in 1912.

Nevada had her name changed to *Rogday* by the Russians.
As things worked out, the steamer never actually did get to the
homeland of her owners. After passing through the Panama Canal,
she ended up in San Francisco, where she was involved in a collision with a U. S. Destroyer. On orders from the United States
Navy Department, she was seized by a U. S. marshall and held for
damages. In 1921 she was purchased by the Pere Marquette Line
Steamers Company of Milwaukee. Her original name *Nevada* was
restored and again she made the long trip through the Panama
Canal en route to her original home, Lake Michigan.

For several years she operated in the cross-lake service be-

S.S. NEVADA — Her fate is sealed. She is shown here sinking off the
Carolina coast.

Courtesy : Manistee Historical Society

tween Milwaukee, Ludington, and Manistee. In 1942 *Nevada* was taken over by the Federal Government for service in the Atlantic. She ended her career by foundering off the coast of South Carolina after losing a five-day battle with a violent north-Atlantic storm. Of the sixty-four member crew, the Coast Guard cutter *Comanche* was able to rescue only twenty-nine men.

Nevada was the last steamship to be built for the Goodrich line. Other ships were discussed and even planned but all future acquisitions were purchased or secured by merger with other companies.

On May 9, 1918, the Goodrich Transit Company purchased the iron side-wheeler *State of New York* from the Detroit & Cleveland Navigation Company of Detroit. This gallant old queen had been constructed in 1883 by the Detroit Dry Dock Company at Wyandotte, Michigan. Her dimensions were as follows: hull, iron; length, 203 feet; beam, 32 feet 6 inches; draft, 10 feet 6 inches; gross tonnage, 807; net tonnage, 564; propulsion, side-wheel; en-

S.S. STATE OF NEW YORK — This is how she looked in the D & C colors. Later she became the *S.S. Florida* for the Goodrich Line.

Courtesy: Marine Collection, Milwaukee Public Library

gines, vertical beam, 36-78-44 x 120; horsepower, 950; revolutions per minute, 30; speed, 16 mph.

When launched, this popular boat was christened *City of Mackinac*. For many years she served on the Detroit-Mackinac Island route. In 1893 she was sold to Cleveland & Buffalo Transit Company and was renamed *State of New York*.

After her purchase by Goodrich she was sent to the shipyard at Manitowoc and given a light overhaul. When this work was completed she was painted in the traditional Goodrich colors and renamed *S. S. Florida*.

On June 14, 1918, *Florida* was placed in excursion service out of Chicago on the Michigan City route. Evenings, on her return from a day trip to Michigan City, she was used for moonlight trips on Lake Michigan from the Municipal Pier. She remained in this service for the next three years without too much success. In May of 1922 *Florida* was sold to W. H. Cochrane, who was representing the Western Transportation Company of Chicago.

Courtesy: Dowling Collection

S.S. FLORIDA — Here she is shown entering Michigan City harbor as a Goodrich steamer.

For a few more years *Florida* continued to be used in the excursion traffic from Municipal Pier and then was finally dismantled. Her hull became a floating clubhouse for the Columbia Yacht Club, at the foot of Randolph Street and the Lake in Chicago. In 1954 she was badly damaged by fire. In 1955 she was rebuilt and is still in service as headquarters for this well-known Yacht Club.

The purchase of *Florida* was the last steamship deal engineered by Albert W. Goodrich as president and chairman of the board of the Goodrich Transit Company.

THE GOODRICH HOME — This lovely old house in Chicago was located at 1474 South Michigan Avenue.

Courtesy: Dora B. Goodrich

Chapter Twelve

END OF THE GOODRICH DYNASTY

W HEN MAKING A STUDY AND REVIEW OF THE GOOD-
rich steamboat operation over the years, one is immediately impressed with the consistency and steadfastness of purpose that
went into the management of this enterprise throughout its history.
The infinite attention that was given to details is obviously one important key to the success enjoyed by the Goodriches for so long a
period.

A good example of this careful attention to detail and the
consistency with which tradition was observed within the company
can be found in the story and history of the Goodrich house flag.
Designed by Captain A. E. Goodrich in 1868, it was a pure-white,
dovetail pennant with the letters "G.T.Co." shown in the same
bright red color used on the stacks of the steamers in the fleet.
This pennant varied somewhat in size through the years, as flags
generally became smaller after the 1920's, but never did this well-
known and highly respected house flag vary from its original design. When the name changed in 1906 from Goodrich Transportation Company to Goodrich Transit Company, the new name was
selected so that it was not necessary to alter the "G.T.Co." design
in the pennant. The same flag marked Goodrich steamers, offices
and docks from its inception in 1868 until the very end, a span of
sixty-six years!

Stack colors, a bright red with an orange cast topped with a
broad black band at the very top of the stack, remained unchanged

throughout the seventy-seven-year life span of the Goodrich operation. Shortly after *Huron* was actually purchased from Captain Ward, her single tall stack was so painted as was every single Goodrich steamer to follow through the years. There is no record of any steamer owned by the Goodrich line that did not proudly carry this well-known stack color.

There is mention throughout the history of the line that Captain Goodrich obtained this color first from the same source that supplied the famous transoceanic Cunard Line of England. This could well be true because the stack colors are identical in shade.

Some of the early Goodrich boats, including the immortal *Huron*, were painted entirely white. Gradually a hull painted black to the main deck and white above with white cabins and topsides won favor with Captain A. E. Goodrich. About the time of the incorporation of Goodrich Transportation Company these hull colors were adopted as standard. Steamers as early as *Northwest, Alpena* and *Corona* carried this color scheme.

In 1890 there was a slight change in this standard color arrangement. After that year the hulls were painted all black with white cabins and topsides. This slight change was the only variation in the original concept as adopted by the founder. Late in the life of the company the *Roosevelt* was permitted to operate as an excursion steamer with an all-white hull but her stacks were in the standard Goodrich tradition. Actually *Roosevelt* was owned by the Chicago & Manitowoc Transportation Company and leased to Goodrich Transit Company. She and the *City of Benton Harbor* were the only two steamers to fly the Goodrich banner with their hulls painted white after the adoption of black as standard.

The very opposite was true with many of the other Great Lakes steamship companies. One is amazed at the continual changes that went on within some of the lines. Stack colors, with and without insignia, were frequently changed and often mixed within the same fleet. Hull colors were often changed almost from season to season and it was not at all unusual to find steamers of the same line with different color schemes in the same season. Typical were the changes that took place during the history of Graham & Morton, Detroit & Cleveland and Cleveland & Buffalo lines.

Early vessels built by Captain Goodrich had wooden pole masts. Always the forward mast, even when the steamer only carried one, was equipped with a gaff-rigged boom. The Goodrich pennant was always flown from this gaff. In later years the pole masts were of steel, yet the gaff boom was always present and from it proudly flew the white "G.T.Co." house flag.

Yet another example of the careful attention that was paid to

Courtesy: Dora B. Goodrich

ALBERT WHALING GOODRICH

details was the steam whistles used on all Goodrich steamers throughout the life of the company. These whistles were carefully chimed and emitted a melodious, pleasant tone unlike that used by any other Lake steamship line. Not only was the tone quite pleasant to the ear but it possessed excellent carrying qualities. When

ALBERT E. GOODRICH II — He is shown here proudly wearing the fire badge which Chief Horan of the Chicago Fire Department gave his father.

sounded, upon entering the pier heads or approaching a dock, the whistles announced in a most thrilling manner that the Goodrich boat was "in" and many a footstep would then be turned toward the Goodrich dock. At night, across many a sleepy Wisconsin or Michigan town, the long blast of the sonorous whistle would let all know that the "night boat" would be casting off in just fifteen minutes.

With some Lake lines the routes and scheduling changed almost every season. Many of these changes were due to changes in management and ownership but it is significant that Goodrich served, generally speaking, the same routes on the same approximate schedules at the death of the company that were being served in the late 1800's. The exception to this was the merger with Graham & Morton in 1925 when the ports at the southern end of the east shore of Lake Michigan were added. The service to the west-shore ports and the Muskegon-Grand Haven route remained very consistent throughout the years. Not only was this a tribute to consistent management but this regularity of the same service also made untold friends for the Red-Stack line.

Captain A. E. Goodrich was a firm believer in high maintenance standards. There was no such thing as an ill-kept, shabby-appearing Goodrich steamer. The early establishment of a shore base of operations at Manitowoc for the purpose of supply and maintenance was a living testimony to the captain's awareness of the need of proper care of the steamers. During winter lay-up a staff of painters, carpenters and shipwrights went through each ship so that when it was time for the season to open, the steamers were spic and span and ready to make more new friends for Goodrich among those that availed themselves of the passenger service. No deviation in these high standards of maintenance was permitted throughout the history of the Goodrich line.

After the passing of Captain A. E. Goodrich, the new president, Captain Thomas Butlin, permitted no changes in the operating policies that he and Captain Goodrich had agreed upon during the many years of their close association. Captain Butlin, a famous shipmaster in his own right, had always been a strong advocate of keeping the ships of the line in top condition. During the time he trained and guided young Albert W. Goodrich to take over the presidency, he taught him the value of good consistent operation and high standards of maintenance well.

The complete story of the exciting career of Albert Whaling Goodrich would make a book in itself. The third child of Captain A. E. Goodrich, and born after the untimely death of his two older sisters in one year, he was the pride and joy of the illustrious captain. As his life unfolded he proved to be indeed a "chip off the old block" and he fully justified the pride and confidence expressed in him by his famous father.

As a youth Albert was raised in the old homestead at 1474 Michigan Avenue. On the corner of Fourteenth Street and Michigan Avenue was one of the oldest fire engine houses in the history of the city of Chicago. During the Chicago Fire of 1871 the famous pumper "Sherman" was housed there. In the early 1900's this station was the headquarters for Battalion Chief Tom O'Connor who later became fire marshall of Chicago under Mayor Carter H. Harrison.

The closeness of the Goodrich home and this famous fire engine house meant that young Albert, early in his life, became a real dyed-in-the-wool fire fan. This enthusiasm for the fire department carried over into his adult life. When still a young man about town, he became a close friend of Chief James Horan. In Albert Goodrich's personal effects there is still a gold fire shield given him by Chief Horan on his birthday. When Horan was killed by a falling wall while fighting a serious fire in the Chicago Stock Yards in 1911, Albert was deeply shocked.

In 1909 Albert became an active member of the Fire Fans' Association and had a joker alarm box installed in both his office and his home. Some of the famous Chicago names in the Fire Fans' Association were E. L. Brand, George Gilman, Fred Sykes,

Special Notice to Passengers

◆◆◆◆◆◆◆◆◆◆◆◆◆◆◆◆◆

LIFE PRESERVERS

may be found under lower berth in staterooms, also triced overhead on Promenade Decks, and in each Lifeboat.

CHILDREN'S LIFE PRESERVERS

may be found in each Cabin in Boxes, Racks or Lockers, so marked.

DIRECTIONS FOR ADJUSTING

Put the Life Preserver on in the same manner as you would a Vest or Jacket, one arm through each shoulder strap, bring the ends of Life Preserver together IN FRONT and fasten.

BAGGAGE

This Company will not be responsible for BAGGAGE unless checked and in charge of Porter, nor for any hand baggage, Wearing Apparel or Valuables left in Cabins or Staterooms.

To guard against errors, have your baggage checked, and claim it before leaving boat.

NO CHARGE FOR CHECKING OR HANDLING BAGGAGE.

LEAVE VALUABLES WITH PURSER OF BOAT, OR COMPANY WILL NOT BE RESPONSIBLE FOR SAME.

No Rooms or Berths given until tickets are procured.
Passengers damaging Boat, Furniture or Bedding will be made to pay for same.
Blankets or other Stateroom Equipment must not be taken from Stateroom.
Children traveling Free or on Half-fare Tickets not allowed to sit at the First Table.
Smoking will not be allowed in Cabins or Staterooms.
Passengers are strictly forbidden to use Oil or Spirit Lamps in the Staterooms.
Dogs or other Live Pets not allowed in Staterooms.

GOODRICH TRANSIT COMPANY.

83   THE FRED J. RINGLEY CO., CHICAGO

Author's Collection

A GOODRICH NOTICE TO PASSENGERS—This notice was taken from the stateroom of an old Goodrich steamer at about the turn of the century.

Charles H. Hermann, W. J. Carney, D. J. Cahill, James Thorne, Bill Corbett and many others. During a big fire on Wabash Avenue on a cold night in 1911, Albert opened his Michigan Avenue home to serve the half-frozen firemen hot coffee and sandwiches. One of the earliest photographs of Albert E. Goodrich II, only son of A. W. Goodrich, shows him in a cute little fireman's outfit complete with helmet. Proudly pinned to his little red shirt is the gold fire badge given to his father by Chief Horan, just before the chief was killed in the Chicago Stock Yards fire.

The fire-fighting equipment aboard all Goodrich steamers was standardized to coincide with the hose and fitting sizes of the Chicago Fire Department equipment. In this manner any Goodrich ship, near the scene of a waterfront fire, could relay water to the land companies in the area.

So rabid a fire fan was Albert that once, while in the middle of signing the Goodrich line payroll checks, the joker alarm box in his office ticked off an extra alarm blaze. Off to the fire dashed the president of the Goodrich line and as a result pay day was a day late for many of the employees.

This great interest in fire fighting was climaxed in 1927 when Mayor William Hale Thompson appointed Albert W. Goodrich to the post of fire commissioner of the city of Chicago. When he assumed this title he became Chicago's first fire commissioner.

He had his personal Rolls Royce equipped with a regulation fire engine bell, red and green headlight lenses and the body of the car painted in regulation fire-engine red. Shortly thereafter the Chicago Fire Boats appeared in the red stack and standard colors of the Goodrich steamers.

About 1912 Mr. Goodrich had all of the steamers in the fleet equipped with a steam siren to be used in emergencies. Later the captains began to sound salutes on these sirens as they departed from the docks of the summer-resort stops much to the enjoyment and thrill of both the passengers and the spectators.

Superstition clung to the steamboat business for a long time. One such was the belief that any trip started on a Friday was a bad omen. No one in his right mind would launch a new ship or begin a new season on a Friday!

It was not until the launching of the *Nevada* in 1915 that anyone other than a girl or a woman was permitted to christen a new ship at launching. When the *Nevada* was ready to slide down the ways Albert Goodrich dared superstition and tradition and designated his young son, Albert E. Goodrich II, as the one to do the christening. There was nothing unlucky about the *Nevada*. She was sold to the Russian Government as an icebreaker at a handsome profit at a time when the company could well use the funds.

Author's Collection

A GOODRICH ADVERTISEMENT—This advertisement was taken from *Beeson's Marine Directory* of 1920, the year A. W. Goodrich sold his holdings in the Red Stack fleet.

A. W. Goodrich was a firm leader. He had a slogan regarding accidents of the steamers while underway that went something like this, "The first time a captain puts a boat ashore it is his fault. The second time that happens with the same captain it is my fault." It was not until the accident of the *Carolina* while under the command of Captain D. J. McGarity that he relinquished the severity of this rule.

Beginning with the renaming of *City of Ludington* to *Georgia* in 1898, all Goodrich steamers received names that ended in "A." This is alleged to be a whim of A. W. Goodrich because his first initial was "A." This practice was dropped after his sale of the Goodrich Transit Company in 1920.

The 1917 issue of the *Book of Chicagoans* had this to say about Albert W. Goodrich: "President and Chairman of the Board of Directors of the Goodrich Transit Company. Second Vice President and Director of the Chicago City Railway Company. Secretary and Director of the Chicago and Milwaukee Transportation Company. Director of the Manitou Steamship Company."

His home address in 1917 was given as 920 Lincoln Parkway. The office address was given as "Foot of Michigan Avenue."

As the year 1920 began, Albert W. Goodrich was celebrating his thirtieth year as president of the Goodrich line, although he then was only fifty-two years of age. His beloved wife Elizabeth McKay Goodrich had passed away in September of 1918 and as a result he was a widower as this eventful year began.

The LaFollette Seaman's Bill still rankled Mr. Goodrich. Even in the press release describing the launching and christening of *Nevada* on September 15, 1915, he made reference to the fact that she would have been a large, half-million-dollar passenger ship were it not for the LaFollette Act and its implications and restrictions that brought about much higher operating expenses. He never avoided an opportunity publicly to bring attention to the fact that this law was, in his opinion, harmful to Lake shipping in general and to the Goodrich line in particular. He could never see the justification of the necessity of larger crews needed to comply with the new law.

On February 11, 1920, Albert W. Goodrich was married to Anna M. Ambrose. They continued to make their home at 920 Lincoln Parkway in Chicago.

After weighing all the factors involved, Mr. Goodrich decided that he would sell his majority interest in the Goodrich Transit Company and step down from the presidency. He also decided to retain as his personal holdings some of the dock properties and real estate held in various locations by the company.

The first step was to dissolve the Goodrich Transit Company organized in May of 1906. This was accomplished by a court order issued in July of 1920. With the issuance of this court order Mr. Goodrich was now free to sell any segment or portion of the company he so desired.

Near the end of 1920, a group of local investors known as the Maritime Securities Company of Manitowoc, Mr. Harry Thorp, and a small group of key personnel and their friends purchased most of the Goodrich Transit Company from Mr. Goodrich.

Among the properties retained as personal holdings by Mr. Goodrich were the Goodrich dock property in the outer harbor at Manitowoc, the docks, sheds, and the office at Muskegon and the facilities at Sheboygan. These properties were then leased to Goodrich Transit Company.

Negotiations went quite smoothly, and satisfactory terms to all concerned were finally agreed upon. The sale was officially consummated on December 15, 1920. On December 24, 1920, a new company by the same name was incorporated under the laws of the state of Delaware.

Officers of the new company were Harry W. Thorp, President; Elias Gunnell, Vice President; W. J. Thorp, Secretary and Treasurer.

All details of office locations, names on the steamers, ship colors, ports of call and shore-based shops remained exactly as they were under the leadership of Mr. Goodrich. Elias Gunnell, listed as the Vice President, was also president of the Manitowoc

WHITEHALL, MICHIGAN — The Goodrich dock at Whitehall, Michigan, was located at the foot of Colby Street and White Lake. This photo was taken July 15, 1914.

Courtesy: Arthur Ruggles

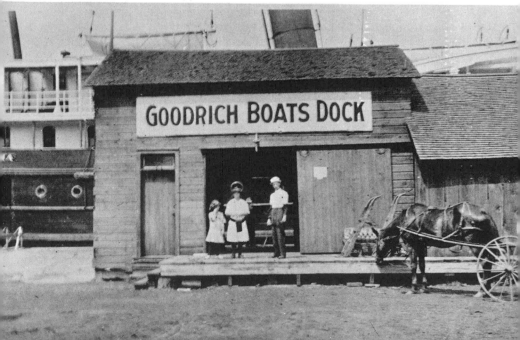

Shipbuilding & Dry Dock Company. He was one of the original group that came up from Chicago and bought out Burger & Burger, thus establishing the present Manitowoc Shipbuilding & Dry Dock Company in 1903. It was Mr. Gunnell who designed both the *Alabama* and the *Nevada*.

The ship roster at the time of this change reads as follows: *Alabama, Arizona, Carolina, Christopher Columbus, Florida, Indiana,* and the tug *Arctic*.

With only six passenger steamers in the fleet, the Goodrich roster was at the lowest level it had been since the founding of the Goodrich Transportation Company in 1868.

After World War I, passenger travel on the Lakes began to decline. The railroads began to offer attractive rates to vacation travelers, but more important, the automobile really began to come into its own at this time. It became quite fashionable to "motor" to the summer home or the vacation spot selected. "Touring" became a common word and all this contributed to a lower passenger traffic volume. Most of those connected with the Lake passenger business thought that the loss could be offset by larger freight volume and that the trend in lower passenger volume was only temporary. In view of A. W. Goodrich's keen insight in business affairs and the later developments, one cannot wonder whether or not he felt he saw the handwriting on the wall at the time of his selling his holdings.

After his resignation as president of Goodrich Transit, Mr. Goodrich continued his residence in Chicago and later became quite active in city politics. He passed away in Chicago on March 6, 1938, at the age of seventy.

HARRY W. THORP, SR. — The Goodrich General Manager is shown here at his desk in the Chicago office. Note the interesting painting of the *Virginia* as she appeared when first built.

Courtesy: Harry W. Thorp, Jr.

Chapter Thirteen

THE ROARING TWENTIES

THE NEWLY APPOINTED PRESIDENT OF GOODRICH, Harry Walter Thorp, was born in Chicago on April 26, 1865. His father was Henry T. Thorp and his mother Louise Melitzer before her marriage.

Early in his marriage, Mr. Henry Thorp decided that he could best pursue his trade of carpentry and painting in Manistee, Michigan. As a result, Harry Thorp attended the public schools of Michigan's famous Salt City.

Except for two years with the Flint & Pere Marquette Railroad, Harry Thorp spent his entire working career with the Goodrich line.

His first position was at Manistee in 1883, when he worked as a part-time clerk while attending high school. At that time Fred C. Reynolds was agent for Goodrich at Manistee. Later Reynolds became general manager for the Pere Marquette Line steamers with offices at Milwaukee. He and Harry Thorp remained lifetime friends as a result of this early relationship.

After leaving school, Harry Thorp went to work aboard the boats and in 1888 he was listed as clerk, or purser as they were later known, aboard the old reliable side-wheeler *Chicago*. Later he served as purser aboard the new *Indiana*.

About 1893 he came ashore to work in the Chicago office as personal secretary to Mr. A. W. Goodrich. This was the beginning of a long and close association between the two. On February 9, 1897, he married Grace Decker, of Chicago. Two sons, Harry W., Jr., and Richard W., were born to this marriage. The couple made their home in Chicago and later moved to 808 Sheridan Road in Evanston, Illinois.

In October, 1897, Harry Thorp was promoted to the position of general manager. When the Goodrich Transit Company was incorporated early in 1906, Thorp was named secretary and general manager of the new company. At the reorganization of 1912 he was appointed vice president and general manager. In this capacity he was second in command to A. W. Goodrich and retained this position until Mr. Goodrich stepped down in 1921 and he assumed the presidency of the new company. It is interesting to note that in 1917 Thorp was listed as a director of the Manitowoc Shipbuilding Company.

During the period from 1906 to 1920 that Mr. Goodrich owned and ran the Goodrich Transit Company no operating figures were released to either the public or to financial rating services such as *Moody's Analyses of Investments*. As a result the actual profit or loss status for the company in 1920 is not known.

S.S. NAOMI — The ship is shown here at the dock in Grand Haven, Michigan, after the fire in mid-lake. She was later rebuilt and again acquired by Goodrich who restored her original name *Wisconsin*.

Courtesy: Edward N. Middleton

Courtesy: Father Edward J. Dowling, S.J.

S.S. PILGRIM — The ship carried this name for two years prior to Goodrich's changing it back again to her original name, *Wisconsin*.

The first year of operation under the new management seems to have gone well. No new vessels were added to the fleet and the gross revenues for 1921 are shown as $1,934,508. Operating expenses for that year were shown to be $1,709,831. The total net income after federal taxes of $48,529 was given as $180,035. The total bonded debt as of December 15, 1920, was shown to be $700,000. At this point Goodrich Transit Company was in good shape financially and its earnings were excellent. The general prosperity that eventually swept the nation and caused the era to be branded the "roaring twenties" was just beginning.

On March 22, 1922, Harry Thorp completed a deal whereby the Goodrich Transit Company purchased outright the assets and properties of the Chicago, Racine & Milwaukee Steamship Company. The properties of this smaller line included two steamers, the *S.S. Illinois* and the *S.S. Pilgrim*. These two steamers ran from Milwaukee to Chicago with a stop at Racine. This service was in direct competition with the Goodrich route between the same points.

The acquisition of this company raised the bonded indebtedness of Goodrich by $325,000, bringing the total to $1,025,000 with interest at 8% payable on July and January 1 of each year.

S. S. Illinois was a heavy steel, combination freight-and-passenger steamer. She was built in the yards of the Chicago Shipbuilding Company at South Chicago, in 1899, for the Northern Michigan Transportation Company. These were her principal dimensions: hull, steel; length, 240 feet; beam, 40 feet; depth, 26 feet; gross tonnage, 2427; net tonnage, 1468; propulsion, single screw; engine, triple expansion 20-32-54 x 36; horsepower, 1250; revolutions per minute, 114; fuel, coal.

In designing the *Illinois*, special emphasis was placed on her bow and hull construction to equip her for cross-lake winter service. As a result she enjoyed over the years an excellent reputation as an icebreaker.

She was placed on the Chicago-Mackinac Island route with stops at Ludington, Manistee, Frankfort, Traverse City, and Charlevoix. For many years the sturdy *Illinois* was a familiar sight in these Lake ports.

Inspection of *Illinois* after her acquisition by Goodrich revealed her to be in excellent condition. Except for painting her in the standard Goodrich colors, no other overhaul or remodeling was found to be necessary to prepare her for Goodrich service.

S.S. Pilgrim was not a stranger to the Goodrich flag. Launched on October 11, 1881, as the *S.S. Wisconsin,* she and her sister ship *S.S. Michigan* were built by Captain A. E. Goodrich for use on the very lucrative cross-lake route from Ludington to Milwaukee in the package freight and passenger service for the Flint & Pere Marquette Railway. When Captain Goodrich lost this profitable contract to the steamers operated by the railroad in 1883, both ships were sold to the Detroit, Grand Haven & Milwaukee Railroad for use between Grand Haven and Milwaukee. This service was the forerunner of the present Grand Trunk Car Ferry Line.

All went well with the Grand Haven-Milwaukee service until the winter of 1884-1885. Even by yesteryear standards, this was a very severe winter. *S.S. Michigan,* while trying to gain entrance to Grand Haven, became locked in the icy grip of a huge ice field. The struggle to free her went on for four long, cold weeks without success. Finally, when the ice started to run, the *Michigan* suffered severe hull damage and sank with no loss of life. *Wisconsin,* also caught in the ice for over two weeks, survived but had to be sent to the shipyard for extensive repairs to her damaged hull. Afterwards she returned to her regular route in the cross-lake service until 1896.

In that year she was sold to E. G. Crosby and his associates of Muskegon. This new steamship company was known as the Crosby Line. They took over the Grand Haven-Milwaukee route, formerly operated by the Detroit, Grand Haven & Milwaukee

Railroad, and then added regular scheduled service to the port of Muskegon. In 1898 *Wisconsin* had her name changed to *S.S. Naomi* in honor of Mr. Crosby's daughter by the same name.

On the night of May 21, 1907, at 1:00 A.M., *Naomi* became the victim of a raging fire in mid-lake. When the fire was discovered she was approximately twenty-eight miles west of Grand Haven and en route to Milwaukee. All aboard seemed doomed until the bulk freighter *S. S. Curry*, seeing the smoke and flames, went to the assistance of the frantic people aboard. At first it seemed as if there was no way for the *Curry* to get close enough to do much good. The flames precluded the use of small boats and the Lake was much too cold at that time of the year for swimmers to survive. Finally, by heroic and remarkable seamanship, *Curry* was able to wedge her bow against the stern of the flaming *Naomi*, thus enabling a quick transfer of those aboard to safety. By this outstanding effort all but four of the crew and passengers lived to tell the tale of horror. The four that lost their lives were crewmen that were trapped below decks and burned to death. After the fire burned itself out, the *Naomi* was towed to Grand Haven by the steamer *Kansas*. What had been her superstructure, with its cabins and public rooms, was reduced to a mass of twisted steel railings and stanchions.

Naomi was towed to the shipyard at Manitowoc where she underwent a complete rebuilding. Her main deck was widened by about six feet. To accomplish this, a bustle was added to her hull. The plates forming the bustle were started well above her fully loaded water line. A superstructure, entirely constructed of steel, was built over her main deck. When this extensive program was completed, she had one hundred fine cabins located on two decks. The usual elegant parlors and public rooms were added, all decorated in the high style of the day. Wood paneling was used freely throughout. The total cost of her rebuilding was approximately $200,000, and when she returned to her regular cross-lake route she was considered one of the finest steamers on Lake Michigan.

In 1912 Mr. Crosby lost his life in the sinking of the ill-fated *Titanic* on her maiden voyage. Shortly thereafter, *Naomi* was renamed *E. G. Crosby* in honor of his memory. She continued in the railroad cross-lake traffic until July of 1918, when the United States Shipping Board took her over and she ended up in New York harbor. Now named *General Robert M. O'Reilly*, she served as a convalescent-hospital ship. At the war's end she was declared to be surplus to the needs of the Government and put up for sale. She was purchased by the Seymour Line and returned to Lake Michigan. Renamed *Pilgrim*, she sailed the Milwaukee, Racine and Chicago route. The Seymour Line failed and this later became the Chicago, Milwaukee & Racine Steamship Company until purchased by the Goodrich company in 1922.

Just two days after her purchase by Goodrich, *Pilgrim* was dispatched to the shipyard at Manitowoc. Again she was given an extensive overhaul and her overnight accommodations were further improved. She was then returned to the Chicago-Milwaukee route and ran as the night boat opposite the *Illinois*. In 1924 Goodrich restored her original name, *S.S. Wisconsin*.

In 1923, while under the command of Captain D. J. McGarity and en route from Chicago to Milwaukee, a storm from the northeast was encountered. The seas were so heavy that the captain decided he would pass up his regular stop at Racine and proceed directly to Milwaukee. Before morning it was found that a lot of water had made its way into the engine room, boiler room, and coal bunkers. The *Pilgrim* had assumed a heavy list to the port side.

She finally gained Milwaukee harbor. In spite of the heavy list to port, the drawbridges were negotiated without assistance and the *Pilgrim* brought to dock at her regular berth. A thorough inspection was made and it was found that water had entered the hull through the forward portion of the bustle on the starboard side. The natural trim of this steamer caused her to have a tendency to be down at the stern. This caused the water to work its way aft to the boiler and engine rooms. Extensive welding was done to the bustle plates, where they joined the hull, and it was thought that the problem was solved.

S.S. WISCONSIN

Courtesy: Marine Historical Collection, Milwaukee Public Library

The fall of 1929 was stormy on Lake Michigan. On October 27 the Grand Trunk Car Ferry *Milwaukee* sailed from Milwaukee harbor about 1:00 P.M. bound out for Grand Haven. Caught in a ferocious gale, the ship disappeared from the face of the Lake, carrying with it to a watery grave all fifty-two souls aboard. That same evening the *Wisconsin* was making her regular trip from Chicago to Milwaukee and took a terrific beating. She passed her normal stop at Racine and arrived in Milwaukee with her cargo shifted and again with a bad list to port.

On the evening of October 29, just two days after the tragic and unbelievable loss of *Milwaukee*, *Wisconsin*, with four passengers and a crew of sixty-four men aboard, departed Chicago on her regular run to Milwaukee. A northeasterly gale was beginning to make itself felt as she rounded the Chicago harbor pier heads and started north on her regular course. Captain D. H. Morrison was in command.

As the wild night progressed the winds shifted to east-northeast and increased to gale force. The huge seas began to pound the ship unmercifully on her starboard bow. Holding her head up was a difficult task and the old ship was taking a terrible beating as she fought her way in the mountainous seas.

About midnight, when she was off Kenosha, the seas seemed to become even more wild and powerful. All the while the ship had been subjected to ceaseless pounding and this extra effort on the part of Mother Nature caused her cargo to shift. In her holds were iron castings, automobiles, and a large quantity of boxed freight.

The engine-room crew became aware of the presence of large quantities of water in the aft end of the ship. This information was quickly relayed to Captain Dougal Morrison on the bridge. When the pumps failed to handle the incoming water properly it was apparent to her master that the ship was in serious trouble.

At 12:50 A.M. the first message indicating that all was not well aboard the gallant old steamer crackled out into the stormy night. This message was received by the *Illinois*, who ran opposite the *Wisconsin* on the Milwaukee-Chicago route, as she lay docked at Racine. The master of the *Wisconsin* inquired about docking conditions in Racine harbor. Upon being told by the *Illinois* that the harbor was crowded with vessels seeking refuge from the storm, Captain Morrison sent this terse reply: "In serious trouble. Must make Racine harbor."

As the water gained on the laboring pumps, Captain Morrison decided that he would heave to, and in that manner all of the steam from the boilers could be used to supply the big pumps. *Wisconsin's* head was then brought into the wind and her port anchor was let go.

Loose coal, washed from the bunkers, made its way to the screened intakes for the pumps and began to slow down the intake capacity. As the rate of flow to the pumps began to decrease, the water rose more rapidly in the engine and boiler rooms. It was now evident that the fires would soon have to be pulled to avoid an explosion in the boilers.

At 1:30 Captain Morrison sent his first request for assistance: "Position four miles east-northeast of Kenosha. Five holds flooded. Stay with us, we may need help soon."

The wireless on the doomed ship came to life again at 2:15 A.M.: "SOS. SOS. SOS. In sinking condition. For God's sake send help."

There was no letup in the force of the storm. The *Wisconsin* pitched and bucked at the end of her anchor chains. With her engines and dynamos down, the ship was plunged into total darkness. In spite of all action taken the water continued to rise in the holds. At 2:35 A.M. the wireless again crackled its terse message into the teeth of the storm: "Fires out. No steam. Rush boats for tow before it is too late. We may save her."

Then a passenger gangway on the starboard side gave way. This gave the seas direct access and the water poured into the foundering ship in torrents. This prompted another message: "Can stay afloat about thirty minutes. Is help coming?"

Shortly thereafter another: "Can see Coast Guard coming to us. They are about halfway from Kenosha."

This Coast Guard motor surfboat arrived alongside the stricken ship at about 4:00 A.M. Because of the tremendous seas the crew dared not approach too close to the side of the *Wisconsin* for fear of having their small boat dashed to pieces, so they bravely stood by.

When the first message revealing the plight of the *Wisconsin* was received ashore, feverish activity broke out in several places. The Coast Guard went into immediate action. Motor boats from the lifeboat stations at both Racine and Kenosha were immediately launched and started for the stricken vessel. A small fishing tug, *Search*, manned by the Chambers brothers of Kenosha, heard of the SOS call and immediately started for *Wisconsin's* position. They fought a valiant battle with the storm and managed to arrive alongside the *Wisconsin* at just about daybreak!

Aboard the *Illinois*, moored to the dock at Racine, preparations were immediately made to go to *Wisconsin's* assistance. Steam was raised and efforts were made to secure the services of a tug to assist in turning the *Illinois* in the narrow Root River. The high wind was going to make this a precarious and difficult undertaking. The large tug *Butterfield* and her tow had taken refuge in Racine harbor from the gale. Her master agreed to assist in turning *Illinois,* although a tug her size was hardly the craft to use for this task.

The job was started. Between the high wind and an apparent misunderstanding in signals, the stern of the *Illinois* was jammed against a bridge abutment and the dock, badly damaging her rudder. This made it impossible to take her to sea to aid her sister ship.

At 4:30 A.M. Captain Morrison gave the order to "abandon ship." The crew, aided by some of the passengers, began the perilous task of launching the port lifeboats. Due to the heavy list of the steamer to port, the starboard lifeboats were rendered useless. After two and one-half hours of dangerous and difficult effort, two boats pulled away from the sinking steamer with forty-nine persons aboard. Ten swimmers were plucked from the storm-tossed waters, making a total of fifty-nine that owed their lives to the brave men on the tug *Search* and the members of the Coast Guard that manned the little surfboats. It was now 7:00 A.M. and the waves were mountainous.

S.S. ILLINOIS—This picture conveys what a fine steel steamer the *Illinois* was.

Courtesy: Henry Barkhausen

At 7:10 A.M. *Wisconsin* began her final plunge. As the ship sank beneath the waves her entire superstructure lifted clear of the hull and scattered wreckage over a large area. The gallant old steamer was gone and she carried Chief Engineer Julius Buschman, from Manitowoc, age seventy, and three or four others with her. Captain Morrison was rescued but he died shortly thereafter from shock and exposure. A total of nine lives were lost in the sinking.

Four bodies that were recovered when the storm subsided remained unidentified and were buried in a cemetery at Kenosha as Bodies Number One, Two, Three and Four. Body Number One was later identified as Peter Reskus, a deck hand, by his brother, from photographs taken by the coroner before burial. The other three remain there, the graves identified only by their numbers.

In the years since the foundering of the *Wisconsin* there have have been two known explorations of the sunken steamer. The first was in 1932 and 1933 and was done by a hardhat diver, Frank Hefling. The second visit to the wreck took place in 1963 and 1964 by a scuba diver named Richard T. Race.

Hefling's objective in reaching the sunken ship was one of concerted effort at salvage. He succeeded in locating the *Wisconsin* and actually gained admittance to the hull by blasting one of her cargo gangway doors open. His efforts did not produce much of value and when he found he was faced with legal problems over the right of salvage, he gave up the project. Frank Hefling lost his life in southern Lake Michigan while performing a routine inspection of a pipe line in only thirty feet of water. The vessel from which he was working fouled his lines and the propeller severed the all-important air hose. This accident happened in September of 1963.

Richard T. Race from Chicago became interested in the *Wisconsin* story in 1961. He made a careful study of the newspaper accounts and Coast Guard records and talked with many people whom he thought might have information on the subject. Among these was Captain McGarity, the only surviving Goodrich master.

After a great deal of research and a very systematic search of about three square miles of Lake bottom off Kenosha, the wreck of the *Wisconsin* was finally located and buoyed. Mr. Race, a competent skin diver in his own right, then began a careful exploration of the hulk.

He found the vessel was down in about 125 feet of water. Her position was 6.49 miles east-southeast of Kenosha. The hull was sitting squarely on her keel in a very nearly upright position. She had settled down in the mud and softer sand almost to her light-load marks. The bow was pointed almost due north.

Her port anchor chain was bent around the stem and carried off in an east-northeasterly direction to where her mushroom anchor is still down deep and firmly imbedded in the bottom. The anchor chain was taut.

The steel superstructure was nearly all swept away. The tangle of supporting I-beams were all that remained. Her stack was down on the deck and lying lengthwise of the ship with quite a lot of her bright-red paint still showing.

Upon entering the hull Race found three automobiles in a remarkable state of preservation. One was a Hudson, one an Essex and the third was a Chevrolet touring car with its fabric top still intact! Race also found the remains of three persons. Two of these were in the crew's quarters area and the third in the wheelhouse area. These remains were not disturbed.

The starboard anchor was still in place on the deck. After the tremendous task of cutting through the heavy anchor chain with a hack saw, Race was able to recover this 2,500-pound navy-type anchor and bring it to the surface. It now adds maritime charm to his back yard in Chicago.

Many mementos were brought to the surface by this very capable scuba diver. Among them were the steering wheel, her main whistle, several items from the purser's office, including a ledger, some reporting forms, stateroom keys and the purser's safe. This contained $8.00 in nickels and a batch of tickets. The amazing thing is that the combination of this safe is still in working condition.

It was the author's very great privilege personally to view several hundred feet of colored movie film taken during one of Mr. Race's visits to the sunken steamer. This film is clear, sharp, and clears up beyond any doubt any previous points of controversy about the old ship.

The preservative qualities of fresh water are sharply brought home in viewing this remarkable film and examining some of the mementos Dick Race has brought up from the depths of Lake Michigan. For example, the engine-room clock hangs on his wall and is in perfect operating condition. The hands of this sturdy clock are of steel and the case is nickel plated. A thorough cleaning and the replacement of a broken spring were all that was necessary to restore the timepiece after being submerged for thirty-five years! The same is true of the steam gauges, revolution counter and other items of extreme interest.

Action of the water had worn away some of the black hull paint in the bow area, revealing a white hull beneath. There, on the white hull, for all to see clearly, is the name *General Robert M. O'Reilly*, given her when she served the United States Government during 1918!

The melodious chimed whistle that served the proud old *Wisconsin* for so many years was recovered and shows no sign of erosion whatsoever.

Because of the depth of the water where she lies, the age of the hull, and the relative low value of her cargo on today's market, *Wisconsin* will undoubtedly be permitted to rest forever where she now lies, at the bottom of the Lake she so proudly sailed for nearly a half-century.

About 1922, Goodrich gave very serious thought to the construction of a new and deluxe combination freight and passenger steamship. The proposed new ship was to be quite similar to *Alabama* in general appearance and characteristics but Goodrich hoped to build her quite a lot larger than her illustrious predecessor.

The new ship was a very personal project of Elias Gunnell, president of Manitowoc Shipbuilding and the designer of both *Alabama* and *Nevada*. Mr. Gunnell spent a lot of time during the winter of 1921-1922 riding the *Alabama* so that he could observe her problems and performance in the ice and at the ports under true winter conditions.

Plans called for the new vessel to be powered by an electric drive. Reversing her presented some engineering problems but Mr. Gunnell indicated by 1922 that he felt certain that problem could be licked.

THE NIGHT BOAT IS IN — Here the *Alabama* is discharging her overnight passengers from Chicago at the Muskegon dock.

Courtesy: Muskegon County Museum

The name *Michigan* was chosen for the new steamer but unfortunately she never progressed beyond the blueprint stage, although plans for the new ship were near the consummation stage by 1923.

With a length of approximately four hundred feet and a beam of over fifty feet, she would have truly been the queen of all Goodrich steamers had her plans only become a reality.

GRAHAM & MORTON DOCK AT ST. JOSEPH — The steamers *City of Milwaukee* (foreground) and *City of Chicago* and the tug *Andy* at the old G & M dock in 1896.

Courtesy: Dowling Collection

Chapter Fourteen

G & M STEAMERS CHANGE COLOR

BUSINESS CONTINUED TO BE RELATIVELY GOOD
throughout the years 1922 and 1923. The line showed a profit
in 1923 but reported a deficit of $59,627 at the end of 1924.

As time went on, some of those in the Goodrich management
were becoming convinced that one possible solution to the problems besetting the steamship business on Lake Michigan was to
place all of the remaining lines under a single management. By
so doing it was felt that costly duplications of service and ad-
ministrative expense could be eliminated. The economies thus
effected would make it possible to operate the Lake Michigan
steamboat business profitably.

The purchase of the Chicago, Racine & Milwaukee Steamship
Company was a step in this direction. The next merger move was
a major one for it involved Graham & Morton, the second largest
operator on Lake Michigan. From the standpoint of size and number of years in the passenger steamship business, Graham and
Morton ranked second only to Goodrich Transit Company. This
merger was the largest ever attempted on the Great Lakes.

Founded in 1875 by John Graham, with the financial back-
ing of J. Stanley Morton of Chicago and Benton Harbor, the G & M
Transportation Company served the ports on the southern half of
Lake Michigan's eastern shore for forty-nine years.

When John Graham established the new steamboat operation in 1875, he secured docks and sheds located on the south

253

Courtesy: Edward N. Middleton

S.S. CITY OF GRAND RAPIDS — The former flagship of the Graham & Morton Line is shown here leaving Chicago. She is painted in the standard Goodrich colors.

bank of the Chicago River. This property extended westerly from the Rush Street bridge to Dearborn Street. The fruit and produce market extended westerly on South Water Street from Rush to Clark Streets. The location of the G & M docks meant that the South Water market was just a very short distance from their sheds. This reduced time and handling from the G & M boats to the market to an absolute minimum. As the years went on, the G & M Line became the largest fruit carrier on the Lakes. At harvest time they often had to make extra trips across the southern tip of the Lake to accommodate the hundreds of tons of baskets and crates of fresh Michigan fruit piled on their docks at Benton Harbor and Saugatuck.

Courtesy: Marine Historical Collection, Milwaukee Public Library

S.S. CITY OF GRAND RAPIDS — This photo shows the havoc that was wrought when she accidentally nudged a Milwaukee River bridge.

Shortly after the end of World War I the city of Chicago drew plans for the improvement of the south bank of the Chicago River. Wacker Drive, a new street named after one of the early city planners, was to follow the river from Congress Street to Michigan Avenue. The familiar old landmark, the Rush Street bridge, was doomed and its place to be taken by the new Michigan Avenue link bridge.

Mayor William Hale Thompson was, in 1924, pushing hard to complete this huge project of civic improvement. The South Water market was to be moved to a new location on Randolph Street running west from Halsted for several blocks. Wacker Drive, an impressive double-decked thoroughfare, would replace the ramshackle sheds and docks that had served the Lake lines for so many years. The property, owned for so many years by Graham & Morton, had to be sold to the city of Chicago.

To add to their woes, the G & M management was finding it increasingly difficult to operate the line at a profit. This and the other problems caused the directors of G & M quickly to agree to a merger with Goodrich Transit Company. Aside from the fact that Goodrich was in a good position financially at this time, the company also possessed good dockage to the east of Michigan Avenue, and this location was entirely free of bridges. In addition, Goodrich had leased space on the mile-long Municipal Pier at the foot of Grand Avenue and the Lake.

Upon completion of the merger, Goodrich was the surviving corporation and the name Graham & Morton was entirely dropped. Ship colors, house flag, corporate offices and all letterheads, trademarks, etc., were to remain Goodrich and entirely unchanged. Mr. Thorp was elected president of the combined companies. The officers and directors were as follows: William A. Smith, Chairman; Harry W. Thorp, President; Elias Gunnell, Executive Vice

S.S. CITY OF HOLLAND — She and her twin *City of Saugatuck* were two of the five steamers that were transferred to the Goodrich fleet when the two lines were merged in 1924.

Courtesy: Great Lakes Historical Society

Courtesy: Great Lakes Historical Society

S.S. SAUGATUCK

President; L. E. Geer, Vice President; J. Stanley Morton, Vice President; W. J. Thorp, Secretary and Treasurer; E. E. Taylor, General Manager.

The directors elected were: W. A. Smith and L. E. Geer of Grand Rapids; H. W. Thorp and W. J. Thorp of Chicago; Elias Gunnell of Manitowoc; J. Stanley Morton of Benton Harbor, and Nathaniel Robbins of Grand Haven.

So passed from the face of Lake Michigan one of its truly great steamship lines. When considering the thousands upon thousands of passengers carried in the nearly half-century of its operation, even the unfortunate loss of the *Chicora* with all on board did not prevent the Graham & Morton Line from compiling a really remarkable safety record. No one has ever attempted to calculate the millions of tons of fresh Michigan fruit carried to market by G & M steamers, but it must be a staggering sum. The cheap transportation afforded by the water route certainly made it possible for a great industry to grow and thrive in southern Michigan's fruit belt. The travel by boat by hundreds of thousands of Chicagoans to the summer resorts of the western shore of the beautiful state of Michigan stamped that state as a delightful summer resort area, a distinction that it very profitably enjoys today. Tourism and resorting is today Michigan's second largest source of income, exceeded only by the great giant, the automobile business.

In the merger five ships of "The Steel Fleet of White Flyers" hauled down the G & M house flags forever. They were replaced with the familiar Goodrich white pennant, and the following five well-known Lake Michigan steamers next appeared in the traditional Goodrich standard colors: *City of Benton Harbor, City of Grand Rapids, City of St. Joseph, City of Holland* and *City of Saugatuck*.

All of these, except the *City of Grand Rapids*, were side-wheelers and relatively old. The *Grand Rapids* was the flagship of the G & M Line and was the last steamer they had built. Her keel was laid at the Cleveland Yards of the American Shipbuilding Company in the year 1911. Her launching took place in early spring of 1912. She was completed and began service for G & M in June of the same year.

Grand Rapids had one stack, just about amidships, and two pole masts, all very nearly vertical. While she was a large combination freight and passenger steamer, she did have a relatively light draft to enable her to enter some of the ports served by G & M. Her general dimensions were as follows: hull, steel; length, 315 feet overall; beam, 48 feet; draft, 12 feet; gross tonnage, 3061; net tonnage, 1572; propulsion, single screw; engine, 4 cylinder triple expansion, 26-42-51 x 42; horsepower, 4,500; revolutions per minute, 135; service speed, 21 mph.

From her building until the merger of 1925, G & M kept the *Grand Rapids* on their various routes from Chicago to southern Michigan ports. For years she provided a fine overnight service from Chicago to Holland at which point connections by rail for Grand Rapids were made.

The big ship had elaborate accommodations for her overnight passengers. Her public rooms were quite elegant, in keeping with the decor of the day. During the years she sailed for G & M she made many friends among the Michigan travelers and was a very popular boat. When acquired by Goodrich, there was very little that needed to be done to bring her up to Goodrich standards. After repainting and the usual pre-season refurbishing, she was placed on the Chicago-Grand Haven-Muskegon route where she ran opposite *Alabama* in the cross-lake overnight service. This action placed two of the finest steamers on Lake Michigan on this popular and well-traveled route during the summer season.

During her entire career, *Grand Rapids* was a very lucky ship and she was never involved in a serious accident or mishap. After Goodrich ceased operations, *Grand Rapids* was owned by several different groups, the last being the Cleveland & Buffalo Steamship Company in 1946. The Coast Guard inspection of 1951 specified that certain major repairs were deemed necessary before she could be certified and approved for future service. As a result she was laid up at Benton Harbor, Michigan. On May 24, 1951, she was sold to the scrap firm of Hyman Michales Corporation of Chicago. In September, 1952, all equipment and furniture were sold at Benton Harbor at a public auction. Soon afterwards the Chicago firm sold the steamer to the Canadian Salvage Company of Hamilton, Ontario.

On Monday, October 27, 1952, the sea-going tug *Helena* and the local tug *Clara B* moved the *Grand Rapids* through the Blossomland and C & O R.R. bridges en route to the pier on the south side of the Lake Michigan channel at Silver Beach. This was done amid the tooting of factory whistles, among which was the former whistle of the *Grand Rapids* herself, now used by the Industrial Rubber Goods Company. The move from the Consumers Company dock to a berth on the south side of the channel was the first step in preparation for the start of a thousand-mile tow by the *Helena* to Hamilton, Ontario, where the former Lake queen was destined to be cut up for scrap.

As though the proud old gal was reluctant to leave the place that had been her home port for over forty years, she put on quite a show before the long journey finally got underway.

After the two tugs had nosed her alongside the pier, lines were made fast fore and aft. The tug *Clara B* had started back to her berth when she was frantically recalled by the *Helena*. It seems that the bow line became unfastened inside the ship and her bow began to swing across the channel. To avoid damage at the stern it was necessary to let go on the stern and this permitted the big ship to swing completely across the channel and block the inlet from Lake Michigan. In spite of a stiff inshore wind, the two tugs finally managed to get the former queen back in position and properly moored.

The weather conspired further to keep the *Grand Rapids* "home." West-northwesterly winds thirty-two to thirty-eight miles per hour made it impractical to start for another three days. On Saturday morning, while nosing up close to the steamer, the tug accidently parted the stern mooring line and again the old gal swung out into the channel. This time *Helena* was able to return her to position with only a few splintered pilings being the result of this escapade.

At 8:15 A.M. on Sunday, November 3, 1952, the tug and her tow put in at Ludington to await better weather. It was just twenty hours from the pier heads at St. Joseph to the pier head at Ludington so the tow was making an average of six miles per hour. After that the long trip was without further incident and the proud old G & M flagship finally fell victim to the cutting torch.

The newest of the four side-wheel steamers that went over

to Goodrich in the merger was the *City of Benton Harbor*. An outstandingly beautiful and very well-appointed steamer of her day, she had been built by G & M at Toledo, Ohio, and launched in March of 1904. Delivery to G & M took place in June and the new ship was placed on the Chicago-Benton Harbor route where she served on the "dustless route to happy land" for the twenty years she sailed under the G & M house banner.

This steel-hulled side-wheeler was 260 feet in length and was one of the finest examples of her type ever built. Equipped with feathering paddles, she was a quiet, fast, comfortable and very easy ship to handle, even in a brisk sea.

Built as a combination freight and passenger steamer, she did a huge business during the harvest of the fruit crop. By loading in the late evening she could leave Benton Harbor as late as midnight and still deliver her cargo at Chicago the next morning in time for the opening of the South Water market.

After the merger the *Benton Harbor* continued on the same route for Goodrich and so remained until the very end. When the ships were sold at auction, *Benton Harbor*, along with three of her former running mates, were purchased by Captain John Roen of Sturgeon Bay.

S.S. CITY OF ST. JOSEPH — This photo shows her in the Graham & Morton colors and docked at Benton Harbor, Michigan.

Courtesy: Great Lakes Historical Society

S.S. CITY OF BENTON HARBOR — Here she is docked at Mackinac Island on her maiden voyage from the builder to Benton Harbor, Michigan.

Upon arrival at Sturgeon Bay, Captain Roen decided that the *Benton Harbor* was in too fine a condition to be scrapped. She was converted into a "show boat" by her new owner. Painted and refurnished in a manner befitting her new role as a glamour ship, she was indeed a splendid sight when completed. Unfortunately the venture failed to be profitable and she was laid up at the Roen Yard. In 1938 the fine old steamer was gutted by fire and in 1940 she was completely scrapped, thus ending the life of another glamour lady of Lake Michigan.

The third of the five G & M steamers actually built by Graham & Morton was the side-wheeler *City of St. Joseph*. Built at Bay City, Michigan, this steel-hulled steamer was christened *City of Chicago* when she was launched in 1890. Originally she was 226 feet in length and had a beam of thirty-four feet. Equipped with side-by-side smoke stacks she was a very graceful and handsome steamer of the era.

In 1905 she was sent to the shipyard for a complete rebuilding. She was lengthened to 254 feet and no expense was spared to make her a truly luxurious steamer. Her staterooms were large and comfortable and every effort was made to assure her overnight passengers a comfortable night's rest. Her grand saloon was really magnificent to see with its rare wood paneling, brass fittings and fixtures, and capped by a skylight with imported stained-glass windows throughout. Extra thick red velvet carpet, laid wall to wall, set off to the fullest advantage the heavy black walnut and mahogany furniture. Many early movies that required a shipboard background were filmed aboard the lavish *Chicago.*

Among her many attractive staterooms and parlors was a special deluxe suite known as the "honeymoon suite." This truly elegant suite was famous and many a wedding and honeymoon trip was planned around the groom's ability to book space aboard the *Chicago* and latch on to the "honeymoon suite" for the crossing. The author's parents made their honeymoon trip on this elegant old side-wheeler.

For the most part the *Chicago* led a very uneventful existence. Except for a few minor groundings on the sand spits that so frequently formed around the entrance to St. Joseph harbor, the steamer had a very accident-free career. The major disaster came on September 1, 1914. When only a short distance off Chicago harbor fire was discovered in her hold. Rather than try to abandon ship in the open Lake, O. C. Bjork, her master, decided to run for the pier at Chicago where he could get assistance and put his passengers off on land. To avoid any delay in this action he actually ran the steamer into the breakwater adjacent to the Chicago Harbor Lifesaving Station. The crew of the station saw her coming and had ladders ready to take the passengers off the ship in a hurry.

When everybody was safely off the ship the Lifesaving crew devoted their entire attention to fighting the fire which was finally extinguished, but with very severe damage to the steamer. Most of her upper works and cabins were completely destroyed. Her hull, however, was found to be sound and she was towed to the shipyard at South Chicago where she was completely rebuilt.

The twin smoke stacks were replaced by a single stack. Her boat deck was redesigned and additional lifeboat capacity was added. Her original luxurious interior was fully restored. When all work was completed she was renamed *City of St. Joseph* and returned to her old route. She remained there until the cessation of all operations in 1934. Following her purchase by Captain Roen, she was again the victim of a fire while moored in Benton Harbor. She was finally towed to Sturgeon Bay and converted into a pulpwood barge in 1938. On September 21, 1942, while being towed by the tug *John Roen,* she and another barge, *Transport,* had to be cut adrift in a big blow. Both barges were wrecked on the shores of Lake Superior with one life being lost on the barge *St. Joseph.* That person was the wife of the barge captain; her body came ashore amidst many of the logs that had been carried by the former gallant old side-wheeler.

The remaining two side-wheelers were not originally built by Graham & Morton. These "twins" were built to identical specifications at Wyandotte, Michigan, in 1893. When launched, they

Courtesy: Edward N. Middleton

S.S. ROOSEVELT — This photo shows her early in her career, departing from Saugatuck, Michigan, in tow of the tug *B. F. Bruce.*

were named *City of Mackinac* and *City of Alpena.* They were built for the Detroit & Cleveland Steam Navigation Company as combination passenger and package freighters. They were 266 feet in length and measured sixty-nine feet wide over the guards. Their paddle wheels were of the feathering type and they were both excellent seaboats. An innovation on these boats was the installation of bow rudders to enable them to maneuver in and out of tight harbors such as they encountered at Alpena and Cheboygan.

D & C kept the "twins" on the Toledo-St. Ignace route until business on that route fell off in 1919. The steamers were then laid up at Detroit. They remained there until they were purchased by Graham & Morton in 1921. After their purchase they were completely overhauled and placed opposite each other on the Chicago-Saugatuck route. The *City of Mackinac* was renamed *City of Holland* and the *City of Alpena* was renamed *City of Saugatuck.*

After their purchase by Captain Roen they were both towed to Sturgeon Bay. In 1936 the *Saugatuck* was cut down and con-

Courtesy: Marine Historical Collection, Milwaukee Public Library

S.S. ROOSEVELT — This is how she appeared when running the Milwaukee-Chicago route for Goodrich.

verted into a tow barge. Renamed the *Leona* she spent the next ten years in the pulpwood service. In 1946 *Leona* was sold to Canadian owners and renamed *Normil*. Again she was used in the pulpwood trade until 1956, when she was finally scrapped.

The *Holland* remained at Sturgeon Bay as no good use for her seemed to present itself. In 1940 she was scrapped and another Great Lakes steamer died under the cutting torch.

In 1924 gross revenue for Goodrich Transit was $1,886,759. Operating expenses for this year amounted to $1,743,088 with a gross profit of $143,671. After deduction of all expense and dividends the deficit amounted, as previously stated, to $59,627.

Gross revenue in 1925, the first full year of operation after the merger with Graham & Morton, rose to $2,744,332. Operating expense in this year was $2,487,052 leaving a gross profit of $257,280. After addition of other income amounting to $35,616 and the deduction of all expense and dividends the profit amounted to $5,623. The significant thing about 1925 is that this was the last profitable year in Goodrich history!

The very next year, 1926, ended up with a deficit of $119,683. Gross revenues dropped to $2,581,661 while the operating expense remained nearly the same as the previous year with a total of $2,434,661.

There are those who strongly believe that Goodrich Transit would have remained much stronger and perhaps fared much better if the merger with Graham & Morton had never taken place. The above figures do lend some credence to this reasoning.

The year 1927 brought the second highest gross revenue figure in Goodrich history. In this year the total was $2,618,458 but the operating expense soared to $2,642,132 so the gross "profit" was a red figure of $23,674. The final deficit amounted to $279,856 and that proved to be the biggest loss in Goodrich history. The sad part about the 1927 figures is that business across the nation was booming and the nation's general economy was at an all-time high in our history. This was also the year a new passenger excursion steamer joined the fleet.

In the year 1906, the Craig Shipyard at Toledo, Ohio, launched a beautiful steel-hulled, twin-stacked excursion steamer. Constructed for the Indiana Transportation Company she was christened *S.S. Theodore Roosevelt*. This great and fast steamer proudly bore the same name throughout her entire career on the Great Lakes. At the same time she was built, the Indiana Transportation Company also owned a slightly smaller but quite similar ship, the *S.S. United States*.

S.S. Theodore Roosevelt, long hailed as the speed queen of the Lakes, had the following dimensions: hull, steel; length, 289 feet; beam, 40 feet; draft, 16 feet; height, 52 feet from keel to bridge; gross tonnage, 1955; net tonnage, 1330; propulsion, single screw; engines, 4 cylinder, triple expansion, 30-48-56 x 40; horsepower, 4,500; revolutions per minute, 140; speed, 24 mph (28 mph on trials); passenger capacity, 3,500.

Equipped with seven Scotch boilers, they delivered a huge supply of steam at a pressure of two hundred pounds per square inch. With a relatively high shaft speed of 140 revolutions per minute, the big steamer had a top speed of twenty-four miles per hour. With a double bottom and seven watertight compartments, *Roosevelt* was promptly labeled "unsinkable" by her proud new owners.

When completed, *Roosevelt* had two silver stacks and two tall pole masts, all slightly raked. Between her two stacks was a large sign brightly displaying her name in electric lights. This was a very striking feature as she plied her way on Lake Michigan at night. Her hull and topsides were all painted white and she was very sleek and striking in general appearance.

Her first duty for Indiana Transportation Company was on the Chicago-Michigan City route. Due to her speed, she was able to do two round trips a day. She remained on this very profitable route until the outbreak of World War I in 1917.

During the war she was taken over by the Government and

Courtesy: Father Edward J. Dowling, S.J.

S.S. ROOSEVELT — Photo of the stripped-down hull at Jones Island, Milwaukee.

served as an officers training vessel. When the war was over she was declared surplus and was purchased by Lake Erie interests. For the next few years she was engaged in the excursion trade on Lake Erie.

Late in 1926, *Roosevelt* was purchased by a group incorporated as the Chicago and Manitowoc Transportation Company. Some of the officers of Goodrich were involved in this company and a lot of the operating capital came from local Manitowoc persons. After her purchase by this group, *Roosevelt* was chartered to the Goodrich Transit Company.

During the winter of 1926-1927 *Roosevelt* underwent extensive remodeling at the Manitowoc Shipbuilding Yards. On March 26, 1927, it was announced in the Milwaukee press that the renovation of the big excursion steamer had cost Goodrich $300,000 and that on that date the program was rapidly nearing completion.

On June 23 the ship began service on the Chicago-South Haven route. Under her announced schedule she departed from

Navy Pier at 10:00 A.M. with arrival in South Haven at 2:00 P.M. Return from South Haven was at 4:30 P.M. with arrival in Chicago at 9:45 P.M. Fare was $1.50 for the round trip. On Saturday the "Big White Flyer," as she was referred to in Goodrich advertising copy, departed from Chicago at 2:00 P.M. and stopped at Benton Harbor en route. Return to Chicago was at midnight on Saturday.

On June 22, 1929, the *Roosevelt* began service on the Milwaukee-Chicago excursion route where she ran opposite the *Christopher Columbus*. Under her announced schedule, she departed from the Goodrich dock at Michigan Street bridge at 9:00 A.M., arriving at Chicago at 2:00 P.M. Returning, she departed Chicago at 5:00 P.M., arriving at Milwaukee at 10:00 P.M. This schedule was one hour faster in each direction than that of the somewhat slower *Columbus*. At this time the round-trip fare was $1.50 weekdays and $2.00 on Sundays and holidays. During her entire career with Goodrich *Roosevelt* continued as an all-white steamer but she did have her stacks painted in the standard Goodrich bright red.

Roosevelt remained with Goodrich until the very end. When the line went bankrupt she was not subject to the various court orders affecting the line, as she remained the property of the Chicago & Manitowoc Steamship Company. Later she was sold to other interests and continued to operate as an excursion boat on Lake Michigan until 1942. During that year she was used on the Bob-Lo Line out of Detroit. The very next season she again returned to Lake Erie and ran from Cleveland to Cedar Point for several summers.

In the late 1940's *Roosevelt* was taken out of service and returned to Benton Harbor, Michigan, where she was laid up. On May 21, 1950, she was delivered to the Cream City Wrecking Company at Milwaukee in tow of a tug. Immediately after her arrival, the big excursion steamer fell victim to the cutting torch and she was broken up for scrap. Thus ended the career of one of the fastest and most popular excursion steamships ever built. Not only was she the fastest of her class ever to sail the Lakes, but she also carried untold thousands of pleasure-seeking passengers with never a serious accident to mar her long and glorious record.

For some time prior to the beginning of 1928, Mr. Thorp had been the victim of failing health. In the early spring of that year he decided, on advice of his physician, to retire from the presidency of the Goodrich Transit Company, the position he had so capably filled since December 24, 1920.

At the time of his retirement on April 1, 1928, he elected to retain his stock in the company and his seat as a director. He continued in this capacity until all activities of the Goodrich Transit Company were stilled by the bankruptcy action in 1934.

Harry W. Thorp was taken by death on January 30, 1941, following a paralytic stroke. He was seventy-six years old. He had served faithfully and capably in one capacity or another with the Goodrich organization for a half-century. He left behind a host of friends and admirers both in and out of the steamboat company that had been his very life all these years.

S.S. PETOSKEY — This was the largest of the four steamers that joined Goodrich in the merger with the West Ports Steamship Company, and the only one equipped to carry passengers.

Chapter Fifteen

THE DEMISE

ON RECEIPT OF THE RESIGNATION OF HARRY W. Thorp, effective April 1, 1928, a special meeting of the board of directors was convened on April 16, 1928. At this meeting Mr. Thorp's resignation was accepted with regrets and the following officers and directors were elected: William A. Smith, Chairman; Captain E. E. Taylor, President & General Manager; Major F. K. Heath, Assistant to the President; Charles C. West, Executive Vice President; L. E. Geer, Vice President; J. Stanley Morton, Vice President; W. J. Thorp, Secretary and Treasurer.

The duly elected directors were: W. A. Smith of Grand Rapids; H. W. Thorp, W. J. Thorp, L. E. Geer, J. W. Alder and E. E. Taylor of Chicago; J. S. Morton of Benton Harbor and Nathaniel Robbins of Grand Haven.

Mr. William Alden Smith, Chairman of the Board, was a former senator from the state of Michigan. He had been a substantial shareholder in the Graham & Morton Line, thus becoming affiliated with Goodrich Transit at the time of the merger.

Captain Edward E. Taylor, the new president and general manager, also came into the Goodrich organization at the time of the merger. Earlier in his career he had been a shipmaster for Goodrich when Mr. A. W. Goodrich was president. When the *Alabama* was first placed in service, Captain Taylor was her first master and sailed her for about two years before leaving the company.

After leaving Goodrich, Captain Taylor worked for others on Lake Michigan and finally became associated with Graham & Morton as general manager. He held this position at the time of the merger and assumed the same title and duties in the merged company.

Captain W. E. Franklin was superintendent of operations and Harry Meyering was freight traffic manager. Mr. Park Robbins was passenger traffic manager and a city ticket office was maintained at 104 South Clark Street in downtown Chicago.

The year before, the last of the Chicago River operations had been moved to Navy (Municipal) Pier so that now all the general offices and all operating departments at Chicago were centered at the huge pier. Only the *Christopher Columbus* continued to arrive and depart from the old dock location at the Michigan Avenue bridge.

As the season of 1928 began, the following twelve passenger steamers comprised the Goodrich fleet. All of these were active that year: *Alabama, Carolina, Columbus, City of Benton Harbor, City of Grand Rapids, City of Holland, City of St. Joseph, City of Saugatuck, Illinois, Indiana, Theodore Roosevelt,* and *Wisconsin.*

Goodrich offered regular scheduled sailings to ten ports on the east shore and twelve ports on the west shore. Ship assignment was as follows:

Columbus continued on the daily excursion route between Chicago and Milwaukee. Her Chicago dock was at the Michigan Avenue bridge but all other sailings were from Navy Pier.

Wisconsin and *Illinois* served on the overnight route between Chicago and Milwaukee. These steamers made a stop at Racine in both directions.

Carolina was on the Chicago, Green Bay, and Mackinac Island route. Departing Chicago on Mondays at 2:00 P.M., she stopped at Milwaukee, Sturgeon Bay, Ephraim, Sister Bay, Washington Island, Fayette, and Mackinac Island, arriving there at 7:00 A.M. on Wednesday. Departure from Mackinac was at 6:00 P.M. on Wednesday and St. Ignace was the first stop. Fayette, Washington Island, Sister Bay, Ephraim, Sturgeon Bay, Manitowoc, and Milwaukee were ports of call on the southbound trip. Arrival at Chicago was at 4:30 P.M. on Friday. The continuous round trip, including meals and berth, was $40.00.

Carolina also handled the Chicago-White Lake route on weekends. Her first trip began at 7:00 P.M. on Friday evening and her last trip departed from Montague at 8:00 P.M. Sunday night, arriving at Chicago at 6:00 A.M. on Monday morning.

Alabama and *City of Grand Rapids* ran opposite each other on the Chicago, Grand Haven, and Muskegon route giving an overnight service in both directions. Departure from Chicago was

10:30 P.M. with arrival in Grand Haven at 6:30 A.M. and in Muskegon at 7:40 A.M.

City of St. Joseph and *City of Benton Harbor* handled the cross-lake route at the southern end of Lake Michigan. There were two trips each way daily between Chicago and Benton Harbor. These reliable old side-wheelers did a huge fruit business during the harvest season.

City of Holland and *City of Saugatuck* were on the Chicago to Saugatuck and Holland route. They also provided two sailings each way daily and did a big freight business during the fruit season.

Theodore Roosevelt was assigned to the South Haven route. On week-ends Benton Harbor was also a port of call for the big, white express liner.

To encourage the summer auto tourist to use Goodrich for at least part of his trip, the timetables and other literature of the year 1928 quoted port-to-port rates on automobiles. A feature of the 1928 timetable was a photograph of a 1927 Buick being driven aboard a Goodrich steamer at Navy Pier. The published one-way rate from Chicago to Muskegon varied from $5.00 to $12.00 depending on the length of wheelbase. A flat rate of $5.00 was quoted on all automobiles from Chicago to Benton Harbor.

A tribute to the foresight of Harry Thorp was the slogan "wireless service on all steamers" that appeared frequently in all Goodrich advertising copy. In the early days of the development of wireless, it was he who strongly advocated its use on Lake steamers. Goodrich was one of the first Lake passenger carriers to have all steamers in their fleet so equipped.

Gross receipts in 1928 amounted to $2,458,185. Operating expense totaled $2,401,580 leaving a gross profit of $56,605. After deducting all expenses the deficit amounted to $171,639. While this deficit figure was over $100,000 less than that suffered in 1927, it was still a far cry from a profitable operation. To add to the seriousness of the situation, all dividend payments were suspended in 1928.

The year 1928 is reviewed in detail because from a standpoint of the number of steamers operated, ports served, and total tonnage handled, Goodrich Transit Company reached its all-time peak. The sad part of all this is that even with the operation being the largest in the history of the glorious old line, it was not possible to make money. In spite of the nation's booming economy 1927 and 1928 were years of huge deficits for Goodrich, and the handwriting was on the wall — the line seemed doomed to financial failure!

Early in 1929 a small Lake carrier known as the Benton Transportation Company found itself in financial difficulties. Its principal asset was the small package freighter *Bainbridge*. To

Courtesy: *Edward N. Middleton*

S.S. ALGOMAH II — She was the former *Bainbridge* and a familiar sight
to thousands who sailed her between Mackinac Island and the mainland
when she was an Arnold Line boat.

acquire this steamer, Goodrich agreed to purchase the Benton
Transit Company outright. This transaction was completed on
June 18, 1929.

S. S. *Bainbridge* was a small packet freighter built at East
Boothbay, Maine, in the year 1922. When originally designed, she
was intended for coastwise trade from Hawkesbury, Nova Scotia,
to Newfoundland. Actually, she was never delivered to her originally intended owners and was purchased new by the Benton Transit
Company.

Benton Transit used the new steel freighter in cross-lake
service from Benton Harbor to Chicago. In this role she did a good
business in the fruit traffic. Dimensions of *Bainbridge* were as
follows: hull, steel; length, 139 feet; beam, 30 feet; draft, 12 feet;
gross tonnage, 704; net tonnage, 413; propulsion, single screw;
engine, triple expansion, 12¼-21½-35 x 24; horsepower, 550; revolutions per minute, 118; fuel, coal.

After her purchase some work was done on her at Grand Haven. She was used on various Goodrich routes. When Goodrich ceased operations *Bainbridge* was laid up at Manitowoc where she remained idle through the 1933 season.

From 1934 to 1936 she operated on charter as a ferry between Beaver Island and Charlevoix, Michigan. In 1936 she was acquired by the Island Transportation Company and her name was changed to *Algomah II*. In 1948 she was purchased by the Arnold Transit Company and placed in their fleet of ferries between the mainland and Mackinac Island. In this service she handled thousands upon thousands of summer tourists to this famous Michigan beauty spot.

About 1960 *Algomah II* was laid up at Cheboygan, Michigan, and kept in condition as a stand-by boat for the busy Arnold Line, who was now converting to a one hundred percent diesel operation. In 1964 she was sold to Wasac Waterways, Inc., of Cleveland. After

S.S. BAINBRIDGE

Courtesy: Father Edward J. Dowling, S.J.

some remodeling she was renamed *Erie Queen*. Intended for charter service for special parties, the new venture did not meet with complete success. As this is written, she is again laid up and her fate is uncertain.

The year 1929 brought no improvement in the financial picture for Goodrich. In this year gross revenues totaled $2,612,957 but again operating expenses exceeded the gross revenues by approximately $14,000 and the net result for the year was a deficit of $239,289. As in 1928, the payment of all dividends was suspended. The tragic loss of the *Wisconsin* did nothing to help the financial picture for 1929.

The year 1930 found the depression settling like a pall of gloom all over our great country. The Lake steamers were no exception and traffic began to fall off at an alarming rate. Gross revenues for Goodrich fell approximately 30%, to $1,820,000. The number of employees dropped from 760 in 1928 to just over four hundred in 1930. This plunge in gross revenue signaled the beginning of serious troubles for the Goodrich Transit Company.

On November 13, 1930, Federal Judge James H. Wilkerson, of the Court at Chicago, granted a federal receivership on the basis of a claim of $39,000, filed on behalf of the Consumers Company of Chicago. Judge Wilkerson appointed Captain E. E. Taylor, president of the company, and George F. Getz as receivers. In their petition the Consumers Company set forth the fact that a $100,000 first mortgage was due on January 1, 1931, but because of frozen assets the Goodrich company would be unable to meet the payment due.

The company's assets were placed at $2,000,000 and their liabilities at $1,300,000. The liabilities were made up of $800,000 in mortgages and $500,000 in other debts.

At the hearing Captain Taylor blamed the situation the company found itself in on general business conditions resulting from the industrial depression that was sweeping the nation. He further indicated that he looked for an increase in business during the year 1931. He expressed the hope that this increase would be large enough to carry the company out of its financial troubles without loss to anyone. Mr. L. M. Bowden, attorney for the plaintiff, concurred in Captain Taylor's belief.

A proposed merger of Goodrich, Pere Marquette Line, Wisconsin & Michigan Transportation Company and West Ports Steamship Company was cited by Captain Taylor during the hearing. This proposed merger, first announced in the Chicago and Milwaukee papers on September 27, 1929, would, according to Captain Taylor, reduce operating overhead and give the proposed combine a better earnings picture.

While the merger of the four companies was never actually

accomplished, the merger between Goodrich and the West Ports Steamship Company took place on January 1, 1930.

In this merger four small steamers joined the Goodrich operation. *Sheboygan*, *Waukegan* and *Kenosha* were small freighters and the fourth, *Petoskey*, was a small combination freight and passenger vessel. The first three were originally converted sea-going tugs.

This new company was known as the Goodrich-West Ports Steamship Company. The Goodrich portion involved only the west-shore division of the company. The freighters involved continued to use the former West Ports Line dock at Broadway bridge in Milwaukee and the regular Goodrich docks were used at Sheboygan, Manitowoc and Chicago. The steamer *Illinois* was used to augment the service provided by the smaller vessels.

On January 5, 1930, Mr. C. L. Dunlop, general agent for Goodrich at Milwaukee, announced that the freight sheds on the old Goodrich docks on the Milwaukee River at Michigan Street were to be abandoned and razed. All the freight operations, formerly handled at Michigan Street, would be transferred to the West Ports Line docks at Broadway. The passenger ships, however, would continue to use the Goodrich docks at Michigan Street. In abandoning the freight sheds at Michigan Street, it was pointed out by Mr. Dunlop that these sheds represented Milwaukee's oldest industry in one location. When these buildings were razed, they had served the very same purpose for Goodrich for over seventy years!

Mr. Dunlop's career with Goodrich covered a span of over twenty-five years. He had started with Goodrich in 1905 as a freight solicitor and continued with the line until he was promoted to general agent some years later. With the new arrangement, Mr. Dunlop assumed the title of local passenger manager.

Business conditions across the country became steadily worse. The anticipated upturn in Lake traffic, predicted so hopefully by Captain Taylor in the hearing before Judge Wilkerson in November, 1930, failed to materialize. On Thursday, May 14, 1931, Mr. Beverly Vedder, Chicago attorney, representing the Bondholders Protective Committee, announced that foreclosure action was to be started immediately in the Federal Court at Chicago, to acquire five of the ships. The targets of this action were the *Alabama, Columbus, Illinois, Carolina* and *Arizona*.

On June 17, Circuit Court Judge John C. Kleczka, at Milwaukee, took under advisement a petition of the First Union Trust & Savings Bank of Chicago, for permission to begin proceedings in the Admiralty Courts to foreclose mortgages on *Columbus, Carolina* and *Arizona*.

Judge Kleczka had jurisdiction over all the Goodrich property in the state of Wisconsin. At the same time Federal Judge Charles E. Woodward, of Chicago, was taking under advisement a similar plea by the same bank to foreclose on the *S. S. Alabama.*

Senator William Alden Smith, of Michigan, represented the trustees Captain Taylor and Mr. Getz. During the course of the hearing, Senator Smith made a dramatic plea to the court to save the ships and thereby permit the Goodrich line to try and regain its feet. Said he: "The Goodrich company has paid its just debts for over sixty years. It is only this debacle that has come over the world like a pall, that has forced it into difficulties. The future looks bright for the company. It will cripple the company to lose these boats at this time. There ought to be a closed season against rapacious creditors."

On July 25 a glimmer of hope came in the form of the rulings by Judge Kleczka of Milwaukee and Judge Woodward of Chicago, to the effect that the steamers were not to be sold at that time. In rendering his opinion Judge Kleczka pointed out that it would be better to sell all the assets of the company together, rather than sell piecemeal. The sale of the vessels separately would preclude any opportunity the line might have of recouping their lost traffic. Judge Kleczka reached his decision prior to Federal Judge Woodward's similar decision in the hearing at Chicago against the *Alabama,* but he did cite the Chicago decision in support of his own opinion.

S.S. WAUKEGAN — This is one of the three small package **freigh**ters that were involved in the merger with the West Ports Steamship Company.

Courtesy: Dowling Collection

This reprieve, staying the immediate sale of the steamers, was indeed good news to those trying so desperately to pull the company out of the red. Unfortunately the welcome reprieve proved to be only short-lived. The death blow to the Goodrich Transit Company came on December 20, 1932! On that fateful day E. W. Sims of Chicago, attorney for the receivers, filed a voluntary petition in bankruptcy.

The petition was heard by Federal Judge George A. Carpenter at Chicago. In the petition the receivers set forth that the company was losing money constantly and as a result was insolvent and therefore could not continue operations. At the hearing Judge Carpenter indicated that prompt action in the matter would be forthcoming.

On the next day, December 21, not a wheel turned on any of the floating property of the Goodrich Transit Company. These bankruptcy proceedings did not, however, affect the operation of the Goodrich-West Ports Steamship Company. At this date they were operating the Goodrich-owned *Illinois* on a charter and the three small freighters *Waukegan*, *Sheboygan* and *Kenosha*, formerly of the West Ports Steamship Company. The service still operated from Chicago to Manitowoc with stops at Milwaukee, Racine, and Sheboygan.

At the time the petition was filed there were three Goodrich Transit boats at Manitowoc. They were *Christopher Columbus*, *Carolina* and *Bainbridge*. The *Bainbridge* was then under lease to Goodrich and not affected by the bankruptcy petition. *Alabama* and *Illinois* were at Chicago and Milwaukee. The five former Graham & Morton steamers were at Benton Harbor. On March 9, 1933, all nine of these steamers were seized by federal marshals.

A "Notice of Trustee's Sale" published by Garfield Charles, Referee in Bankruptcy, under Numbers 51,950 and 46,061 announced that a hearing would be held before him in his courtroom at 11:00 A.M. on Monday, March 20, 1933, at 100 West Monroe Street, Chicago, Illinois.

This notice of sale listed all the Goodrich properties in Holland, Grand Rapids, Saugatuck, Milwaukee, Racine, Sturgeon Bay, and several other locations, as well as the nine steamers, the tug *A. W. Luebke* and all shop equipment, inventories, and office equipment.

On April 28 Referee Charles ordered the company's property sold at a series of public auctions beginning on May 10, 1933. The first auction was held in the courtroom of Referee Charles at 10:00 A.M. on Wednesday, May 10. The room swarmed with lawyers and other interested persons. Sprinkled among the crowd were several grizzled, old Lake veterans some of whom had been masters of the very steamers to be sold. To these men this was a sad day indeed!

Courtesy: Dowling Collection

S.S. KENOSHA — This is another package freighter that joined Goodrich in the West Ports merger. It was originally converted from a seagoing tug.

During the auction the nine ships were sold to the highest bidder. The five steamers of the old Graham & Morton Line had a combined bonded debt of $550,000. B. P. Merrick, counsel for the Michigan Trust Company of Grand Rapids, bid $3,500 as trustee for the bond issue. Steamer *Illinois* was sold to attorney Francis Bloodgood, Jr., of Milwaukee for $1,500 and the bond issue amounting to $60,000. *Alabama, Carolina* and *Christopher Columbus* were sold to attorney Beverly Vedder, representing the First Union Trust & Savings Bank of Chicago as trustee for a bond issue of approximately $200,000. The price for this lot was $2,500.

Indiana and *Arizona* had previously been sold to a construction firm by the receivers for $16,200 each. With the receipt of the paltry $7,500-bid in cash at the auction, the famous Goodrich fleet was now all gone. For the first time after seventy-seven years of continuous service on the Lakes, the stately Goodrich house flag no longer flew from the gaff boom on the foremast of a proud Goodrich steamer!

In the next five days other auctions were held to dispose of Goodrich property and real estate. The final auction was held at Manitowoc on Monday, May 15, at 10:00 A.M. The equipment at

UNITED STATES OF AMERICA
NORTHERN DISTRICT OF ILLINOIS } SS
EASTERN DIVISION

In the District Court of the United States
for the Northern District of Illinois
Eastern Division.

In the matter of
GOODRICH TRANSIT COMPANY,   } In Bankruptcy.
                          Bankrupt.   No. 51,950 and 46,061

Notice of Trustee's Sale

HERBERT A. LUNDAHL   FRED E. HUMMEL
and HENRY F. TENNEY   TRUSTEE IN BANKRUPTCY
ATTORNEYS FOR TRUSTEE   100 W. Monroe Street
120 S. La Salle Street   Telephone State 2710
Chicago, Illinois   Chicago, Illinois

Courtesy: Marine Collection, Milwaukee Public Library

NOTICE OF TRUSTEE'S SALE — Reproduction of the sad news as it
appeared in official form.

Muskegon, Sheboygan, and Sturgeon Bay had all been transferred to Manitowoc for this last event. Although the public auction was well attended, the net proceeds amounted to just a little over $36,000!

Goodrich, at the time of bankruptcy, did not own any real estate in Manitowoc. The upriver shops at the foot of State Street were located on land owned by the city and leased to the company. The lower Goodrich offices, warehouses, and docks were the property of Mr. Goodrich, who had retained them at the time he sold his interest in the company. He had leased these facilities to Goodrich Transit Company. The Manitowoc property, owned by Mr. Goodrich, was sold in 1935 to Arthur C. Sullivan for $15,000.

On July 10, 1933, Mr. W. F. Grohan, general manager of Goodrich-West Ports Steamship Company, notified its local agents that the service offered by that line was to be immediately discontinued.

Agent Ray Luecke, at Manitowoc, received word that the two freighters of the line still in operation, the *Sheboygan* and *Kenosha*, would arrive in Manitowoc with freight destined for local delivery. Upon delivery of this cargo he was to close the Manitowoc office and discontinue doing business.

The other freighters of the line had been previously taken out of service. The *Illinois* was laid up at Milwaukee, the *Waukegan* at Sturgeon Bay, and the *Petoskey* at Manitowoc.

When *Sheboygan* and *Kenosha* arrived at Manitowoc they discharged their freight and were then laid up at that port along with *Petoskey*. With the discontinuation of service Manitowoc found itself without a package freight service for the first time in over sixty years.

For a short time there was talk of a resumption of service by Goodrich-West Ports but nothing came of it and the little package freighters remained idle until the assets of the company were finally disposed of.

The life of the Goodrich Transit Company was now ended. In 1934 the bondholders disposed of the steamers, but we have already covered the ultimate fate of each steamer in its individual story.

Following the demise of Lake Michigan's oldest steamship company, other lines tried to operate some of the former Goodrich steamers in their attempt to stay in business. Eventually, each fell by the wayside in the attempt and one by one they sailed away over the horizon of progress and changing times, until today the Lake passenger steamer is, with only a very few exceptions, a thing of the past. An exciting, challenging, and wonderful era is now gone forever. But fortunately, for some, the memory still strongly lingers on!

APPENDIX

GOODRICH CAPTAINS

No steamship line is better than the masters that take its ships to sea. Once a vessel leaves her dock all decisions regarding her course, speed, conduct of her crew, safety of her passengers, and the ship itself are the responsibility of her captain. He alone is the master of the little world within the confines of the ship under his command.

Goodrich, over the long years of its glorious history, was most fortunate in having for masters of its steamers some of the most competent and courageous men in the history of the Great Lakes. Had this not been the case, the line could never have achieved its long and enviable operating record.

Navigation history was written by these men. With nothing more than a good pocket watch, an oil-dampened compass, and the courage and determination to reach their destination, these men compiled an amazing record of dependability over these many years.

From the scant records still available and from the memory of just a few, the following alphabetical list of Goodrich captains has been compiled, plus the names of the steamers on which these brave men served.

Baldwin, T. G.	*Georgia, Alabama*
Bjork, Oscar C.	*City of Saugatuck*
Bronson, Charles	*Georgia*
Brookheyser, George	*Arizona, Florida, Georgia*
Butlin, Thomas G.	*Planet, Orion, City of Racine*
Carrigan, Joseph	*Indiana, Carolina*
Carus, Edward	*Muskegon, Sheboygan, Georgia*
Chamberlain, L.	*Planet*
Chatterson, C. B.	*Lady Franklin*
Clark, Alexander	*Navarino*
Clark, Hugh	*City of Ludington*
Clark, William A.	Tug *Arctic*
Cochrane, David M.	*Georgia, Arizona*
Cook, F. J.	*Iowa*
Cottrell, William	*Chicago*
Crawford, J. C.	*Arizona, Illinois*
Crosson, Michael	*Indiana, Arizona*
Delatre, Henry	*Indiana, Illinois*
Dority, Frank A.	*Menominee*
Dorsey, Edward W.	*Iowa*
Dougal, W. (lost)	*Sunbeam*
Douglas, W. E.	*Wabash Valley*
Edwards, Joseph	Tug *Arctic*
Finefield, A.	*Orion*
Flood, W. E.	*Ogontz*
Fowler, Chris C.	*Chicago, Arizona*
Franklin, W. E.	*Georgia, Alabama*

Gain, Andy H.	*Muskegon, Shebyogan*
Gallagher, Anthony	*Corona, Indiana*
Gaylord, F. D.	*Comet*
Gee, John	*City of Racine*
Gehen, John H.	*Oconto*
Gilman, John M.	*De Pere, St. Joseph*
Goodrich, A. E.	*Huron, Ogontz, Comet*
Johnson, Ace	*Georgia*
Jones, S. R.	*Chicago*
Kirkland, Chas. E.	*Menominee, Ottawa, Orion*
Larson, Louis	*City of Ludington*
MacDonald, D. A.	*Columbus, City of Holland*
Mackey, Mel D.	*Georgia, Arizona, Illinois*
McCauley, Cornelius ("Con")	*Chicago, Atlanta, Carolina*
McDonald, Thomas	*Truesdell*
McGarity, Daniel J.	*Chicago, Carolina, Alabama*
McGinn, James	*Ottawa, Truesdell*
McHenry, H. ("Archie")	*Seabird, Alpena.*
McIntire, A.	*Sheboygan*
McIntosh, Charles	*Sheboygan*
McSweeny, John	*Sheboygan*
Moody, Charles	*Christopher Columbus*
Morgan, M. F.	*City of Grand Rapids*
Morgan, Sanford N. ("Shanty")	*Huron, Comet, Ogontz*
Morris, John (lost)	*Comet, Sunbeam, Seabird*
Morrison, Dougal (lost)	*Wisconsin*
Muccunk, John F.	*Alpena*
Munger, Joseph	*Atlanta*
Napier, Nelson (lost)	*Corona, Alpena*
Nicholsen, William	*Atlanta*
Pabst, Frederick	*Huron, Comet, Planet*
Pardee, George	*Virginia*
Perrit, John	*Truesdell*
Pheatt, Harvey D.	*Menominee*
Plummer, William	*Iowa*
Pittman, A. F.	*De Pere*
Prindeville, Redmond	*Michigan*
Raleigh, John	*City of Ludington, Iowa*
Redner, Elmer E.	*Virginia, Indiana, Nevada*
Richardson, Frank	*Georgia, Indiana*
Richardson, John	*Orion*
Rossman, Charles A. W.	*Menominee*
Russel, John	*Manitowoc*
Simmons, A. J.	*City of Benton Harbor*
Smallman, H. C.	*City of Milwaukee*
Smith, James	*Indiana, Chicago*
Smith, Robert	*Christopher Columbus*
Sniffin, Berl	*Tug Arctic*
Snow, James	*Huron, Alpena*
Spafford, Friend W.	*Oconto, Truesdell*

Stannard, W. M.	*Alpena*
Stenes, Henry E.	*De Pere, Truesdell, Virginia*
Stufflebeam, Gerald	*Iowa, Indiana, Alabama*
Sweeney, Barney	*Manitowoc, Chicago*
Sweet, B. G.	*Chicago*
Taylor, Edward E.	*Atlanta, Indiana, Alabama*
Thayer, Chan R.	Tug *Arctic*
Vaughn, W. J.	*City of Racine,* Tug *Arctic*
Voight, A. E.	*Sheboygan*
Walsh, Thomas	*Alpena*
Wilkins, Ben	*Planet, Northwest, Comet*
Wilson, John A.	*Sheboygan, Arizona, Indiana*
Wittie, George S.	*Chicago*

Although the author has spent much time and care to make the above list as accurate as possible, he is fully aware of the fact that it may contain omissions and errors, due to the lack of complete information. To the relatives and friends of those omitted or listed erroneously the author offers his sincere apologies.

LIST OF STEAMERS OWNED AND OPERATED BY CAPTAIN A. E. GOODRICH

GOODRICH TRANSPORTATION COMPANY
GOODRICH TRANSIT COMPANY

HURON

Side-wheel steamboat, 348-36/95 tons burden. Built at Newport, Michigan, 1852. Bought of Captain E. B. Ward, August 10, 1856. Sold to Trowbridge and Wilcox. Cost $16,000. Sold for $10,000.

OGONTZ

Propeller steamer, 343-37/95 tons burden. Built at Ohio City, 1848. Bought of J. D. Smedly and A. T. Spencer, May 1, 1858. Dismantled 1861. Engine put in propeller *Union,* hull sold to W. Crostin for a barge. Cost $5,600. Sold for $500.

COMET

Side-wheel steamboat, 350-80/95 tons burden. Built at Newport, Michigan, 1860. Bought of E. B. Ward, May, 1860. Dismantled November, 1869. Engine put into *Corona,* hull sold to Cobb for barge for $10,000. Cost $32,000.

WABASH VALLEY

Propeller steamer, 600 tons burden. Bought of Clinton Bank of Buffalo, May, 1860. Wrecked November 23, 1860, at Muskegon, Michigan. Boiler and furniture used in steamer *Sunbeam.* Cost, $19,000. Insurance $14,831.67.

UNION

Propeller steamer, 465 tons burden. Built at Manitowoc, Wisconsin, 1861. Sold to James H. Mead and J. F. Kirkland, August 1, 1862. Cost $19,000. Sold for $28,000.

SUNBEAM

Side-wheel steamboat, 400 tons burden. Built at Manitowoc, Wisconsin, 1861-1865. Wrecked on Lake Superior, August 28, 1863. Cost $50,000. Insurance $20,-000. Sold engine for $1,000.

LADY FRANKLIN

Propeller steamer, 341-16/95 tons burden. Built at Chicago, Illinois, 1861. Bought of John T. Edwards, January, 1863. Sold to Eber Ward in trade for steamer *May Queen,* May, 1865. Cost $24,000.

SEABIRD

Side-wheel steamboat, 638-42/95 tons burden. Built 1859. Bought of E. B. Ward and others, April, 1863. At 6:00 A.M., April 9, 1868, burned off Waukegan. Cost $36,000. Total loss. No insurance.

PLANET

Side-wheel steamboat, 993-62/95 tons burden. Built at Newport, Michigan, 1855. Bought of E. B. Ward and Owen Patten, June, 1863. Dismantled, June, 1866. Engine put into *Northwest,* hull made into barge. Cost $38,000.

MAY QUEEN   Side-wheel steamboat, 694-27/95 tons burden. Built at Trenton, Michigan, 1853. Bought of Eber Ward, May 22, 1865. Wrecked at Sheboygan, Wisconsin, towed to Milwaukee, Wisconsin, and burned in river in 1865. Engine put into steamer *Manitowoc*. Hull sold to Galen Eastman for a barge. Cost $34,000. Hull sold for $600.

MICHIGAN   Side-wheel steamboat, 642-41/95 tons burden. Built at Detroit, Michigan, 1847. Bought of Joel Ellis, July 17, 1865. Dismantled 1865. Engine put into *Orion*. Hull made into barge. Cost $6,000.

ORION   Side-wheel steamboat, 449-79/100 tons burden. Built at Manitowoc, Wisconsin, 1865-1866. Wrecked at Grand Haven, October 16, 1870. Engine put into *Muskegon*. Cost $68,000. Insurance $24,000.

MICHIGAN   Barge built at Manitowoc, Wisconsin, May, 1866, from hull of steamer *Michigan*. Sold to Ballentin Lawrence & Company, June, 1866. Cost $10,800. Sold for $14,000.

PLANET   Barge built at Manitowoc, Wisconsin, May, 1867, from hull of steamer *Planet*. Sold to Peshtigo Company, September, 1867. Cost $9,800. Sold for $15,000.

NORTHWEST   Side-wheel steamboat, 1109.19 tons burden. Built at Manitowoc, Wisconsin, 1866-1867. Sold to Detroit & Cleveland Steamboat Navigation Company, July, 1868. Cost $117,000. Sold for $115,000.

G. J. TRUESDELL   Propeller steamer, 498.87 tons burden. Built at Chicago, Illinois, 1864. Bought of Martin Ryerson, March, 1867. Sold to Lyon & Company, Ludington, Michigan, April 7, 1881. Cost $50,000. Sold for $20,000.

OTTAWA   Propeller steamer, 578.14 tons burden. Built at Cleveland, Ohio, 1854. Bought of Martin Ryerson, March, 1867. Dismantled and made into barge *Ottawa*, March, 1871. Sold to Hackett & Walsh, Detroit, Michigan, for $6,000. Cost $20,000.

ALPENA   Side-wheel steamboat, 653 tons burden. Built at Marine City, 1866. Bought of Gardner, Ward & Gallagher, April, 1868. Left Grand Haven, Michigan, Friday evening, October 15, 1880, for Chicago, and encountered the great "Windstorm," from southwest direction, about 2:00 A.M. Saturday morning, fifteen to twenty miles off Kenosha, Wisconsin, and totally wrecked — so reported by vessel captains. Cost $80,-000. Insurance $20,000.

Goodrich Transportation Company organized April 18, 1868. A. E. Goodrich, President; J. M. Goodrich, Vice President; T. G. Butlin, Superintendent; W. H. Wright, Secretary and Treasurer.

MANITOWOC	Side-wheel steamboat, 569.60 tons burden. Built at Manitowoc, Wisconsin, 1867-1868. Dismantled, 1873-1874. Hull converted into a barge. Engine put into steamer *Chicago,* cabin transferred to steamer *Chicago.* Cost $91,300.
SHEBOYGAN	Side-wheel steamboat, 623.96 tons burden. Built at Manitowoc, Wisconsin, 1868-1869. Sold for scrap to the Manitowoc Iron & Metal Company, Manitowoc, Wisconsin, August 4, 1914. Thursday, September 24, 1914, towed out into Lake Michigan by tug *Arctic,* Captain B. N. Sniffin, beached about two miles north of Manitowoc harbor, and set fire to at 4:25 P.M. and burned. William Schroeder, carpenter foreman of Goodrich Transit Company had charge of starting fire under the direction of Captain David M. Cochrane, superintendent. Cost $93,300.
ST. JOSEPH	Propeller steamer, 477.93 tons burden. Built at Buffalo, New York, 1867. Bought of I. Irving Pearce, March, 1869. Sold to Charles Chamberlin and others, Detroit, Michigan, April 22, 1873. Cost $26,000. Sold for $30,000.
CORONA	Side-wheel steamer, 470.23 tons burden. Built at Manitowoc, Wisconsin, 1869-1870. Sold to John J. Warde, Chicago, Illinois, January 30, 1892. Cost $42,000. Sold for $7,500.
OTTAWA	Steam barge, 1870. Hull of propeller *Ottawa.* Sold to R. J. Hackett and others, March 1, 1871. Cost $11,300. Sold for $6,000.
WYOMING	Steam barge, 1870 (scow). Wrecked and sold 1871. Cost $8,600.
PLYMOUTH ROCK	Barge built from hull of schooner *Plymouth Rock,* 1870. Sold to R. J. Hackett and others, March 1, 1871. Cost $5,875. Sold for $7,000.
CONTEST	Barge built 1870. Sold 1872. One-third interest only.
NAVARINO	Propeller steamer, 760.64 tons burden. Built at Manitowoc, Wisconsin, 1870-1871. Burned in great Chicago Fire, October 9, 1871, at 9:00 A.M. Cost $60,104.51. Insurance $16,112.00.
SKY LARK	Propeller steamer, 90.18 tons burden. Bought of Thomas L. Parker, February 1, 1871. Dismantled on November 26, 1871. Engine put into propeller steamer *Oconto.* Cost $6,000.
MUSKEGON	Side-wheel steamer, 618.21 tons burden. Built at Manitowoc, Wisconsin, 1871. Wrecked in the Milwaukee Dry Dock Company's dock at Milwaukee when block-

ing gave way, September 22, 1896. Cost $69,460.44. Wreck sold to H. B. Burger for $250.00 at an auction.

OCONTO

Propeller steamer, 505.35 tons burden. Built at Manitowoc, Wisconsin, 1871-1872. Sold August 15, 1883, to Caldwell. Cost $42,204.50. Sold for $13,500.

MENOMINEE

Propeller steamer, 796 tons burden. Built at Manitowoc, Wisconsin, 1872. Sold hull, etc. to *S.S. Iowa*, 1896. Cost $60,599.32. Sold to *Iowa* for $45,000.

DE PERE

Propeller steamer, 736.22 tons burden. Built at Manitowoc, Wisconsin, 1873. Sold to S. B. Grummond, Detroit, Michigan, December 31, 1891. Cost $57,200. Sold for $9,000.

CHICAGO

Side-wheel steamer, 746.85 tons burden. Built at Manitowoc, Wisconsin, 1873-1874. In 1915 steamer was operated July and August only and as a freight boat only. 1915 was last year steamer was operated by Goodrich line. In 1916, steamer was dismantled by the Goodrich Transit Company. Hull and upper works sold to Manitowoc Shipbuilding Company, Manitowoc, Wisconsin, for use as a dining hall and for the housing of shipyard employees. Cost $85,000.

BARGE MANITOWOC

Barge built at Manitowoc, Wisconsin, from hull of steamer *Manitowoc*, 1879, 507 tons burden. Sold March 2, 1880, to McLane and others, Buffalo, New York. Cost $12,806. Sold for $18,000.

CITY OF LUDINGTON

Propeller steamer, 842.33 tons burden. Built at Manitowoc, Wisconsin, by G. S. Rand, 1880-1881. Rebuilt 1890. Rebuilt and lengthened 1898. Name changed to *Georgia*. Cost $60,000.

CITY OF MILWAUKEE

Iron side-wheel steamer, 1148.72 tons burden. Built at Wyandotte and Detroit, Michigan, by Detroit Dry Dock Company, 1881. Launched February 11, 1881. Sold May 1, 1883, to D.G.H. & M. Railway Company. Later steamer came into possession of the Graham & Morton Transportation Company of Benton Harbor, Michigan. Name was changed to *Holland* and operated between Chicago and Holland, Michigan. Graham & Morton Line sold steamer to the Crosby Transportation Company of Milwaukee who changed name to *Muskegon* and operated her between Milwaukee and Muskegon, Michigan. In attempting to make piers at Muskegon, Michigan, early morning of October 28, 1919, steamer struck south pier and foundered. About twenty lives lost. Cost $179,100. Sold for $180,000.

MICHIGAN

Iron propeller steamer, 1183.19 tons burden. Built at Wyandotte and Detroit, Michigan, by Detroit Dry

Dock Company, 1881. Launched August 20, 1881. Sold May 1, 1883, to D.G.H. & M. Railway Company. Cost $159,212. Sold for $160,000.

WISCONSIN

Iron propeller steamer, 1181.66 tons burden. Built at Wyandotte and Detroit, Michigan, by Detroit Dry Dock Company. Launched October 11, 1881. Sold May 1, 1883, to D.G.H. & M. Railway Company. Later owned by Crosby Transportation Company of Milwaukee, Wisconsin, and named *Naomi*. Burned on Lake Michigan en route from Milwaukee to Grand Haven, Michigan. Several lives lost. Was rebuilt at Manitowoc, Wisconsin, and named *E. G. Crosby*. In 1918 taken to the Atlantic coast and eventually taken over by the United States Government and named *General R. M. O'Reilly*. Steamer sold in 1919 by the Government to the Chicago, Racine & Milwaukee Line of Chicago and renamed *Pilgrim*. Reacquired by Goodrich and again named *Wisconsin*, she was lost off Kenosha, Wisconsin, on October 29, 1929, with loss of nine lives. Cost $152,212. Sold for $160,000.

ARCTIC

Tug built at Manitowoc, Wisconsin, by G. S. Rand. Engine and boiler by Excelsior Iron Works, Chicago, 1881. Tonnage 52.97. Lengthened. Rebuilt 1919. Beached north of Manitowoc. Cost $16,015.68. Rebuilt at a cost of $21,097.98.

CITY OF
RACINE

Propeller steamer built at Manitowoc, Wisconsin, by H. B. and G. B. Burger, 1888-1889. Launched April 18, 1889. Tonnage 1041.02. Name changed to *Arizona* in 1909 after a thorough rebuild. Last operated as a passenger steamer in 1926. Cost $125,000.

INDIANA

Propeller steamer built at Manitowoc, Wisconsin, by H. B. and G. B. Burger, 1889-1890. Launched April 5, 1890. Tonnage 1177.71. Steamer cut in two and pulled apart, rebuilt, reboilered and lengthened twenty-two feet in 1915. Steel bulkheads also installed. Work done by Manitowoc Shipbuilding Company, Manitowoc, Wisconsin. Tonnage increased to 1979 tons gross. Last operated as a passenger steamer in 1928. Used 1931-1932 as powerhouse and hotel for workmen on deepening job in West Neebish Cut, St. Mary's River. Taken to Livingstone Channel, Detroit River, for same use in 1932. Cost $135,000.

VIRGINIA

Steel twin-screw steamer built at Cleveland, Ohio, by Globe Iron Works Company, 1890-1891. Launched May 2, 1891. Tonnage 1606.66. Due to war with Germany, commandeered by United States Government April 16, 1918, and renamed *U.S.S. Blue Ridge*.

Part of the second- and third-tier staterooms removed. Side ports or gangways sealed, fitted with surface condensers, etc. Part of bow removed in order to be taken through locks and canals to Atlantic Ocean. Probable intended use, transporting troops across English Channel from England to France. Sold by the United States Navy Department to William Wrigley, Jr., of Chicago, Illinois. New upper works put on. Renamed *Avalon* and sent to Pacific coast. Operated from San Pedro, California, to Catalina Island. Scrapped about 1959-1960. Cost $301,163.89.

ATLANTA

Wooden screw steamship built at Cleveland, Ohio, by Cleveland Dry Dock Company, 1890-1891. Launched April 25, 1891. Tonnage 1129.11. Burned off Amsterdam, Wisconsin, March 18, 1906, at 12:30 P.M. Total loss. Cost $108,678.41. Insurance $82,680.

IOWA

Built at Manitowoc, Wisconsin, by H. B. and G. B. Burger, 1896. On February 4, 1915, *S.S. Iowa*, Captain G. E. Stufflebeam, arrived off Chicago 8:00 A.M. in company with *S.S. Racine* of the Chicago, Racine & Milwaukee Line. Attempted to make way through heavy ice blocking Chicago harbor. Wind southeast fresh. Ice started running and caught *S.S. Iowa*, crushing and sinking steamer. Total loss of steamer and cargo. All of crew saved by walking ashore over ice. Cost $145,000.

GEORGIA

Formerly *City of Ludington*. Rebuilt at Manitowoc, Wisconsin, by H. B. and G. B. Burger, 1898. Sold to Crosby Transportation Company of Milwaukee, Wisconsin, November 1, 1920. Last operated as a passenger steamer in 1924. Later condemned. Sunk off Summer Island, Green Bay, as breakwater for stone quarry. Cost $120,000. Sold for $75,000.

CHRISTOPHER COLUMBUS

Steel whaleback, single-screw steamer purchased by Chicago & Milwaukee Transportation Company from A. W. Goodrich in 1898, who purchased steamer from the Columbian Steamship Company. In 1899 chartered from the Chicago & Milwaukee Transportation Company. Last operated 1932. Cut up for scrap iron 1937 and scrap sent to Japan. Cost $290,000.

CAROLINA

Iron steamer *C. H. Hackley*, twin-screw, purchased from Hackley Transportation Company. Name changed to *Carolina*. Last operated 1931. Cut down to main deck 1937. Hull sold to Roen of Sturgeon Bay. Cost $80,000.

Goodrich Transit Company organized in 1906. A. W. Goodrich, President; E. L. Upton, Vice President; H. W. Thorp, Secretary; W. S. Willard, Assistant Secretary; W. J. Louderback, Treasurer.

ARIZONA   Formerly *City of Racine.*

ALABAMA   Steel screw steamer built at Manitowoc, Wisconsin, by
                     Manitowoc Shipbuilding & Dry Dock Company; cabin
                     by Manitowoc Building Supply Company. Launched on
                     Saturday, December 18, 1909. Tonnage, gross 2626,
                     net 1684. Steamer was built for Grand Haven and
                     Muskegon route and winter service. First trip to
                     Grand Haven and Muskegon Wednesday, June 29,
                     1910. Cut down to main deck at Holland, Michigan,
                     1961. Converted to work barge *Alabama of Bay City.*
                     Cost $386,272.74.

NEVADA   Steel freight, single-screw steamer built at Manitowoc
                     Wisconsin, 1915, by Manitowoc Shipbuilding Company.
                     President's room and private dining room built by
                     Manitowoc Building Supply Company. Launched
                     Wednesday, September 15, 1915, at 9:00 A.M. De-
                     parted Manitowoc yards Monday, December 6, 1915,
                     at 10:40 A.M. Tonnage, gross 2122, net 1078. On
                     February 8, 1917, the Goodrich Transit Company con-
                     tracted with the Imperial Russian Navy Department
                     through Captain I. Mishtowt, to sell *S.S. Nevada* to
                     the Imperial Russian Navy Department for $725,000,
                     steamer to be delivered at Montreal, Quebec. Steamer
                     departed Manitowoc, Wisconsin, May 10, 1917, under
                     command of Captain D. J. McGarity, for Montreal.
                     Russian Government renamed steamer *Rogday.* In-
                     volved in a collision with a United States Navy
                     Destroyer, *Rogday* was impounded in San Francisco
                     for the duration of World War I. Later returned to the
                     Great Lakes and finally lost off the Carolina coast
                     during World War II. Cost $411,000.

FLORIDA   Iron-hull side-wheel steamer, formerly *City of Mack-
                     inac.* When purchased by Goodrich Transit Company,
                     name of steamer was *State of New York.* On May 9,
                     1918, purchased from Detroit & Cleveland Navigation
                     Company, Detroit, Michigan. During first season of
                     1918 operated in the day-excursion business between
                     Chicago and Michigan City, Indiana, and for moon-
                     light excursions on Lake Michigan from Municipal
                     Pier, Chicago. Hull is now clubhouse of Columbia
                     Yacht Club, Chicago. Cost $25,000.

ILLINOIS   Steel propeller built by the Chicago Shipbuilding Com-
                     pany at South Chicago, Illinois, in 1899. Built for the
                     Northern Michigan Transportation Company, she was
                     a very sturdy combination freight and passenger
                     steamer. Gross tonnage was 2427; net, 1468. She was
                     acquired by Goodrich on March 22, 1922, the date of
                     the purchase of the Chicago, Racine & Milwaukee
                     Steamship Company by Goodrich.

CITY OF   Steel side-wheeler built by the Craig Shipbuilding
BENTON   Company at Toledo, Ohio, for Graham & Morton, in
HARBOR   1904. Being a combination freight and passenger
                     steamer, she was one of the finest of her type ever
                     built. Gross tonnage, 1286; net, 811. Acquired by
                     Goodrich in the merger with Graham & Morton.

CITY OF   Steel propeller built by the American Shipbuilding
GRAND RAPIDS   Company at their Cleveland yards in 1912. Built for
                     Graham & Morton, she remained in their service until
                     the merger with Goodrich in 1924. Gross tonnage,
                     3061; net, 1572.

CITY OF   Steel side-wheeler built by F. W. Wheeler & Company
ST. JOSEPH   at West Bay City, Michigan, for Graham & Morton.
                     She was launched in 1890, and christened *City of
                     Chicago*. Following a bad fire and rebuilding in 1914,
                     she was renamed *City of St. Joseph*. Gross tonnage,
                     1439; net, 1012. Acquired by Goodrich in the merger.

CITY OF   Steel side-wheeler built by the Detroit Dry Dock Com-
HOLLAND   pany at Wyandotte, Michigan, in 1893. Built for the
                     Detroit & Cleveland Steam Navigation Company, she
                     was christened *City of Mackinac*. In 1921 she was
                     sold to Graham & Morton and renamed *City of Hol-
                     land*. Gross tonnage, 1749; net, 1277. She was ac-
                     quired by Goodrich in the merger with Graham &
                     Morton.

CITY OF   This steel side-wheeler was a twin to *City of Holland*.
SAUGATUCK   Built from the same set of plans, she was named
                     City of Alpena upon her launching in 1893. Gross ton-
                     nage, 1735; net, 1277. She was sold to Graham &
                     Morton in 1921 when her name was changed to *City
                     of Saugatuck*. Acquired by Goodrich in the merger
                     of 1924.

THEODORE   Steel propeller built by Craig at Toledo, Ohio, in 1906
ROOSEVELT   for the Indiana Transportation Company. Gross ton-
                     nage, 1955; net, 1330. She was never actually owned
                     by the Goodrich Transit Company, but was chartered
                     from a group known as the Chicago & Manitowoc
                     Transportation Company, in 1926.

BAINBRIDGE   This steel-propeller package freighter was built at
                     East Boothbay, Maine, in 1922. Purchased new by
                     Benton Transportation Company, she had gross ton-
                     nage of 704 and a net of 413. Acquired by the Good-
                     rich company when it purchased the Benton Trans-
                     portation Company on June 18, 1929.

PETOSKEY   Wooden propeller built by Burger & Burger in Mani-
                     towoc, Wisconsin, in 1888. Originally built for the

Seymour Transportation Company, this sturdy combination freight and passenger steamer was owned, at one time or another, by almost every steamship operator on Lake Michigan. Gross tonnage, 770; net, 544. She was acquired by Goodrich in the merger with the West Ports Steamship Company on January 1, 1930.

KENOSHA

Wooden propeller built by the Universal Shipbuilding Company of Sturgeon Bay, Wisconsin, in 1919. Originally built as a large tug, she was converted to a package freighter after the end of World War I. Gross tonnage, 763; net, 519. Acquired by Goodrich in the merger with West Ports Steamship Company.

SHEBOYGAN

A twin to *Kenosha,* this wooden propeller was built by the Sturgeon Bay Dry Dock Company in 1919. Later she was converted to a small package freighter and acquired by Goodrich in the merger with West Ports Steamship Company.

WAUKEGAN

Built to the identical plans of *Kenosha* and *Sheboygan,* this wooden propeller was also converted to a package freighter at the end of World War I. She was operated by the West Ports Steamship Company, and later acquired by Goodrich in the merger of 1930.

GOODRICH TRANSIT COMPANY

Preferred Shareholders — June 27, 1925

Name	Address	Shares	Dividend
Osborn & Lange, Inc.	Insurance Exchange, Chicago	200	$ 350.00
J. T. Davis	Austin Ave., Chicago, Ill. .	20	35.00
John A. Brown	Goodrich Transit, Racine, Wisconsin	10	17.50
R. A. Handel	Goodrich Transit, Manitowoc, Wisconsin	45	78.75
Joseph Peroutka	Goodrich Transit, Manitowoc, Wisconsin	20	35.00
Irma Grasse	c/o M. A. Grasse, Goodrich Office, Chicago	17	29.75
Beatrice Grasse	Goodrich Office, Chicago ..	13	22.75
W. J. Thorp	Goodrich Office, Chicago ..	25	43.75
W. L. P. Althouse	17 Battery Place, New York City	50	87.50
James R. D. Stevenson	560 Hawthorne Place, Chicago	25	43.75
James D. Lynch	National Bank of Republic.	450	787.50
Louis Kunz	Manitowoc, Wisconsin	50	87.50
Clark W. Hawley	30 N. Michigan Ave., Chicago	10	37.50
W. E. Elliot	718 St. Clair St., Manitowoc, Wisconsin.	8	14.00
Maritime Securities Co.	Manitowoc, Wisconsin	1565	2,738.75
Harry W. Thorp, Jr.	808 Sheridan Road, Evanston, Illinois	1	1.75
Richard W. Thorp	808 Sheridan Road, Evanston, Illinois	1	1.75
Nathaniel Robbins	Grand Haven, Michigan ...	410	717.50
M. H. Dempsey	First National Bank, Manitowoc, Wisconsin.	30	52.50
William Alden Smith	Grand Rapids Savings Bank	392	686.00

Walter Killen	Manitowoc, Wisconsin	30	52.50
Hilda and Anna Nelson	Benton Harbor, Michigan .	10	17.50
Marjorie Jameson	162 Cedar St., Oberlin, Ohio	8	14.00
J. Stanley Morton	Benton Harbor, Michigan .	70	122.50
Ferry K. Heath	Houseman Bldg., Grand Rapids	343	600.25
E. E. Taylor	Goodrich Office, Chicago ...	10	17.50
Noyes L. Avery	Michigan Trust Co., Grand Rapids, Michigan	17	29.75
George C. Wittey	516 Buffalo St., Manitowoc, Wisconsin	20	35.00
O. H. Lueps	830 N. 10th St., Manitowoc, Wisconsin	40	70.00
T. W. Gray	Manitowoc, Wisconsin	10	17.50
	TOTAL	3900	$ 6,825.00

NOTE: *This list bears the official stamp of "Goodrich Transit Company, Chicago, No. 1, President and General Manager." The stamp is dated July 20, 1925.*

GOODRICH TRANSIT COMPANY

Common Shareholders — November 17, 1924

Name	Address	Shares	Par Value
Harry W. Thorp	Goodrich Office, Chicago ..	1650	$ 165,000
Grace D. Thorp	808 Sheridan Rd., Evanston, Illinois	12	1,200
W. J. Thorp	Goodrich Office, Chicago ..	487	48,700
Maritime Securities Co.	Manitowoc, Wisconsin	3345	334,500
J. T. Davis	315 E. Ohio St., Chicago ..	65	6,500
W. E. Franklin	Goodrich Office, Chicago ..	16	1,600
D. M. Cochrane	3530 Ellis Ave., Chicago ..	32	3,200
Jules Dixon	Goodrich Office, Chicago ..	32	3,200
Park Robbins	Goodrich Office, Chicago ..	32	3,200
H. P. Bloodgood	Goodrich Office, Chicago ..	16	1,600
Joseph Peroutka	Goodrich Transit, Manitowoc	32	3,200
R. A. Handel	Goodrich Transit, Manitowoc	32	3,200
Anna R. O'Connor	22 - 34th St., Milwaukee ...	16	1,600
W. E. Elliott	718 St. Clair St., Manitowoc	7	700
Charles V. Howard	104 So. Clark St., Chicago .	16	1,600
William L. Ross	108 So. LaSalle St., Chicago	16	1,600
W. L. P. Althouse	17 Battery Place, New York	162	16,200
John A. Brown	Goodrich Transit Co., Racine, Wisconsin	16	1,600
Charles B. Hopper	American Hawaiian S.S. Co., Chicago	16	1,600
M. H. Dempsey	National Bank, Manitowoc .	81	8,100
N. A. Knudson	Maritime Securities, Manitowoc	81	8,100
James R. D. Stevenson	560 Hawthorne Place, Chicago	40	4,000

James Sullivan	228 Lake Ave., Duluth, Minnesota	1	100
J. W. Alder	133 W. Washington St., Chicago	81	8,100
M. A. Grasse	Goodrich Office, Chicago . . .	16	1,600
W. M. Herbst	Goodrich Office, Chicago . . .	5	500
Harry W. Thorp, Jr.	808 Sheridan Rd., Evanston, Illinois	103	10,300
Richard W. Thorp	808 Sheridan Rd., Evanston, Illinois	27	2,700
William Alden Smith	Grand Rapids Savings Bank	1093	109,300
Ferry K. Heath	Houseman Bldg., Grand Rapids	959	95,900
Nathaniel Robbins	Grand Haven, Michigan . . .	612	61,200
Hunter Savage Robbins	Grand Haven, Michigan . . .	572	57,200
J. Stanley Morton	Benton Harbor, Michigan .	245	24,500
Noyes L. Avery	Michigan Trust Co., Grand Rapids, Michigan	49	4,900
Edward E. Taylor	Goodrich Office, Chicago . .	10	1,000
Goodrich Transit Co.	Goodrich Office, Chicago . . .	9	900
	TOTAL	10,000	$1,000,000

NOTE: *This list bears the official stamp of "Goodrich Transit Company, Chicago, No. 1, President and General Manager." The stamp is dated December 31, 1924.*

BIBLIOGRAPHY

Beeson Marine Directory, Years 1899 to 1907.

Chamberlain, Henry, Article from John Otto Collection.

Chicago Evening Post, December 10, 1909; December 12, 1909.

Chicago Historical Society, Obituary files, General newspaper files, Shipwreck records.

Chicago Times Herald, September 15, 1860; November 24, 1861.

Chicago Tribune, December 11, 1909; December 12, 1909; June 6, 1910; September 4, 1915; November 3, 1915; July 15, 1918; December 1, 1920; October 17, 1924; August 10, 1926; December 13, 1929.

Chicago Graphic News, Years 1898, 1899, 1902, 1905; December 14, 1929; June 1, 1930; April 12, 1932; December 21, 1932; May 11, 1933; June 8, 1934; January 4, 1937.

Dictionary of Wisconsin Biography, 1960.

Edward (Captain) Carus Collection, courtesy of Henry Barkhausen.

Great Lakes Maritime Institute, *Telescope*, Vol. 13, No. 10.

Historic Grand Haven and Ottawa County by Leo C. Lillie.

History of Great Lakes by Mansfield—Beers, Vols. I, II.

History of Manitowoc County by Dr. Louis Fagle.

History of Manitowoc County by Ralph G. Plumb.

History of Muskegon County, Muskegon Public Library.

History of Wisconsin by Usher, Vol. VIII.

Inland Seas, Quarterly Journal of Great Lakes Historical Society: Volume 7, Number 4, Winter; Volume 13, Number 4, Winter; photo files at Cleveland Public Library.

Inter-Ocean of Chicago, December 19, 1909.

Lake Michigan by Ralph G. Plumb.

Lake Michigan by Milo M. Quaife.

Lake Carriers Association Annual Report of 1929.

Lake Superior News and Journal, September 4, 1863.

Manitowoc News, November 8, 1916.

Manitowoc Herald News.

Marquette County Historical Society.

Michigan, The Wolverine State by Willis Frederick Dunbar.

Marvyn Scudder Manual of Obsolete or Extinct Companies, July 1, 1926.

Moody's Analyses of Investments, Years 1920 to 1933.

Milwaukee Sentinel, July 20, 1852; March 18, 1864; June 30, 1864; **March 4, 1865**; November 17, 1865; March 5, 1866; May 22, 1866; June 1, 1866; June 27, 1866; June 29, 1866; September 4, 1866; April 10, 1867; July 2, 1867; August 12, 1867; August 23, 1867; November 11, 1867; April 8, 1868; July 2, 1868; July 3, 1868; July 16, 1868;

August 24, 1868; September 7, 1868; November 16, 1868; November 10, 1868; November 24, 1868; March 8, 1869; April 12, 1869; April 15, 1869; May 3, 1869; May 4, 1869; May 12, 1869.

Muskegon Chronicle, May 7, 1964.

Muskegon Reporter, May 4, 1860.

Our Inland Seas by J. C. Mills.

Polks Marine Directory of Great Lakes, Years 1888 to 1908.

Recollections of Life and Doings in Chicago by Charles H. Hermann.

Red Stacks in the Sunset by Rev. Edward J. Dowling, S.J.

The Goodrich Anchor, May, 1928.

The Great Chicago Fire by Robert Cromie.

20th-Century History of Berrien County by Judge Orville W. Coolidge.

The Region of Three Oaks by Edward K. Warren Foundation.

United States of America, Northern District of Illinois, Notice of Trustee's Sale in Bankruptcy, Nos. 51,950 and 46,061.

Wisconsin Marine Historical Society, *Soundings,* Vol. 5, Nos. 2-3.

INDEX OF NAMES

Note: Page numbers with * refer to entries found in captions with pictures.

Adler, J. W. 271
Admirality Courts 277
A. D. Patchin 16, 19*
Advance 206
Alabama, 120, 149, 151, 168*, 174, 180*, 181, 182, 183, 184, 185, 186, 187, 188, 189, 190, 191, 192, 193, 194, 195, 196, 203, 207*, 208, 209, 210, 215, 216, 237, 250, 258, 271, 272, 277, 278, 280
Alabama of Bay City 195*, 196
Albany, N. Y. 15
Alexander McDougall 154
Algomah II 274*, 275
Algomah, Wisc. 204
Alice Stafford 172, 174
Allis Chalmers 84
Allis, Edward P. 84
Alpena, 52, 53, 59, 71, 74, 78, 79, 80, 167, 228
Amazon Knitting Mill 52
Ambrose, Anna M. 235
Americans 195
American Shipbuilding Co. 258
American Steam Vessels 129
American Steel Barge Co. 154
Ann Arbor Line 83
Ann Arbor No. 4 192
Antelope 110
Arctic, 17, 63, 75, 81, 82, 83, 86, 87*, 97, 98, 106, 112, 166, 206, 237
Arizona, 107*, 108*, 111*, 119, 120, 123, 185, 201, 237, 277, 280
Arnold Line 274*, 275
Arnold Transit Co. 275
Astor Planing Mill 71
Atlanta, 119*, 122*, 123, 124, 125, 127, 128, 142, 166, 170, 174, 200, 201
Atlantic Ocean 27, 135, 223
Atlantic Seaboard 172, 173
Augusta 35
Augusta, Maine 169
Avalon 136
A. W. Luebke 279

Bainbridge 273, 274, 275, 279
Bank, Clinton 31
Banta, Jacob W. 41
Barge No. 101 154

Barker, Jacob A. 13
Barry, Capt. Miles 172
Barry Line 76, 171*, 173, 174
Bates, John 36
Bates Shipyard 36, 37, 49
Bates, Stephen 36, 37, 118
Bay City, Mich. 261
Bayfield 178
Beaver Island 221, 275
Belmont Ave. 190, 191*, 192*
Benton Harbor, Mich., 253, 254, 257, 259, 260, 261*, 262, 267, 271, 273, 274, 279
Benton Transit Co. 273, 274
Berman, Harry 175
Best, Jacob & Sons 29
Best, Marie 29
Best, Philip 29, 30
Big Point Sauble 85, 109
Big Point Sauble Lifesaving Station, 85
Big Rapids, Mich. 199, 202, 267
Big Storm 78, 148
Bjork, Capt. O. C. 262
Blodgett & Byrne 52
Blodgett, Judge 45
Bloodgood, Francis, Jr. 280
Blossomland Bridge 259
Blue Ridge 135, 136
Bob-Lo Line 267
Bondholders Protective Committee, 277
Book of Chicagoans 235
Boston, Mass. 135, 170
Boston Navy Yard 135
Bowden, L. M. 276
Boy Scouts 179
Brand, E. L. 232
Bristol, Catherine 102
Broadway Bridge 277
Buel, Alex W. 110
Buffalo, N. Y., 13, 14, 15, 31, 59, 64, 194
Buick 273
Burger & Burger 87, 94, 118, 120, 237
Burger, George 118
Burger, Henry 118
Burnham, Daniel 142
Burnham Harbor 142
Burnham & Root 141
Buschman, Julius 248

Butlin, Capt. Thos. G., 48, 58, 59, 86, 99, 101, 105, 106, 107, 110, 111, 112, 115, 117, 118, 120, 169, 231

Butterfield   246

Caldwell, Mr.   72
California   136
Camp Owassippi, Mich.   179
Camp Randall   30
Canada   106
Canadian Salvage Co.   259
Canal Lifesaving Station   204
Carney, W. J.   214
Carolina, 170, 171*, 173*, 174, 175, 176*, 177, 178, 179, 192, 198*, 202*, 203, 204, 205*, 206, 208, 235, 237, 272, 277, 279
Carpenter, Judge Geo. A.   279
Carter Harrison Crib   121, 149
Carus, Capt. Edwin, 43, 71, 72, 88, 144
Catalina Island   136
Catalina Navigation Co.   136
Cedar Point   195, 267
Central Wharf   52, 124
Central Wisconsin   110
Challenger   78, 79
Chamberlain, A. C.   43
Chamberlin, Chas.   60
Chambers Brothers   246
Charles, Garfield   279
Charles H. Hackley, 170*, 171*, 173, 174
Charlevoix, Mich.   242, 275
Chauncey Davis   51
Cherry Street Bridge   71
Chesapeake & Ohio   64
Chesapeake & Ohio R.R. Bridge   259
Chevrolet   249
Chicago City Railway Co.   235
Chicago, Duluth & Georgian Bay Line, 194
Chicago Fire   68*, 69
Chicago Fire Boats   233
Chicago Fire Dept.   230*, 233
Chicago Graphic News   115, 138, 140
Chicago Harbor, 121, 147, 157*, 159, 215, 262
Chicago Harbor Lifesaving Station, 262
Chicago Harbor Light   177, 203
Chicago, Ill., 7, 12, 14, 15, 16, 17, 18, 21, 22, 24, 26, 27, 28, 35, 38, 39, 40, 41, 43, 45, 49, 51, 53, 54, 57, 59, 63, 64, 69, 72, 74, 77, 78, 79, 80, 83, 88, 98, 99, 105, 106, 109, 114, 115, 117, 118, 119, 120, 124, 125, 130, 138*, 149, 151, 155, 157, 159, 162, 165, 166, 169, 172, 175, 177, 179, 183,

184, 185, 186, 189, 190, 191, 194, 195, 201, 202, 203, 206, 208, 210, 216, 217, 219, 224, 225, 226*, 237, 238*, 239, 240, 241, 242, 243, 244, 245, 248, 249, 254*, 255, 256, 257, 258, 259, 260, 261, 262, 266, 267, 270, 271, 272, 274, 276, 278, 280
Chicago & Manitowoc Trans. Co., 228, 266, 267
Chicago & Milwaukee Trans. Co., 156, 235
Chicago & Muskegon Trans. Co.   172
Chicago Outer Harbor   121
Chicago, Racine & Milw. S. S. Co., 149, 241, 244, 253
Chicago River, 7, 22, 24*, 29*, 62, 66, 81*, 92*, 144*, 147, 148, 149, 157, 158, 169, 170*, 254, 255, 272
Chicago Shipbuilding Co.   242
Chicago Stock Yards   232
Chicago Stock Yards Fire   233
Chicago Tribune Dock   147
Chicora   87, 257
Christopher Columbus, 128, 130, 131, 134, 152*, 153, 154, 155, 156, 157, 158, 159, 160, 161, 162, 163, 164, 165, 166, 167*, 200, 201, 237, 267, 272, 277, 279, 280
City of Alpena   263
City of Benton Harbor, 228, 258, 260, 261, 272, 273
City of Chicago, 73*, 76, 77, 78, 80*, 81*, 92*, 112, 201, 252*
City of Grand Rapids, 192, 254*, 255*, 258, 259, 272
City of Holland, 256*, 258, 263, 272, 273
City of Ludington, 83, 84, 85, 86, 93, 112, 117, 144, 235
City of Milwaukee, 78, 95, 96*, 97, 98, 252*
City of Mackinac   224, 263
City of Racine, 99*, 106*, 107*, 118, 120, 124, 142, 149, 150, 151, 166
City of St. Joseph   258, 260*, 261, 262
City of Saugatuck, 206, 256*, 257*, 258, 272, 273
Civil War   47, 49, 58
Clancy, Chief   127
Clara B   259
Clark, Capt. Alexander   64, 66
Clark Street   254, 272
Clement, Capt. S.   17, 18
Clement Steamboat Line, 17, 18, 21, 23, 24, 26
Cleveland & Buffalo S. S. Co., 228, 258
Cleveland & Buffalo Transit Co., 195, 224

Cleveland Dry Dock Co. 123
Cleveland, Ohio, 16, 17, 18, 30, 49, 123, 127, 128, 133, 136, 195, 267, 275
Cochrane, Capt. D. M., 144, 145, 146, 148, 169
Cochrane, W. H. 224
Columbian Exposition, 64, 130, 141, 153, 154
Columbian Whaleback S. S. Co., 156, 157, 167*
Columbian Yacht Club 225
Comanche 223
Comet, 20*, 24*, 26, 27, 29, 30, 31, 32, 33*, 59, 64
Congress Street 255
Connelly Contracting Co. 116*, 122
Consumers Company 276
Consumers Company Dock 259
Cook, Capt. J. C. 25, 147, 148
Copper Harbor 38, 39
Corbett, Wm. 233
Corliss Engine 87
Cornelia 43
Corona, 31, 63, 64, 66*, 67*, 72, 73*, 117, 228
Cowan, John S. 102
Craig Shipyard 265
Cream City 22, 133, 157
Cream City Wrecking Co. 267
Crosby, E. G. 242, 243
Crosby Line 89, 98, 242
Crostin, W. 26
Cunard Line 128, 228
Curry 243
Cutler House 114
Cuyuga 128

Dearborn Street 254
Decker, Grace 240
DeKoven Street 66
Delaware 236
De Pere, 74, 75, 76, 77*, 86, 99*, 112, 117
Detroit 105
Detroit & Cleveland Steam Nav. Co., 49, 61, 223, 228, 263
Detroit Dry Dock Company 94, 223
Detroit, Grand Haven & Milw. R. R., 32, 93, 97, 98, 242
Detroit, Mich., 12, 14, 15, 16, 17, 22, 25, 27, 32, 48, 49, 50, 60, 61, 76, 87, 106, 123, 194, 223, 224, 263, 267
Detroit River 120, 123
Detroit Street Dock 145
Door County 115, 166
Dorsey, Capt. Edward 145
Dougall, Capt. Wm. 37, 39, 40

Douglas, Capt. 31
Dowling, Edward J., Father 68*, 94*
Drew & Goodrich 23, 27
Drew, George C. 18, 21, 23, 54, 167
Dry Dock Engineering Co. 87
Dunlop Reef 88
Duluth, Minn. 90, 154, 169, 194
Dustless Route To Happyland 260

Eagle Harbor 36, 38
East Boothbay, Maine 274
Eastern S. S. Co. 171
Eastland 136, 158
Eastman, Galen 48
East River 71
East Water Street 22
East Western Ave. 51
Edwards, John T. 41
E. G. Crosby 243
Eighth Street Bridge 88
E. K. Collins 106
Elevator "A" 67
Elevator "B" 67
England 128, 228
Ephraim, Wisc. 272
Episcopal Church 57
Episcopal Church of Chicago 102
Erie Canal 15
Erie Queen 276
Escanaba & Garden Bay Trans. Co., 206
Escanaba, Mich. 86, 117
Essex 249
Europe 128
Evans, Capt. 32
Evanston, Ill. 34*, 35, 72, 132, 240

Fairman, Louisa 60
Fall River Line 171, 172
Fall River, Mass. 170, 171
Favorite 206
Fayette, Wisc. 272
Federal Court 277
Federal Gov't. 59, 169, 201, 223
Ferris Wheel 142
Fire Fans Association 232
First Union Trust & Savings 277, 280
Fitzpatrick, Thomas 209
Fletcher Engine 54
Flint & Pere Marquette No. 1 85, 96
Flint & Pere Marquette No. 2 85, 96
Flint & Pere Marquette R. R., 64, 84, 85, 93, 107, 239, 242
Flint, Raymond 71
Flood, Capt. 26
Florida 223*, 224, 225, 237

Forestville, Mich.   106
Fox River   71
Frankfort, Mich.   63, 192, 242
Franklin, Capt. W. E.   272
Frazier, Chas.   39, 40
Fredericks, John   30
Fredstorf, Fred   175
Fruitport, Mich.   114

Galien River   12, 13, 14*
Garden City   61
Gardner House   99
Gardner, Ward & Gardner   52
Gartland & Sullivan S.S. Co.   194
Gaylord, Capt.   31
Gazelle   24, 106, 107
Geer, L. E.   257, 271
General Rob't M. O'Reilly   243, 249
General Passenger Agent   117
Georgia, 43, 85*, 86*, 87, 88, 89, 127,
    166, 188, 235
Georgian Bay Line, 185*, 193, 194*, 195
Germany   27, 112, 118
Getz, George E.   276, 278
Gilman, George   232
Gilson, Capt. Joseph   67, 68
Globe Iron Works   127, 133
Globe Shipbuilding Co.   128
Goodfellow, Henry   27
Goodrich, Capt. Albert E., 2*, 11, 13,
    16, 17, 18, 19*, 21, 22, 23, 25, 26, 27,
    28*, 29, 31, 32, 35, 36, 37, 40, 41, 42,
    43, 46, 47, 48, 49, 51, 54, 57, 58, 59,
    64, 66, 67, 68, 74, 80, 84, 89, 90, 94,
    96, 99, 100, 101, 102, 105, 110, 120,
    140, 167, 227, 228, 231, 242
Goodrich, Albert E. II, 215*, 230*, 233
Goodrich, Albert W., 47*, 52, 59, 63,
    86, 100, 110, 120, 131, 136, 140, 141,
    142, 148, 153, 155, 156, 158, 164, 169,
    170, 174, 181, 182, 184, 206, 214,
    215, 216, 217, 220, 221, 225, 229*,
    231, 232, 233, 234*, 235, 236, 237,
    239, 240, 271, 282
Goodrich Captains   284
Goodrich, Catherine   13
Goodrich, Cordellia   13
Goodrich, Cornellia   13
Goodrich Dock, 24*, 28*, 39*, 46*, 47*,
    56*, 66, 70*, 81*, 88, 89*, 100*, 104*,
    119, 144*, 147, 155*, 160*, 186, 199,
    212*, 236
Goodrich, Edgar
Goodrich, Elizabeth, 140, 180*, 182,
    183, 196, 216
Goodrich, Elizabeth McKay   235

Goodrich, Grace   57
Goodrich, Gertrude   57
Goodrich Hotel   13
Goodrich, Jasper   13
Goodrich, Joseph   13, 42, 59, 110
Goodrich Line, 11, 29, 31, 54, 60, 63,
    78, 94, 96, 99, 113, 117, 127, 128,
    138, 142, 145, 147, 148, 173*, 223*
Goodrich Queen   136
Goodrich, Rosamond, 59, 100, 102, 111
Goodrich, Russel   13, 14
Goodrich's Steamboat Line, 2*, 7, 23,
    26, 33, 41, 47, 48, 54, 58, 169
Goodrich Transit Co., 7, 157, 158, 169,
    170, 183, 185, 194, 222, 223, 225,
    226, 228, 235, 236, 237, 239, 240,
    241, 244, 253, 256, 264, 265, 267,
    268, 272, 273, 276, 277, 279, 282
Goodrich Transportation Co., 45, 58,
    59, 60, 71, 79, 80, 82, 90, 93, 96, 99,
    101, 102, 110, 111, 112, 115, 120,
    132, 140, 143, 157, 166, 174, 188,
    200, 210, 227, 228, 237
Goodrich-West Ports S.S. Co.,   277,
    279, 282
Goodrich Yards   57, 145
Gould, Helen   172
Gould, Jay   172
Gov't. Inspectors   206
Graham & Morton, 87, 98, 192, 210,
    215, 228, 231, 252*, 253, 254*, 256,
    257, 258, 260, 261, 262, 263, 264,
    265, 272, 279, 280
Graham, John   253
Grand Ave.   256
Grand Haven Herald   80
Grand Haven, Mich., 24, 26, 32, 49, 51,
    53*, 58, 74, 76, 78, 79, 80, 85, 93, 113,
    114, 117, 120, 121, 124, 134, 135,
    138*, 143, 150*, 166, 174, 179, 183,
    184, 185, 186, 187, 188, 190, 191,
    192, 194, 203, 207*, 208, 209, 210,
    217, 231, 240*, 242, 243, 257, 258,
    272, 273, 275
Grand Rapids & Indiana R.R.   199
Grand Rapids, Mich., 50, 187, 188, 199,
    257, 258, 271, 279, 280
Grand River   24
Grand Trunk Car Ferry Line, 97, 186,
    242, 245
Grand Trunk R.R.   173
Grannis, Cordellia   102
Great Lakes, 11, 36, 37, 43*, 49, 102,
    130, 140, 153, 158, 164, 166, 173,
    179, 201, 203, 214, 216, 265
Great Lakes Dredge & Dock Co.   151

Great Lakes Towing Co. 210
Green Bay, Wisc., 22, 31, 71, 74, 115, 117, 166, 272
Greyhound 49
Grimm, Otto 150
Grohan, W. F. 282
Grosse Point Light 149
Grummond, S. B. 76
Gunnell, Elias, 179, 216, 236, 250, 256, 257

Hackley, Chas. H. 170, 174
Hackley & Hume 174
Hackley Trans. Co. 170, 174
Halsted Street 66, 256
Hamburg, N.Y. 13
Hamilton, Ontario 259
Hanley, Ellen 199
Hartford 172, 173
Hartford & N.Y. Trans. Co. 172
Hawkesbury, Nova Scotia 274
Heath, Major F. K. 271
Hefling, Frank 248
Helena 259
Henneberry, Edwin 43
Hermann, Chas. H. 158, 215, 233
Hickey, Mike 126
Hills Point 145
Hitchcock & Gibson 59
Hodge, S. F. & Co. 154
Holland, Mich., 79, 194*, 196, 215, 258, 264, 273, 279
Home Insurance Co. 31
Honeymoon Suite 262
Horan, Chief 223, 230*, 232
Horseshoe Island 86
Hotel Manitowoc 42
Houghton, Mich. 40
Hudson 249
Hudson River 15
Hull No. 101 154, 165
Hull No. 128 154
Hume, Thos. 174
Huron, 7, 18, 21, 22, 23, 24, 25, 26, 27, 29, 46, 167, 228
Hurson Line 130, 155, 156
Hutchins, J. 18
Hyman, Michales Corp. 259

Illinois 16, 42, 100
Illinois, 240, 242, 244, 245, 246, 247, 272, 277, 279, 280, 282
Illinois Central R.R. 17
Imperial Russian Navy 221
Indiana, 100, 120, 121, 134, 142, 143
Indiana, 112*, 113*, 114*, 115*, 116*, 122, 123, 124, 166, 185, 192, 201, 239, 272, 280
Indiana Trans. Co. 265
Inter-Ocean 182
Iowa 202
Iowa, 62, 74, 87, 100, 134, 141*, 142, 143*, 144, 145, 146, 147, 148, 149, 150*, 151, 166, 174, 201, 202, 203, 215
Island-Bay S.S. Line 195
Isle Royale 194

Jackson Park 64, 141, 155
Japan 165
Japan 153
John Roen 262
Johnston & Hodges 26
Johnston, Robert 78
Johnston's Pier 41
Jones Island 48, 127, 266*
Jones, K. K. 23, 26
Journeys Inc. 194
J. S. Crouse 206

Kalamazoo Land Office 12
Kalamazoo, Mich. 12, 16, 17
Kansas 243
Kellog, L. H. 18
Kenosha 157*, 277, 279, 280*, 282
Kenosha, Wisc., 26, 41, 69, 79, 80, 90, 115, 132, 146, 166, 169, 202, 245, 246, 248
Kewaunee Jim 175
Kewaunee Station 206
Kewaunee, Wisc., 27, 30, 54, 64, 117, 177, 204
Keweenaw Peninsula 39
Kirby, Earl G. 194
Kirby, Frank E. 94
Kirkland, J. F. 37
Kirk's Soap Factory 67
Kleczka, Judge 277, 278
Knapp, Cornelia 102
Knight Templar 159, 161, 163

Lady Elgin 34*, 35, 36, 39, 58
Lady Franklin 41, 48
LaFollette Act 212, 214, 215, 235
LaFollette, Rob't M. 212
Lake Carriers Assoc. 220
Lake Erie 14, 49, 64, 266, 267
Lake Forest, Ill. 132
Lake Huron 17, 22, 61
Lake Macatawa 196
Lake Michigan, 7, 11, 12, 14*, 15, 17, 18, 22, 23, 24, 26, 27, 30, 31, 35, 36, 38*, 42, 51, 52, 58, 63, 64, 66, 69*, 70, 71, 76, 83, 84, 85, 92*, 98, 104*,

106, 107, 108, 109, 110, 117, 125, 126, 129, 131, 132, 134, 136, 145, 147, 148, 154, 155, 159, 165, 166, 167, 178, 182, 188, 195, 196, 199, 203, 204, 217, 219, 221, 224, 231, 243, 245, 248, 249, 253, 257, 258, 259, 261, 267, 273, 282

Lake St. Clair   17, 22
Lake Shore Drive   141
Lakeside Packing Co.   129
Lake Superior, 38, 39, 40, 41, 45, 46, 47, 74, 106, 154, 178, 219, 221, 262
Land Office   12, 13
Lansing   87
LaSalle Street   142
Leannington, Ontario   195
Leigh Valley R.R.   128
LeLand Hotel   99
Leona   264
Leups, Jacob   110
Limitation of Liability Act   45
Lincoln Park   132
Lincrusta-Walton   132
Little Sable River   109
Livingstone Channel   120, 123
London, England   105
Lone Pine Tree Point   75
Long Island Sound   170, 171, 173*
Louderback   169
Lowery, Frank   150
Ludington, Mich., 63, 64, 78, 84, 96, 107, 223, 242, 259
Luecke   282

Mabel Bradshaw   172
Mackinac Island, 38, 43, 85*, 87, 88, 113, 166, 175, 195, 206, 208, 224, 242, 261*, 272, 274*, 275
Madison Street   142
Madison, Wisc.   30
Magnolia   67, 68
·Maine   169
Manistee Lifesaving Station   86
Manistee, Mich., 84, 86, 89, 174, 223, 239, 242
Manistique   117
Manitou S.S. Co.   235
Manitowoc   53, 54, 61, 77
Manitowoc, Wisc., 7, 22, 23, 24, 25, 26, 27, 28*, 30, 31, 36, 41, 42, 45, 48, 49, 51, 54, 57, 59, 60, 61, 62, 63, 64, 66*, 69, 72, 73, 74, 75, 76, 77*, 78, 79, ·82, 83, 86, 87, 88, 89*, 90, 94, 99*, 101*, 104*, 106*, 107, 110, 112*, 118, 119, 120, 121, 122, 123, 125, 129, 135, 142, 143*, 145, 146, 148,

157, 163, 166, 174, 176*, 177, 181, 184, 185, 189, 196, 200, 206, 208, 216, 219, 221, 224, 231, 236, 243, 244, 248, 266, 275, 279, 280, 282
Manitowoc Guards   30
Manitowoc Herald   30, 61
Manitowoc Highlands   110
Manitowoc Metal Co.   62
Manitowoc & Mississippi R.R.   110
Manitowoc River   88, 181*, 182*, 218
Manitowoc Shipbuilding Co., 83, 120, 177, 179, 181, 183, 214*, 216, 236, 240, 266
Marine City, Mich.   21, 52
Marine Review   129, 134
Marin's Reef   61
Maritime Securities Co.   236
Marvin, Comfort   13
Maumee River   111*, 120
Maxon, Capt. F. C.   160
May Queen   41, 48, 53, 77
McCauley, Capt., 125, 126, 127, 145, 175, 177
McDougall, Capt. A., 153, 154, 156*, 167*
McGarity, Capt. D. J., 125, 127, 148, 175, 177, 182, 191, 192, 198*, 199, 200, 201, 202, 203, 204, 205*, 206, 207*, 208, 209, 210, 221, 235, 244, 248
McGrane, Mr.   27
McKay, Elizabeth   140
Mead, James H.   37
Mears   109
Mears Block   88
Menasha, Wisc.   110
Menominee, 68, 74, 99*, 112, 117, 138*, 141*
Menominee River   159
Menominee, Wisc.   61, 117
Merrick, B. P.   280
Meyering, Harry   272
Meyers   206
Michigan, 7, 12, 15, 50, 58, 100, 101, 210, 251, 257, 271
Michigan   48, 94*, 95, 97, 98, 242
Michigan Ave., 22, 29*, 57, 99, 101, 102, 117, 130, 147, 157, 169, 186, 226*, 231, 235, 255, 256, 272
Michigan Central Depot   68
Michigan Central R.R., 15, 16, 17, 18*, 22, 106, 110
Michigan City, Ind.   11, 224, 265
Michigan Pine   68
Michigan Shore   108, 109
Michigan Southern R.R.   17

Michigan Street (Milw.), 22, 56*, 100*, 267, 277
Michigan Transit Co.   190
Midwest   16, 219
Mill Dock   51
Milwaukee   245
Milwaukee, Wisc., 7, 12, 15, 16, 17, 22, 23, 24, 26, 27, 28, 29, 30, 32, 35, 41, 48, 52, 53, 57, 60, 61, 64, 67*, 69, 73, 76, 81, 82, 84, 88, 93, 95, 96, 97, 100*, 106, 115, 117, 119, 120, 125, 127, 130, 131, 132, 134, 144, 145, 146, 147, 149, 157, 158, 159, 160*, 161*, 162, 165, 166, 175, 177, 184, 185, 186, 192, 202, 204, 208, 216, 217, 222, 223, 239, 241, 243, 244, 245, 267, 272, 276, 279, 280
Milwaukee Assoc. of Commerce   177
Milwaukee Bay   133
Milwaukee Clipper   47*, 52
Milwaukee Dry Dock Co., 73, 145, 147
M.F.D. No. 15   127
Milwaukee Harbor, 81, 159, 175, 201, 244
Milwaukee News   27
Milwaukee River, 22, 56*, 70*, 73, 145, 148, 159, 160, 162, 164, 255*, 277
Milwaukee Sentinel   41, 81
Minnesota   110
Minneapolis, Minn.   122
Missouri   190, 192*
Mistowt, Capt.   221
Monarch   86
Monroe, Mich.   123
Montreal, Quebec, 135, 173, 221, 222
Moody's Analysis of Investments   240
Moody, Capt. Chas., 160, 161, 162, 163*, 164
Morgan, Capt. Sanford (Shanty), 24, 27, 32
Morning Examiner   158
Morning Star   49
Morris, Capt. John   41
Morrison, Capt. D. H., 245, 246, 247, 248
Morton, J. Stanley   253, 257, 271
Municipal Pier   224, 225, 272
Muskegon, Mich., 24, 25, 26, 32, 41, 46*, 50, 51, 52, 58, 74, 76, 79, 97, 98, 113, 114, 117, 119*, 120, 121, 124, 126*, 134, 138*, 143, 166, 170, 172, 173, 179, 183, 184, 185, 186, 187, 188, 189, 190, 191, 192, 194, 199, 201, 203, 208, 209, 216, 217, 231, 236, 242, 243, 250*, 258, 272, 273, 282
Muskegon   49, 72, 73, 98, 112

Muskegon Coast Guard   191
Muskegon Harbor   32, 34
Muskegon Lake   51, 189*
Muskegon Reporter   24, 26

Naomi   240*, 243
National City Bank   221
Navarino   64, 66, 67, 68, 69, 74
Navy Pier   121, 267, 272, 273
Neafic & Leavy Shipyard   172
Nevada, 151, 214*, 215*, 216, 217, 218, 219, 220, 221, 222, 223, 233, 235, 237
New Buffalo, Mich., 13, 14, 15, 16, 17, 18*, 19*, 101, 105
Newell, T.   50
New England   16
Newfoundland   274
Newport, Mich., 21, 22, 26, 41, 46, 170
New York City, N.Y., 15, 16, 170, 171
New York Harbor   243
New York House   28
New York State   101
Niles, Mich.   16
Normil   264
North Dock   147
Northern Mich. Trans. Co.   242
North Pier   24, 25, 26, 30.
North Point, Wisc.   144, 145
Northland   165
Northwest, 43*, 47, 49, 59, 165, 228
Norton, James   175
Notice of Trustee's Sale   279, 281*

O'Connor, Tom   232
Oconto   69, 70*, 71, 72, 79
Odgensburg   48
Ogontz   26, 31, 37, 47
Ohio City   26
O'Leary   66
O. McMullen   206
Olsen, Capt. Ingar   96
Oneida   85, 97
Ontonagon, Mich.   38, 39
Orion   42*, 48, 72
Osborne, Rev. L. O.   102
Ottawa   50, 51, 59, 74

Pabst Brewing Co.   30
Pabst, Capt. Frederick, 20*, 24, 27, 28, 29, 30, 33*
Pabst, Fredericka   27, 28
Pabst, Gottlieb   27
Pabst Theatre   30
Pacific   16, 17
Panama Canal   136, 222
Parker, Thos. L.   69

Patten, Owen   46
Patterson, N.J.   50
Pearce, Irving   59
Peninsular Point   86
Pere Marquette Lake, 107, 108, 109
Pere Marquette Line, 89, 222, 239, 276
Pere Marquette, Mich.   110
Pere Marquette River   110
Petoskey   270*, 277, 282
Phelps, W. L.   215
Pierpont & Hall   23
Pig Boat   154, 155*
Pilgrim   241, 242, 243, 244
Pine Street   51
Planet   39*, 40, 46, 106
Platt, Jarvis E.   110
Plummer, Capt. Wm. E.   146, 147
Port Washington, Wisc., 22, 24, 30,
    61, 125, 127, 192
Post Boy   11, 12
Provisional Gov't.   222
Provost Marshall   30
Pullman, Ill.   17
Put-in-Bay   195

Quartermaster Dept.   174
Queen of the Lakes   95, 98

Race, Richard T.   248, 249
Racine Harbor   121, 245
Racine, Wisc., 26, 41, 61, 69, 115, 117,
    119, 120, 121, 132, 145, 146, 147,
    149, 166, 175, 177, 184, 185, 241,
    243, 245, 246, 272, 279
Raleigh, Capt. John C.   144
Rand & Burger   81, 82, 83, 118
Rand, Greenleaf S., 49, 53, 54, 60, 63,
    64, 69, 74, 118
Randolph Street   155, 225, 256
Rand Yard   49, 51, 76, 118
Rathbone Stove Works   67
Redner, Capt.   122, 189
Red Stack Line, 167, 174, 184, 200,
    210, 231
Reliable   201
Reskus, Peter   248
Reynolds-Corliss   84
Reynolds, Fred C.   84
Richardson, Capt. John   48, 121
R. N. Rice   49
Robbins, Nathaniel   257, 271
Robbins, Park   257
Rockland Station   43
Roen, Capt. John, 179, 260, 261, 262,
    263
Roen Yard   261

Rogday   222
Root   142
Rosehill Cemetery   102
Rush Street   254, 255
Rush Street Bridge, 24*, 81*, 132, 212*,
    254
Ryerson & Knickerbocker   50
Ryerson & Morris   50
Ryerson, Martin   50, 51

Saginaw Bay   196
Saginaw, Mich.   22, 110
Saginaw River   22
St. Clair, Mich.   105
St. Clair River   21, 26
St. Ignace   263, 272
St. Joseph   59, 60, 262, 272, 273
St. Joseph, Mich., 12, 15, 16, 58, 60,
    64, 67*, 84, 105, 252*, 259
St. Joseph Harbor   262
St. Lawrence River   135, 173
St. Mary's River, 108*, 116*, 122, 202*,
    220, 221
St. Paul, Minn.   110
Salt City   239
San Francisco, Cal.   222
San Pedro, Cal.   136
Saugatuck, Mich., 79, 254, 263*, 273,
    279
Sault Ste. Marie   38, 105, 113, 121
Schroeder, Wm.   63
Scotch Boilers   265
Scotland   153, 184
Seabird   38*, 41, 42, 45, 58, 167
Search   246, 247
Seymour Line   243
Shanty Bay   86
Sheboygan, Wisc., 7, 22, 24, 25, 43, 45,
    48, 61, 62*, 117, 125, 127, 144, 166,
    236, 279, 282
Sheboygan, 56*, 60, 61, 62, 63, 71, 73*,
    77, 112, 117, 143*, 144*, 146*, 148,
    166, 179, 191, 277, 279, 282
Sheppard's Jewelry Store   42
Sheridan Road   240
Sidney O. Neff   190
Sims, E. W.   279
Singleton, John J.   117
Sister Bay   272
Skylark   66, 68, 69
Smith, Capt. G. H.   125, 126, 127
Smith, Elizabeth   150
Smith, James   175, 177
Smith, Wm. A.   256, 257, 271, 278
Sniffin, Capt. B. N.   63
South American   194

South Carolina   223
South Chicago, Ill.   242, 262
South Haven, Mich.   266, 267
South Philadelphia, Pa.   172
South Point   145
South Water Street   254, 256
Spafford, Capt. F.W.   71
Spanish American War   172
Sprague, A. A.   233
Spring Lake House   114
Spring Lake, Mich.   114
Stanton, Samuel Ward   129
Starke   148
State Creek   11
State of Mich. Ferries   151
State of New York   223, 224
State Street   282
Stender Construction Co.   196
Stines, Capt. George   88
Stines, Capt. Henry E.   87
Stonington, Conn.   173
Stony Creek   204, 208
Straits of Mackinac   151, 221
Stufflebeam, Capt. G.E., 148, 149, 150,
    151, 186, 209, 210
Sturgeon Bay Canal   62, 115, 204
Sturgeon Bay, Wisc., 89, 117, 145, 179,
    195, 206, 260, 261, 262, 263, 264,
    272, 279, 282
Sullivan, Arthur C.   282
Summer Island, Wisc.   90
Sunbeam, 30, 31, 33, 36*, 37, 38, 39,
    40, 58, 84, 167
Superior   14
Superior City, Wisc.   38, 39, 152*, 154
Sweeney, Capt. B.   53, 77
Sycamore Street   22
Sykes, Fred   232

Taylor, Capt. E. E., 185, 257, 271, 272,
    276, 277, 278
Taylor Street   66
Terry   172
Tessler   122*, 125, 126, 127
Theodore Roosevelt, 228, 263*, 264*, 265,
    266, 267, 272
Thompson, John R.   142
Thompson, Wm. Hale   233, 256
Thorp, Harry W., 63, 158, 169, 215,
    236, 238*, 239, 241, 256, 267, 268,
    271, 273
Thorp, Harry W., Jr.   215*, 240
Thorp, Henry T.   239
Thorp, Richard W.   240
Thorp, W. J.   236, 257, 271
Thorne, Janus   233

Thunder Bay Reef   31
Thuringen, Saxony   27
Titanic   129, 193, 243
Toledo, Ohio, 120, 123, 195, 260, 263,
    265
Toledo Shipbuilding Co.   195
Tonwanda, N.Y.   64
Topeka, Kans.   199
Transport   262
Traveler   16, 17, 24
Traverse City   242
Trenton, Mich.   48
Trowbridge   25
Truesdell   50, 51, 59, 74
T. T. Morford   146
Turner, T. A.   18
Two Rivers, Wisc., 22, 23, 27, 29, 30,
    61, 75, 87

Union   40
United States   265
University of Chicago   160
Upton, E. L.   169
U.S. Army   172
U.S. Gov't.   172, 249
U.S. Marshall   280
U.S. Navy Dept.   222
U.S. Senator   212
U.S. Shipping Board   243

Vandura   175
Vedder, Beverly   277, 280
Victor   37
Virginia, 123*, 124*, 125, 126*, 127,
    128, 129, 130, 131, 132, 134, 135,
    136, 138, 142, 153, 155, 157, 166,
    179, 185, 192, 193, 215, 238*
Vladivostok, Russia   221

Wabash Ave.   233
Wabash Valley   31, 32, 33, 35
Wacker Drive   255, 256
Walk-in-the-Water   14
Walker Point Bridge   148
Wallace, Clara   208
Wallace, Ethel   208
Wallace, Wm.   208
Ward, Capt. E. B., 16, 17, 18, 21, 23,
    26, 27, 28, 41, 46, 48, 77, 106, 228
Ward, John W.   64
Ward Line, 15, 16, 17, 18, 21, 22, 28,
    29, 52, 58, 64, 105, 106, 107
Ward Yard   21, 26, 46
Warrenville, Ill.   208
Washburn   178
Washington Island, 31, 90, 121, 166,

272

Waukegan, Ill., 41, 43, 277, 278*, 279, 282

Welcome   145, 146, 159, 160, 161

Welland Canal   173

West, Chas.   271

Western Trans. Co.   224

West Neebish Channel   122

West Ports S.S. Co., 270*, 276, 277, 278*, 279, 280*

West Yard   147

Whaling, Rosamond Frances   57

Wheaton College   208

Whitcomb, F. L.   215

Whitefish Bay   220, 221

Whitehall, Mich.   179, 236*

White Lake, Mich., 76, 88, 175, 236*, 272

White Pigeon, Mich.   12

White Star Line   49

Whittaker, Capt. Harry   16

Whittaker, Capt. Wessel, 11, 12, 13, 14, 19*

Whittaker Propulsion System   37

Wilkerson, Judge James H.   276, 277

Willard, Nelson   13

Willard, W. S.   169

Wilson, Capt. Jack   35

Wilson, Edward   207*

Wind Point   177

Winston, B. M.   215

Wisconsin, 7, 16, 23, 58, 169, 179, 210, 212, 230, 278

Wisconsin, 95, 97, 98, 240*, 241*, 242, 243, 244, 245, 246, 248, 250, 272, 276

Wisconsin Inc. Bill   58

Wisconsin-Mich. Trans. Co.   276

Wolverine State   16, 50

Woodward, Judge Chas. E.   278

Wright, W. H.   59

Wrigley Bldg.   208

Wrigley, Wm.   136

Wyandotte, Mich.   95, 223, 262

Yahr-Lange Drug Co.   161

Yates, Capt.   43

York Street   42